Designing
Classroom
Spontaneity

In the **Prentice-Hall Series in Curriculum and Teaching**
Ronald T. Hyman, *Consulting Editor*

Dempsey/Smith, *Differentiated Staffing*
Morine/Morine, *Discovery Techniques in Teaching*

DESIGNING CLASSROOM SPONTANEITY

Case-Action Learning

WILLIAM C. NUTTING

University of Utah

Prentice-Hall, Inc.

Englewood Cliffs, New Jersey

Library of Congress Cataloging in Publication Data

NUTTING, WILLIAM C.
    Designing classroom spontaneity: case-action learning.

    (Prentice-Hall series in curriculum and teaching)
    1. Education, Elementary. 2. Activity programs
in education. I. Title.
LB1555.N85   372.1'3   72-4450
ISBN 0-13-201988-4
ISBN 0-13-201970-1 (pbk.)

10 9 8 7 6 5 4 3 2 1

Printed in the United States of America

Prentice-Hall International, Inc., *London*
Prentice-Hall of Australia, Pty. Ltd., *Sydney*
Prentice-Hall of Canada, Ltd., *Toronto*
Prentice-Hall of India Private Limited, *New Delhi*
Prentice-Hall of Japan, Inc., *Tokyo*

Contents

Part ONE

Building Scholarship in the Elementary School

v

Part TWO

A Design for Case-Action Learning

Identifying a Potential Case

Basic Criteria for Selecting a Case, 95; *Is the Case Worthwhile?* 95; *Is the Case Learnable?* 95; *Is the Case Interesting?* 95; **Other Criteria for Selecting a Case,** 96; *Coordinating Present Effort with Other Learning Experiences,* 96; *Feasibility of a Selection,* 97; **A Teacher's Responsibility in Selecting a Case,** 98; *Official Courses of Study,* 98; *Seeking the Cooperation of School Principal and Supervisors,* 99; *Coordinating with Other Teachers;* 101; *Capability of a Particular Group of Children,* 102; *Special Needs and Interests of a Particular Group of Children,* 103; *Permanent Value of a Learning Experience,* 104; *Timeliness or Cruciality of a Case,* 105; *Availability of Essential Materials and Equipment,* 106; **Role of the Children in Selecting a Case,** 107; *Making Sure that a Potential Case Holds Interest for Children,* 108; *Giving Children Experience in Decision Making,* 108; *Giving Children a Sense of Commitment,* 109; **Summary,** 109

Getting Interested in a Proposed Case

Drawing Attention to a Potential Case, 111; *Purpose of Attention Calling,* 112; *Planned Techniques and Activities,* 112; *Unplanned Techniques and Activities,* 112; **Considering Possibilities and Merits of a Proposed Case,** 113; *Purpose of More Deliberate Consideration,* 113; *Suggested Techniques and Activities,* 113; **Planning and Using Interest Builders Effectively,** 114; *Reading or Telling a Story,* 114; *Classroom Demonstration,* 115; *Mounted Flat Pictures,* 115; *Display of Objects,* 116; *Samples and Specimens,* 117; *Scale Models,* 117; *Maps and Charts,* 118; *Posters,* 119; *Bulletin Boards,* 119; *Dramatizations,* 120; *Games and Contests,* 121; *Classroom Visitor,* 121; *Special Report,* 122; *Motion Picture Film,* 124; *Filmstrips and Slides,* 125; *Single Concept Filmloops,* 125; *Recordings,* 126; *Transparencies and Overlays,* 126; *Mockups,* 126; *Dioramas,* 127; *Graphs and Diagrams,* 127; *Collections,* 128; *Directed Reading,* 128; *Library Research,* 130; *Interviews,* 130; *Letter Writing,* 131; *Experiments,* 132; *Informal Quizzes,* 132; *Voluntary Homework,* 133; *Field Trip or Excursion,* 133; *Small Group Discussions,* 136; *General Class Discussions,* 138; **Making Good Use of Unplanned Incidents,** 139; *Children's Questions or Casual Observations,* 139; *Unusual Happenings and Coincidences,* 140; *Surprise Visits,* 140; *Gifts and Letters,* 141; *News Events,* 142; *Commercial Television and Neighborhood Movies,* 142; *Accident or Disaster,* 143; **Summary,** 143

Taking on a Promising Case

Purposes, 147; **Procedure,** 148; *Open Discussion to Encourage Asking of Questions,* 148; *Recording Questions and Concerns,* 149; *Editing and Categorizing Questions,*

Organizing for Action on a Case

Developing a Case

Closing a Case

Contents   ix

Part THREE
Planning a Successful Case

Maintaining a Resource File   Chapter Eleven
207

Purposes of a Resource File, 207; **Suggested Filing Procedures,** 208; *Basic Equipment,* 208; *Sources of Ideas and Materials,* 209; *Filing Arrangements,* 211; **Summary,** 212

Design for Success   Chapter Twelve
214

Six Steps to Success, 215; *A Systematic Design for a Spontaneous Happening,* 215; *A Simultaneous Development of All Steps,* 216; *A Fresh Start for Every Design,* 216; **Panic-Free Planning,** 217; *Taking It Easy,* 217; *Making the Most of Long-Range Planning,* 218; **Personalizing Education Through Group Action,** 218; *Case-Action Learning in Various Patterns of School Organization,* 219; *Group Action and Rugged Individualism,* 220; **Case-Action Learning and Subject Matter Study,** 221; *A Needed Complement,* 221; *A Note of Caution,* 222; **A Thought or Two in Closing,** 223

Index   225

Preface

Many teachers have felt a need for increased spontaneity in the elementary classroom. By nature, children are impulsive activists; but the limitations and requirements that have traditionally been placed upon youthful behavior have curtailed much of the exuberance that is normal to childhood. The situation calls for a design that will enable teachers to incorporate group-identified concerns and individual freedom directly into the curriculum.

The recommendation presented in this book carries no automatic demand that everything old be summarily thrown out to make room for the new. In the first place, there is much in the old that is actually quite good. And, in the second place, immediate implementation of the ideas suggested herein need not take up a great deal of space in an already crowded curriculum. Supporting argument, therefore, is not premised upon any spirited cataloging of real or imagined weaknesses in present educational programs. Instead, the proposal calls for blending an obvious, but usually overlooked, dimension of elementary education together with proven elements of standard practices. The intention, specifically, is not to eliminate subject matter in any way from the elementary curriculum, but rather to include the child and his group to an extent that has not generally been thought feasible.

An ultimate goal—perhaps the major goal—of an elementary school ought to be the development of scholarship in every child. But scholarship consists of much more than simply the mastery of subject matter. A genuine love of learning for its own sake is an equally legitimate and reasonable aim. There are sound reasons for building forthrightly from both a knowledge-based, subject-centered approach, and a child-focused, learning-oriented convergence upon curriculum.

In a child-centered approach, the ultimate value of a particular learning activity lies in the quality of the experience as such as it relates directly to the felt needs and personal satisfactions of the learner. Much of the discussion focuses upon the means for achieving just such an end. The fact that subject matter is not examined in equivalent detail should in no way be taken to imply that a disciplinary approach is not vital as one basic dimension of elementary curriculum. But the argument for including significant measures of formalized knowledge in the child's education has already been convincingly demonstrated. There is no reason for viewing the two approaches as being in competition; they simply are not of the same wave length. Certainly, there is abundant need for both.

Despite the considerable evidence, however, that there presently is much of genuine value in elementary curriculum practices, at least two very important qualities are largely missing. First, in consideration of the individual's fundamental drive actually to *do* something significant about his own education, each child should have frequent occasion to determine to an appreciable extent his own course of action in school-based learning experiences. Second, in view of the crucial need to develop positive social attitudes and basic skills in interpersonal behavior within every citizen, it becomes almost mandatory that children be regularly involved in authentic group undertakings. Unfortunately, relatively little of either of these characteristics is observed in even the most modern elementary schools. With the exception of a few isolated instances, children are given insufficient opportunities for realistic self-determination and genuine group interaction.

Case-action learning is proposed as a fascinating and dependable way of getting immediately at both of these considerations. The discussion shows how group-identified concerns may be designed to fit beneficially into existing elementary curricula.

The book is organized in three parts. Part One identifies a unique set of purposes of elementary education and shows the significance of case-action learning in building scholarship and love of learning in young children. It also indicates a proper philosophical and practical relationship between case-action learning and subject matter. Part Two presents several realistic examples of school-based group undertakings and methodically outlines a step-by-step procedure for designing case-action learning for and with children. Part Three summarizes and provides a helpful down-to-earth approach for developing a successful case as an ongoing aspect of the total teaching task.

William C. Nutting

Designing Classroom Spontaneity

Part ONE

Building Scholarship
in the
Elementary School

*The more children study the things they like,
the better they like the things they study.*

Chapter One

Purposes of
Elementary Education

First of all, an elementary school ought to be a happy place. Very probably, happiness is the one ingredient most noticeably abundant in good schools and most obviously lacking in poor ones. The observation is not lightly made; the more closely it is scrutinized the more believable it becomes. Happiness bespeaks a positive outlook: confidence, efficiency, and a zest for the task at hand. It means enthusiastic children and dedicated teachers.

The Curriculum: Happiness, Scholarship, and Subject Matter

In view of the high incidence of happiness observable in quality education programs, it might seem a bit odd that there have been so few candid efforts to fabricate it deliberately into the school. Perhaps this seeming incongruity stems in part from a Puritanical viewpoint that happiness is to be valued in the abstract but not necessarily in the concrete. The historical development of the American elementary school does not abound with expressed concern for the inclusion of joy or pleasure in the curriculum. At best, pleasure has more frequently been tolerated as a deferred, and perhaps incidental, outcome. Even in those excellent schools characterized by a rather high level of happiness, it seems that, more often than not, this precious commodity has been smuggled in under wraps, and any references in the official course of study as to its desirability have been tactfully couched in acceptable euphemisms. Despite the fact that a good many genuinely happy schools are flourishing at this very moment, it really has not been politic to develop one on purpose.

Part of the difficulty has been that curriculum planners have traditionally equated scholarship with subject matter. While subject matter is, of course, an absolute requisite, the real essence of scholarship lies fully as much in the attitude of the learner toward the pursuit of knowledge as in the actual mastery of knowledge per se. Genuine scholarship is more process than product; actually, it is not so much learning *in order to achieve* some specific objective as it is *for the sheer joy* of the learning experience as such. For the true scholar, *what* is learned is often seen as a by-product of the activity; the greater reward frequently comes in the pure delight of the effort and in the resulting satisfaction of having done one's utmost. This is scholarship. And this is happiness. If scholarship and happiness are not identical twins, they certainly are close relatives. Particularly in terms of developing scholarship in children, subject matter should be seen as a means to an end as well as an end in itself.

A careful look at a typical course of study will reveal a curious contradiction. The prefatory statements will often reflect a philosophy that seeks to identify the full range of educational needs of the child as he attempts to relate to the opportunities and hazards in his total environmental situation. The list of aims that may be presented rather glowingly in a sample preliminary statement not only embraces the familiar requirements of the "three R's" complete with innovations, but also points determinedly to learning experiences and educational outcomes that go well beyond the usual subject matter goals. However, in the carefully written sections which follow, in which the scope and sequence of each curriculum area are laid out in minute detail and logical clarity, there is little, if any, hint of concern for values other than mastery of subject matter.

What a frustration for the conscientious teacher! For, despite the strong reassurances in the philosophical statement that there is much more to the elementary curriculum than mastery of subject matter, he too often finds that there are simply no concrete suggestions for implementing any objectives *other than* subject matter. It should not be too surprising, therefore, that some of the most dedicated and hard working teachers have frequent misgivings as to the outcome. The teacher with a real concern for the total educational well-being of each child finds it virtually impossible to reconcile the broad challenge of the course of study preamble with the narrow subject orientation of the specific requirements which are detailed "in the fine print." It is not difficult to understand how some teachers have been driven to a rationalization of subject matter solely as an end rather than equally as a means to an end.

Subject matter is properly both provender and product of elementary education. Every meaningful learning experience has two worthwhile outcomes: first, the acquisition of knowledge—that particular fact, skill, attitude, or appreciation that constitutes the tangible, measurable result of the learning effort; and second, the quality of the actual learning experience as such. Subject matter ought to be used in such a way as to insure both of these outcomes. The means and the end must be kept in careful balance if a genuine love of learning is to be developed in the young child. A reasonable degree of knowledgeableness and an unabashed love of learning are the irreducible essentials of scholarship. And the development of real scholarship in every child ought to be the main business of an elementary school.

School in Society: Heritage of an Image

It may be good to step back and view in some perspective the basic responsibility and function of the elementary school in present-day society. In its evolution over the many decades, elementary education has come to mean a variety of things to different people. Despite a rather significant degree of uniformity across the country, there is today no single, unvarying concept of this vital institution that is so very close to the pulse of every household. In establishing meaningful educational purposes, it will be appropriate to consider briefly some of the possible factors that have contributed to this composite image.

That the elementary school established in colonial America was founded in part for the purpose of teaching immediately marketable vocational skills to a specific segment of the potential labor force has undoubtedly left a lasting impression. In the early school, objectives were simple and straightforward. Incentive and relevance were inherent in the school-to-society relationship. Mastery of subject matter was an obvious virtue, and—like any virtue—was its own reward.

Social structures have, of course, changed a great deal in three centuries. The role of the school has undergone a marked transformation. Elementary education has long ceased to function as a terminal program in vocational training. But the old image fades slowly, and the relative importance of specific skills and factual information remains nostalgically large on the public retina. This, quite possibly, may account in part for a periodically recurring obsession with subject matter as the beginning and end of curriculum.

As society gradually assumed greater sophistication in its operations and interrelationships, the aims of education—particularly elementary education—became less direct and increasingly remote from classroom learning activities. Incentives and rewards became less obvious. Subject matter, in the meantime, was expanding in quantity and developing in logical structure. And, even as relevance of school programs inevitably became more obscure in the daily life of the individual child, the absolute necessity of at least a minimum of formal education for every citizen grew rapidly more pronounced.

The sciences of child study and educational psychology were, in retrospect, noisy latecomers on the scene. It should not seem surprising, therefore, that considerations for the logically oriented content of subject matter consistently loomed disproportionately large in traditional curriculum.

With increasing postponement of ultimate gratification of efforts to learn, there has been a corresponding disenchantment with school on the part of many children. Parental pressures and compulsory attendance laws, however, have guaranteed the school a seller's market. To no small degree has the traditional elementary school held a captive audience. Extrinsic rewards in the form of annual promotions and arbitrary marking systems have generally sufficed as substitute incentives.

Despite the fact that many children, even today, are "being educated" against their own desires, most people don't appear to be particularly upset. It seems to be rather generally accepted that a good many children should just naturally be less than delighted with the character and quality of their school experiences. Neutral toleration, or even mild dislike, of school can be regarded, apparently, as a reasonable price to pay for a knowledgeable citizenry. While most people undoubtedly are genuinely pleased with occasional instances of eager scholarship and youthful enthusiasm for voluntary learning activities, they are not disturbed that the great majority of the younger generation does not display these characteristics to any appreciable degree. Our literature abounds with references of negativism: the "reluctant scholar," the "trudging" to class, the rebellious free soul playing hooky, and the unbridled hilarity that marks the closing of school in the spring. In short, it is rather generally assumed that most children are herded unasked—but for their own good, of course—through the school curriculum like so many sheep through a dipping pit. Even the "good" students, it is further assumed, should probably feel a certain amount of healthy resentment toward the uncompromising institution.

School in Society: A Needed Balance

If a system of education is to function properly in a democratic society, its underlying philosophy must be in tune with the basic tenets of that society. Values deep in our culture need to be clearly identified in school purposes and deliberately nurtured through the curriculum. It is important, also, that these values be cultivated in the curriculum in a consonant and realistic balance.

The individual has traditionally held an exalted position in our democratic society. Both custom and law have firmly established the principle of this relationship. It should, therefore, be seen as reasonable and necessary that programs of education be specifically designed to promote the development of individuality. An inescapable cultural demand is that education in our society be simultaneously a restricting and a freeing experience. Particularly in regard to young children in their yet-formative years, it is essential that an appropriate individual-to-society relationship be carefully developed.

To a considerable extent, it is obviously the function of education to "shape" or "mold" the child. It is accepted that this particular terminology may carry somewhat offensive overtones in that it seems to regard a human soul as just so much modeling clay to be squeezed into whatever form is desired. Nevertheless, the behavior of the individual must, in many ways, conform neatly and obligingly to cultural expectations and requirements. Society sets certain standards and insists that they be met. The welfare of society demands quality performance on the part of the individual. It is quite clear that much of education must be categorized as *training*. Some necessary learning experiences are intended primarily for the well-being of society rather than directly for individual self-fulfillment.

Admittedly, society has a vital stake in the child's education. However, in the enthusiasm of responding to the important requirements of the greater community, the equally crucial needs of the individual must not go unattended. The child's education must include abundant opportunities for finding personal identity and self-enhancement. There must be provision for worthwhile learning experiences by which he may achieve objectives that he sets for himself. The fostering of individuality *for its own merit* must be seen as an essential outcome.

Simply stated, the composite task of elementary education in a truly open society is to discipline the mind and free the spirit. An effective elementary curriculum will reflect a balanced concern for purposes that stem from both individual needs and societal needs.

Identifying Individual Needs

Perhaps individual needs may be most succinctly discussed in terms of total maturity. Maturity, of course, is a relative, everchanging frame of reference for evaluating certain personality characteristics. In general, maturity may be regarded as the appropriate degree of total readiness of the individual to respond effectively to various conditions within his total environment. Rarely, if ever, is readiness an absolute. As the individual grows in capacity to meet certain responsibilities, the environmental conditions relentlessly change both in magnitude and in complexity of interrelationship. Thus, it may be correct, on occasion, to refer to a "mature five-year-old," or an "immature adult." In a sense, maturity is that will-o'-the-wispish goal of education—ever to be closely pursued, but never quite attained. Hopeful pursuit provides a constant challenge to spur renewed effort. But, while individual gratification does not hinge directly upon actually reaching a fleeting goal, frustration is the certain result of being unduly thwarted in the attempt.

Physical Maturity as an Individual Need

Of the various aspects of total maturity that are especially useful in identifying individual needs, perhaps the most observable and most measurable is physical maturity. At a very early age the child develops an awareness of and an interest in his own body. He senses certain assets and liabilities. He has many occasions to compare his own physical adequacies with those of his immediate family and his acquaintances, and he finds these comparisons to be the frequent source of both pride and humility. "When I get big" is some obscure point in the future at which he will cope masterfully with a given situation that is presently beyond his control. The child typically expects his body to serve him more satisfactorily as he grows and develops. He looks forward to becoming taller and stronger, to running faster and jumping farther, to performing with skill and grace, and, in general, to being independent.

While the role of the school in past decades has been relatively minor in helping the child to gain in physical maturity, it is rapidly becoming more significant. Elementary education continues to accept increasingly greater responsibility as changing patterns of family living and more critical public awareness gradually move the matter generally in the direction of the school's domain.

Intellectual Maturity as an Individual Need

The persistent curiosity of the very young child has long been recognized by proud parents everywhere as an encouraging sign of normalcy. Within a few days after his birth, the new baby is unmistakably manifesting the behavior of a seeker and doer. Grasping, chewing, tasting, listening, poking, smelling, feeling, and bumping—he commences a lifelong project of "finding out." Clumsily, but very quickly, he begins to organize his immense, jumbled environment—separating self from nonself, and dividing the nonself into personally-useful categories. Quite definitely, he has set out with great enthusiasm on the long, but exciting, road to intellectual maturity.

Possibly the young child's probing behavior is a result of his insatiable curiosity. Or, perhaps, the growing curiosity develops inevitably out of purely instinctive probing and seeking. There may be as much support for one theory as the other. In either case, these two marvelously human characteristics operate in conjunction. Every contact with some unfamiliar facet of his environment serves to stimulate the individual's curiosity; and, in the process of satisfying the aroused curiosity, new approaches to phenomena within the environment result invariably in further curiosity cravings. If the child is properly encouraged and supported in continuing this ever-enlarging cycle of stimulation and satiation of curiosity, he will ultimately develop an intellectual behavior pattern that becomes an integral and lasting part of his personal way of life. He will surely have acquired an appetite for learning.

Lifelong learning is the breath of intellectual maturity. The intellectually mature person delights in learning. Although a relentless pursuer of knowledge, he is fascinated—even pleased—by the magnitude of his own ignorance. He is really more a seeker of questions than of answers, and he revels more in problems than in solutions. He is not discouraged at the unanswered question, but he is dismayed at the unquestioned answer. To be human is to be a learner. To achieve an equitable measure of intellectual maturity is most assuredly a need of every individual.

Emotional Maturity as an Individual Need

Human beings have feelings. And these feelings are not to be denied. It is not by bread alone that the good life is attained; a full complement of sentient gradations is also requisite. Emotions are influential factors in almost every aspect of living; the individual is moved fully as much by them as by his appetites, and his behavior is guided no less by these intense feelings than by the intellect. Emotions are crucial in the life of every person, for they constitute a power that may result either beneficially or otherwise. The individual must strive to live with his emotions so that he is served by them, rather than destroyed. Emotional maturity is an important individual need.

Social Maturity as an Individual Need

That man is a social creature has been reiterated to the point of dulling the full import of the statement. Truisms inevitably have that effect. Nevertheless, it is appropriate to recognize that, to a great extent, individual behavior is focused upon a multiplicity of interpersonal relationships. The quality of living, therefore, is determined in no small way by the efficacy and relevance of these contacts. Social competence is another of the broad facets of total maturity that must be attained by every individual.

Identifying Societal Needs

In a democratic society, which—theoretically, at least—holds the individual in highest esteem, it might be generally assumed that individual needs and societal needs are not particularly in conflict. But it is understandable that any society—democratic or otherwise—is motivated by certain selfish interests, as well as altruistic impulses. It is really quite fundamental: the society has a consuming passion for life—it needs to prolong its own existence. Survival is a powerful incentive.

Maintaining Basic Social and Political Institutions

People everywhere have traditionally defended their social and political institutions with a firmness scarcely equaled in the whole spectrum of human affairs. The health and vigor of these organs of group life have been found to be as essential in their peculiar functions as is the soundness of the bodily organs in terms of biological vitality. Person-to-person, person-to-group, and group-to-group relationships and behaviors have become ritualized as a result of eons of social evolution; and, even yet, mutations continue to occur. Definitive patterns of marriage and family structure exemplify developments which have unfolded slowly over the centuries and endure to serve the race. Benefits and responsibilities that flow from citizenship in community, state, and nation have been stabilized as cherished aspects of a desirable lifestyle. Through custom, sanction, and legal persuasion, the sanctity of established modes of human interrelationships has been upheld with consistency and determination. Continued maintenance and further development of these and other social and political institutions must be recognized as an important category of societal need.

Preservation of the Culture: A Societal Need

Common usage has caused some confusion as to the precise meanings of the words *society* and *culture*. The terms are sometimes used synonymously; for example, references to "Western *society*" and "Western *culture*" seem to be employed almost interchangeably. The two concepts are so closely related as to make it virtually impossible to consider one except in regard to the other. To differentiate somewhat, culture has occasionally been called "the glue that holds society together"—an obvious oversimplification, but not altogether an inaccurate definition, for mutual customs and values held in common supply much of the cohesiveness that bonds a human aggregate into a people. Or, it may be helpful to think of culture as the rules and regulations by which the game of "Civilization" is played, with society as the players. And just as playing according to accepted rules makes generally for a better game, so does preservation of the culture contribute to social progress.

In a very real sense, the more stable the culture, the more vigorously and creatively may society progress. Clearly visible benchmarks of a well established culture provide essential points of reference to insure constant orientation for controlled experimentation and productive innovation. A living culture, of course, is continually growing and changing to accommodate to ever-developing requirements, but these changes must be purposeful and relatively gradual—or social advancement will be without direction, and civilization will ultimately be lost. Of course, the ubiquitous "generation gap" is, and always has been, a much noticed fact of life. But, within limits, this may connote a generally healthy condition. Each succeeding wave of the youthful element in society needs to reenact, and embellish upon, the experiences of the race in discovering for itself the ancient and honorable truths, and to restate them in the light of a new day.

Economic Development as a Societal Need

The human race does not dwell innocently in a Garden of Eden in which the bounties of a beneficent nature drop conveniently off a nearby vine. While an abundance of goods and services alone does not guarantee happiness, it is quite clear that the good life cannot flourish in a vacuum. Adequate diet and protection from the elements are basic necessities for this good life. And, since the natural resources of the earth are limited, efficient production, distribution, and consumption of the fruits of labor are essential to the advancement of civilization. Wealth is more than a fringe benefit: it is crucial. Economic development necessarily ranks high on the priority list of any progressive society.

Health and Welfare as Societal Needs

An enthusiastic and vigorous population has always constituted a significant element in the total makeup of an influential society. Since the dawn of history, fortune has smiled most upon those peoples with great energy for work and play and a capacity to shrug off the vituperations of a harsh environment. The ultimate strength of a nation grows surely out of the physical and moral well-being of its inhabitants. Attention to individual health and welfare yields definite public benefits.

Safety and Defense as Societal Needs

All is not sweetness and light; and wishing will not make it so. To be oblivious to danger is possibly to be dead wrong. There are conditions, both natural and man-made, that daily threaten our individual and collective security; and these conditions must be identified and corrected by whatever means may be required. Even the maligned ostrich, despite legendary rumor, does not place its faith blindly in the sand. Eternal vigilance and intelligent response are a more realistic approach to continued survival. Society must pledge appropriate and necessary resources to the neutralization and eventual elimination of accidents, natural disasters, crime, environmental pollution, and military aggression at their various sources. Attention will increasingly focus upon long-range resources in developing effective solutions.

Establishing Educational Purposes

Purposes of education are derived principally from two sources: first, the identification of certain human needs—either individual or societal; and, second, the malleability of human behavior. In delineating specific aims, therefore, it is important to concentrate upon those particular aspects of need which might best be satisfied as a result of predictable changes in behavior.

Portions of the preceding discussion have pointed out some of the fairly obvious necessities of the more abundant life. To emphasize the essentiality of equitable balance, an effort has been made to categorize each identified need according to its basic individual or societal orientation. To insure cataloging the full range of human needs, such a separation has been useful. However, in detailing the actual purposes of elementary education, it is assumed that both categories of need may be coincidentally responsive; therefore, there is no special merit in continuing the dichotomy further.

Education is widely recognized as a true form of human growth and development which uniquely embraces chiefly the behavioral factors. Major principles that apply in general to the processes of growth and development also apply to education in particular. Both nature and nurture are necessary ingredients. Maturation and selected learning experiences operate in delicate conjunction to bring about desirable increments in behavioral attainment.

As with all facets of human development, education is a highly individualized process. Since each person has his own unique growth pattern, his education must be very much a private matter. Purposes of education, therefore, ought to be stated in terms of individual attainability and from the peculiar point of view of each child.

For Every Child: Self-Identity and Self-Realization

One of the more persistent of human quests is the never-ending search for self. It begins sometime in infancy and continues throughout life. This fascinating impulsiveness to introspection is a singularly distinguishing attribute of humankind. Man has not only the propensity, but even the necessity, to examine and reexamine the character of his own life. In such subjective-objective reflection, the individual constantly views his own image and passes judgment. Particularly from the standpoint of education, the significance of self-image ought not be underestimated. Indeed, it may be a realistic starting point for any scheme to improve the quality of living.

Almost from the outset, the child's rising awareness of self may stand as both cause and effect of his own behavior. Although the human infant is fundamentally a doer, his earliest behavior is instinctive and generally without purpose or direction. He acts and is acted upon. He thrusts and grasps at his undifferentiated environment, and the environment yields or presses back. As this purposeless behavior is by chance ignored, rewarded, or rebuked, subsequent actions gradually take on both purpose and direction. The child constructs a personal orientation by sorting out the various bits and pieces of his environment; and, simultaneously, he starts to form a self-image that serves as an equally useful referent. Thus, very early in life, the individual conceives an image—with certain assets and shortcomings—which he recognizes as himself. From the advent of individuality onward, his behavior represents a concerted effort to communicate and interact with the environment in ways that are likely to prove enhancing to the self.

There is a striking relationship between personal adequacy and self-concept. As the growing child makes behavioral decisions on the basis of previous successes and failures, he constantly revises his personal evaluations of his own worth. Every satisfaction or disappointment, every pleasure or pain becomes another particle in the composition of a developing personality. With each response to a new confrontation, some earlier judgment is reinforced or undermined to some extent, and the individual's self-esteem waxes or wanes accordingly. Every contact with family, friends, or strangers makes its particular contribution. In the process of exploring his ever-expanding world, the young child inevitably finds out more and more about himself, and he becomes convinced of real or imagined traits and accomplishments within his own being. He presumes himself to be relatively capable in a variety of situations and conditions, and incapable in others. Depending upon the particular circumstances and past experiences, the individual manifests confidence or apprehension; he feels strong or weak. To the degree that the child senses his personal adequacy or inadequacy, a given opportunity may be seen as a challenge or a frustration. The requirement for certain types of behavior on his own part will be enthusiastically sought out or desperately avoided.

Early childhood is marked by phenomenal progress in all aspects of growth, including the development of a vital personality foundation. By the time a child enters kindergarten, he has already formed a rather indelible self-image. But the crucial years are not completely behind him; the quest for self continues throughout the elementary school period and even beyond. Especially in the kindergarten and primary grades—but also to a great extent in the intermediate levels—there can be no more important educational goal than that of building in each pupil an abiding belief in himself and a quiet pride in his own inherent worth. Self-esteem is absolutely basic to the promotion of all facets of desirable behavioral growth.

The school can help the individual attain selfhood in two major phases. First, the curriculum must be attuned to the child's craving for a continuing self-identity. The individual must be encouraged and guided in his ongoing struggle to satisfy that unvoiced, but gnawing, question about his own peculiarly personal existence and the nature of his unique mission in life. Second, having provided the child with additional means for discovering his own true identity, the school program must enable him to realize a measure of personal achievement that is reasonably commensurate with the self-concept that has been established. A major purpose of education, therefore, is the attainment by every child of a dynamic, positive self-identity and an accompanying self-realization.

*For Every Child: The Desire and Ability to Live and Work
Effectively with Others*

As we move into the last quarter of the twentieth century, the urgency for developing functional sociality can scarcely be overstated. Getting along with one's fellow passengers on this crowded planet is essential. The accelerating complexities of our modern world, with exponentially increasing populations and technologies, have multiplied the hazards as well as the opportunities. Both the rewards of intelligent, sensitive social behavior and the hideous consequences of ignorance and callousness in interpersonal relationships are markedly greater than ever before. Brilliant successes of highly motivated and remarkably coordinated teams working in medicine, nuclear energy, space exploration, and communication—to mention only a few obvious fields of endeavor—have been well documented. Equally noted have been far too many searing instances of the chain reaction of misery triggered by even a single malevolent act of a misguided human soul. Surely the matter of developing within each child the desire and ability to live and work effectively with others constitutes an educational purpose worthy of our deepest concern and most imaginative and enthusiastic effort.

Although man exists largely by virtue of participating in various interpersonal and intergroup relationships, he is not born with an operable social apparatus. The infant comes into his world as an asocial creature; but, through a process of personal acculturation, he quickly takes on many of the requisites of active membership in the race. The complete course runs a lifetime. The acquisition of a viable social sense is inextricably interwoven with the development of self. During the early phases, the child is solely a recipient of the manifestations of social dynamism. At first there is much priming: he *receives* the love and warmth of his parents and siblings. It is only after these lavishly bestowed expressions of humanization have been firmly implanted within his being that the individual is capable of responding in kind. It has been observed that, in the sequence of motor development, the infant invariably achieves the ability to *grasp* significantly earlier than he does the ability to *release*. Even so, in the unfolding of a human personality the *getting* must necessarily precede the *giving*.

In social development, too, first things come first. The principle of sequence must be observed in this, as in any other, aspect of individual growth. Since the child can give back only that which he has received, it is vital that a proper foundation be laid. Although everyone has a deep-seated need to co-respond with his fellow human beings, he must learn the method. Social interaction is not contrived from the outside. Mere closeness is not togetherness. Toddlers in a sandbox, for example, may very well be playing *in proximity*, but not necessarily *together*. Perhaps there may even be what superficially seems to pass for conversation. It is entirely possible that, within the playing area, each youngster exists as a definite part of another's immediate environment; yet, in no wise, do the two individuals actually co-respond or share in a common experience. Thus, they are *near*, but not *with*, one another; and their actions do not really constitute social behavior. However, the ultimate value of such situations should not be underestimated, for they do provide an important foundational step in the social growth of each child.

Although the child attains an amazing degree of social maturity during his preschool years, much yet remains for him to achieve. And, if the individual is to reach his full potential, a significant contribution must come through the elementary curriculum. Unfortunately, something of a paradox seems to be developing in regard to the school's proper role in providing appropriate learning experiences leading to social development. At the very moment in the history of the world when the absolute necessity of *social maturity* for every individual is being emphatically underscored, traditional opportunities for *social growth* have been sharply curtailed for millions of children. Changing patterns of family life, commercialized recreation, and increasing dependence upon the mass media have virtually made it possible for today's child to live at home in a socially sterile environment. The resulting combination of circumstances would seem to demand that education rush to fill the breach by creating new occasions for social development through inschool learning activities designed to foster increased interpersonal behavior. In view of the cruciality of the total situation, it is indeed a sad commentary that many of the curriculum innovations recently sweeping the education scene have served even further to insulate the child from direct human contact. Certainly the breathtaking challenges of a technological explosion cannot be ignored by the school, but it is a gross misplacement of values that permits *any* school program, regardless of its particular promise, to jeopardize the possibility of adequate social education. The elementary school curriculum must help every child to become functionally social.

For Every Child: An Understanding and Appreciation
of the Cultural Values

One does not shop around for a culture. He simple accepts it as it is. He takes it with all of its loveliness and its ugliness. He can't deny it; he can't change it; he can't escape it. And there's not much point in fighting it. He might as well become acquainted with it and learn to live with it. The subtle process of acculturation begins in early infancy. Everyone is born into a particular culture; and, unless he is removed from it completely, he will carry its mark.

Culture may be thought of as the cumulative record of a society. Systematic patterns of behavior that typify and characterize a particular social group are reflections of habits, values, and beliefs that have been customized and traditionalized through many generations of living. The catalog of behaviors is without end, but a partial list might include such categories as family and social structure, patterns of industry and commerce, language, mannerisms, food habits, norms of emotional display, spiritual values and religious beliefs, music styles and preferences, artistic expressions, modes of recreation, intellectual skills and attitudes, ethnic biases and prejudices, aesthetic appreciations, and moral and ethical principles. Each succeeding generation receives this largess in all its fullness, is shaped by it, uses it, modifies it—be it ever so slightly—and passes it intact to the generation next in line.

The sometimes embarrassing inability of the generations to share a common viewpoint should cause no real surprise. At any given moment in the unfolding chronology of mankind, there are in immediate vital contact with the culture essentially just two generations: the elder and the younger. The senior ranks, from a modest vantage of some few years of struggle and contemplation, may see culture as another resifting of centuries of trial and error, success and failure, obstinacy and compromise and, thus, adopt a passively possessive attitude toward this heritage. But the hasty inclination of a younger generation is to view all of this, not as the sum total of the ages, but solely as the responsibility and creation of its elders: the generation in charge. For the oldsters, culture is to live with, to tolerate, and—if at all possible—to love. Meanwhile, impatient youth, demanding an accounting in full, is delighted with whatever the proceeds and indignant over the shortages. The business of passing on the culture from generation to generation is not without its risks—or its joys.

While transmission of the culture has traditionally been considered an important aim of education, the greater part of the charge has been directed to agencies other than the school: the home, the community, the church. The school has centered mainly on presenting to the coming generation the accumulated and cataloged wisdom of the world as represented in the scholarly disciplines and disseminated through the familiar subject matter areas. Heretofore, this convenient arrangement has been reasonably satisfactory. In an era of relatively stable social groups, predictable community standards, lasting family attachments, little mobility, and fairly gradual change, it was possible to depend upon these more subtle influences. Recent indications, however, are that this matter is much too crucial to be left to chance, especially in the case of educational philosophies too strongly oriented toward the teaching of that which has immediate practical applicability. The school program, therefore, must be somehow adjusted to pass on some of the rather intangible, but highly significant, aspects of the culture. The curriculum must include deliberate consideration of principles, appreciations, and values, as well as the more objective, concrete elements in the culture.

There is little doubt that the school will take on increased responsibility in this matter. The process of acculturation must be fostered in every child; and, through a fortuitous combination of choice and default, the school stands to be in on the assignment. But a serious note of caution is in order. The very fact that many of the concepts are intangible and highly abstract presents a strong temptation to promote them on a verbal level of communication. *And this is deadly.* Principles, appreciations, and values must be taught by allowing the child to practice them *directly;* they cannot be taught by rote or preachment. A youngster may possibly take for granted that his cultural heritage is exclusively the stock in trade of the previous generation; and, in seeking to identify with his peers, he may break too sharply with the generation of his parents and inadvertently tear himself from the cultural benefits as well.

It is essential, therefore, that every child be helped to associate *with* the culture. He must have a chance to relive to some extent the experience of the race and to discover through his own resources the desirability of certain qualities. There is no point in lamenting that the culture is full of conflicts, contradictions, and double standards that cannot be explained away. The child is likely unaware that many of the very inequities that he questions today were also questioned by his parents and grandparents. He must have opportunity to confront these discrepancies firsthand and to understand that the conflicts and contradictions *themselves* are a real part of his culture. But he must also see that the very notion of change is a cherished cultural value. He needs to sense a basic lack of agreement as to values among various subcultures. He needs to develop the honesty and capacity to look objectively at his own culture even as he examines the inner consistencies and inner contradictions of a foreign culture, and, with genuine respect for each, to realize the similarities and differences. A realistic purpose of education is for every child to experience personally the anguish and the rapture of culture discovery.

For Every Child: Basic Intellectual Development

It would be difficult to imagine any list of purposes of education that did not emphasize development of the child's intellectual potentialities. Acquiring worthwhile knowledge, cultivating attitudes, building skills in communication, improving research and problem solving techniques, fostering critical thinking, promoting creativity, and shaping disciplined thought processes are a few of the highly desirable goals that come immediately to mind when we speak of strengthening the higher mental powers. Most curriculum planners would agree that developing the intellect is the single most important job of the school. A few might even go so far as to insist that it constitutes the school's *only* legitimate task. Certainly, in terms of the several responsibilities distributed among the various educational agencies in society, the intellectual function is most uniquely the school's.

While the advancement of civilization has always hinged closely upon the degree of intellectual vigor in a society, the contingency is definitely becoming more direct and more absolute. Both individual need and societal requirement dictate an increased incidence of cognitive behavior. The approaching dilemma of limited natural resources and rising human aspirations will certainly challenge the all-out effort of our best trained minds. Social, political, and economic factors are multiplying the complications of a maze of sensitive interconnections. And every day adds significantly to the world's dependence upon the unfathomed complexities of a mushrooming technology that calls for numerous kinds and vast quantities of data to be created, organized, stored, retrieved, and evaluated. If mankind is to enjoy the good life, it must pay the price; and a part of that very high price is developing the intellectual powers of every person.

For more than a decade, the expression "knowledge explosion" has been standard in our language. And this is more than just a clever figure of speech, for the rate of acquiring new scientific and technological information, which took a sharply upward turn in approximately 1945, has been accelerating ever since. This truly amazing fact has been so profusely reiterated during recent years that its further restating causes more mouths to drop open in yawns than in astonishment. Nevertheless, the knowledge explosion, a solid fact of life, bears directly upon educational decision making.

Recent reports from various fields of research and development indicate that, at the moment, the total volume of scientific and technological information is doubling and redoubling in periods ranging from eight to fifteen years (depending upon the field and the particular report). This phenomenal growth has two obvious implications for the school curriculum. First, a child just beginning school confronts a world containing twice as much knowledge, at least scientific and technological knowledge, than the individual now completing high school faced at that age. In the second place, the graduate, even before he reaches the age of thirty, will be living and working with ideas and concepts that were totally unknown when he was a student. Such conditions obviously render the traditional approach to curriculum obsolete and even ridiculous. The simple additive method of curriculum planning, in which new requirements are quietly tacked onto the list of those already in effect, will no longer suffice—if, indeed, it ever did. Yet we continue to hear the suggestion that newer conditions demand that the child achieve *more* and *more.* In fact, several popular innovations in recent years have been promulgated on precisely the grounds that they would speed up the child's learning rate *in order that he might assimilate greater quantities of information in a given period of time.* Certainly, there is nothing wrong with forthright efforts to make learning more efficient. But the idea that the learner can continue indefinitely to learn faster and faster and, thereby, soak up more and more and more information in order—somehow—to stay abreast of a growing mountain of knowledge is utterly preposterous. And it is as pointless as gorging oneself into misery at a banquet merely because there is plenty of food.

Fortunately, there are better ways of handling knowledge than simply swallowing it whole. The intellectual development of that child who will be properly equipped to live effectively in his present and future world must be approached systematically. There must be much more selectivity in what the child is expected to master and in how he will be encouraged to go about mastering it. Taba has suggested that knowledge has a sort of hierarchical arrangement of several strata, the lowest and most basic being simple, raw facts, processes, and skills. The second level is a systematic formation of related facts that constitute principles or basic ideas which provide consistency or structure. A third stratum is made up of more complex relationships that form highly abstract concepts. And, at the very top, are the integrating thought systems that render the whole conglomerate viable.[1] Exploring this structural arrangement a bit, it should seem reasonable that the learner not spend all of his effort at the very lowest level of knowledge. While some raw facts are definitely requisite, the essential element in the mastery of knowledge is to gain insight into the pattern and predictability of those interrelationships of integrating thought systems to abstract concepts, of concepts to structural principles, and of principles to simple facts. To understand knowledge and to be able to use it with the sureness that an artisan uses a tool requires that the learner approach it in depth.

The combined effect of various academic disciplines is to embrace the total of the world's accumulated knowledge. Each separate discipline has its unique frame of reference, a peculiar way of regarding phenomena that is shared by the scholars who make up its corps of practitioners. This singular viewpoint results in at least two distinguishing characteristics: first, a recognizable body of knowledge; and, second, a standard repertoire

---

[1]Hilda Taba, *Curriculum Development: Theory and Practice* (New York: Harcourt Brace Jovanovich, Inc., 1962), pp. 175–178.

of procedures and techniques for researching and processing that knowledge.

The traditional school subjects, which were derived from the scholarly disciplines, have been deliberately modified to make them teachable to immature children. Unfortunately, something vital has been lost in the translation. There has been undue attention directed at the unstructured raw facts that constitute the base of the knowledge whole, and too little honest concern for those essential interrelationships of systems of abstract ideas into which the simple facts must be integrated. A serious flaw in the organization of the familiar school subjects has been the tendency to relegate them to a purely receptacle function—to deal with knowledge solely as a finished *product,* and completely to ignore the *process.* If knowledge is to be handled on an intellectual level, it must be a living, growing phenomenon. *It must be happening.*

Much effort of some of the more legitimate subject matter reforms recently introduced into school systems across the country has been devoted to implementing the notions that (1) process and product must be in meaningful balance and that (2) knowledge must be dealt with in terms of structures and interrelationships. These are some of the steps that must be taken if the school is to succeed in helping every child attain basic intellectual development.

For Every Child: A Solid Foundation of Genuine Scholarship—
An Honest Love of Learning

Building a sound foundation of genuine scholarship in every child stands as one of the most important purposes of education, yet relatively few elementary schools over the years have succeeded appreciably. Most schools, it is true, have obviously done very well by a *few* children; but few schools can boast of very remarkable results with *most* children. In past years, perhaps the more limited requirements of society were met adequately by the contributions of a few scholars. But certainly the complex demands of the future—even the immediate future—will call more and more upon the fruits of yet-to-be-developed scholarship. Schools simply cannot rely on fortuitous measures. The development of scholarship in the elementary school must be the rule rather than the exception.

These considerations suggest that the obvious failure of typical elementary curricula to develop real scholarship in every child ought to be a matter of deep concern. What might be done to improve the situation? That the record of the school in regard to scholarship development has been far from impressive is quite apparent. But by no means does this record warrant the drastic action occasionally recommended from some quarters: that the curriculum be "junked." In all fairness, it should also be recognized that the school program may not yet be written off as a total failure, for there have been a few signal successes. And it should not seem unreasonable to assume that some of these successes were because of, rather than in spite of, the not-perfect curriculum.

Perhaps a useful hint on how to proceed in behalf of *every* child may be found in the conditions that seem to have generally obtained in those more singular instances. If some children—even a few—have somehow found the intellectual fare of the curriculum palatable and nourishing, other children may also acquire a taste for it. To speculate briefly upon the school program in terms of its peculiar appeal or lack of it for various children may be helpful.

Many children, including some very bright ones, are simply overwhelmed by the school curriculum. They seem to be slogging uphill through deep mud, carrying noticeable burdens of dead weight. That they ultimately succeed in reaching the top of the grade is by dint of firm discipline and hard work. Some of them master assigned subject matter, receive high marks, and generally are considered good students. But they are not, in any sense, scholars. And their commendable effort to master subject matter is not scholarship but intellectual drudgery. Despite their achievements in acquiring knowledge, these children must be counted among the school's curriculum failures.

The contrast between the study habits of the pupils just described and the approach to learning of that much smaller number of children who truly qualify as scholars is not immediately noticeable. There are bright, ambitious young people in both categories. The difference is much more in the *attitude* toward subject matter than in the degree of mastery of it. Careful observation will reveal that a few children, perhaps only one or two in a sample school group, are not at all awed by the curriculum. Admittedly, these pupils may be no more knowledgeable, intelligent, or hard working than many of their classmates; yet their *feelings* about the learning task are greatly different.

These individuals tend to regard study more as a challenge than as an arbitrarily imposed assignment. They look upon subject matter not as a burden to be laboriously handled, but as consumable material to be used up in the learning process. They seem almost to think of subject matter as having been especially designed for their particular pleasure and benefit. And they view the teacher more as a resource than as a taskmaster. These children are firmly in command of the situation—never at its mercy. There is an obvious zeal for the work. And, upon completion of a given task, far from any sign of relief, there is a nice afterglow—a sort of euphoria mixed with just a twinge of regret that the job has been finished. These children have an honest love of learning. They don't simply *tolerate* learning; they *love* it. And they love learning for itself, not merely for some tangible reward at the end. The pursuit is as valued as the conquest.

Thus, for a relatively few children, the school program has somehow contributed to the development of scholarship. The existing elementary curriculum obviously has much that is commendable. What is desperately needed is an improved curriculum deliberately designed to foster genuine scholarship in *every* child.

Summary

Good elementary education reflects a skillful blending of happiness, scholarship, and subject matter. In view of present and future requirements for effective living, developing genuine scholarship in every child ought to be the main concern of curriculum planners. Unfortunately, scholarship has been equated with subject matter. And, while subject matter obviously constitutes a necessary curriculum ingredient, the real essence of scholarship lies fully as much in the pursuit of knowledge as in the mastery of it. The satisfaction and joy of the learning experience are at least as important as what is learned. A reasonable degree of knowledgeableness and an unabashed love of learning are the sine qua non of scholarship. It is regrettable that circumstances in the historical development of American education have inadvertently screened out much of the vitality from the elementary curriculum to leave an inert residue of subject matter content and an image of the elementary school as a generally dull, uncompromising institution. While some notable achievements in mastery of knowledge have been realized, it must be admitted that, on the whole, both scholarship and happiness are conspicuously missing.

The underlying philosophy of an education system must be in tune with the basic tenets of the society. Cultural values ought to be identified in school purposes and nurtured through the curriculum. Because the individual has traditionally held an exalted position in our democratic society, programs of education must promote the development of individuality. The young child must form an appropriate individual-to-society relationship. The individual must behave in ways that conform reasonably to cultural expectations and requirements. Some learning experiences are intended primarily for the well-being of society rather than directly for individual self-fulfillment. An effective elementary curriculum, therefore, will reveal a balanced concern for purposes that stem both from individual needs and societal needs.

Individual needs may be considered in terms of personal maturity: a convenient frame of reference for regarding the proper degree of readiness of the individual to respond effectively, and to his own ultimate satisfaction, to various conditions within his environment. Four important aspects of total maturity useful in identifying individual needs are:

1. Physical maturity.
2. Intellectual maturity.
3. Emotional maturity.
4. Social maturity.

Although individual and societal needs are not necessarily in conflict, society is motivated by certain selfish interests, particularly in respect to its own survival. Identified as societal needs are:

1. Maintaining basic social and political institutions.
2. Preservation of the culture.
3. Economic development.
4. Health and welfare.
5. Safety and defense.

There are two principal sources of purposes of education: first, the identification of certain human needs—either individual or societal; and, second, the malleability of human behavior. In specifying purposes, therefore, it is important to focus particularly upon these aspects of need which might best be satisfied through predictable behavior changes. Since education is a true form of growth and development and is, therefore, a highly individualized process, such aims should be stated in terms of attainability by each individual pupil. Five major purposes which meet the criteria are established as basic to effective elementary curriculum. The following are essential and applicable in the education of every child:

1. Self-identity and self-realization.
2. The desire and ability to live and work effectively with others.
3. An understanding and appreciation of the cultural values.
4. Basic intellectual development.
5. A solid foundation of genuine scholarship—an honest love of learning.

Chapter Two

Relationship of
Case-Action Learning
to Subject Matter

Fundamental purposes of education don't change appreciably. Sometimes specific aspects of one or more goals may seem especially crucial, but the actual long-range aims endure. The five basic purposes of elementary education identified in Chapter One are appropriate to any time, season, and place. How these purposes may be implemented through the elementary curriculum is a demanding challenge.

The long story of curriculum in the American elementary school has been revealed in part by the swing and counterswing of the pendulum from subject-centeredness to child-centeredness and back again. Many of these changes have occurred with about the same frequency and fervor as new trends in women's fashions—and often, it might appear, with the same depth of commitment. While there has been a great deal of change, we really can point to little in the way of revolution. Perhaps even more than we prefer to admit, there has been a tendency toward faddism. Certainly, fresh ideas in curriculum are not promulgated capriciously, but rather with a reasonable expectation that some observable improvement will result. Nevertheless, it is difficult to view the pageant in retrospect without a disheartening realization that the fads have come and gone—possibly to return at some later time.

No one need argue that schools ought to keep abreast of the times. Vibrant, propulsive curricula in tune with a world on the move are obviously necessary. In education programs, as in other aspects of modern living, ready adaptability is essential to vitality and relevance. But there is also a very good case to be made for stability. Change merely for the sake of change has no legitimate bearing upon curriculum selection. Of course, it would be equally serious to claim too much for the "eternal verities." However, while certain components of curriculum development do involve truly phenomenal change, certain other considerations call for hardly any change at all.

Resolving the Unresolvable

Opposing arguments as to the relative merits of a subject-directed focus versus a child-centered orientation remain largely unresolved in most elementary school curricula. Interestingly, there are few, if any, differences in the basic purposes that have prompted each of the contradicting lines of reason. The chief concern of the elementary school has traditionally been the intellectual development of the child. Both camps of protagonists generally subscribe to this end. It is principally in the means for attaining this mutually regarded aim that opinions differ.

Making Knowledge Teachable

In its pure state, knowledge is not easily assimilated by the immature learner; rather, it must be specially prepared for his sensitive intellectual digestive system. The world's accumulated knowledge is comprised within the various scholarly disciplines, which are not particularly teachable in their unadulterated forms. As mentioned earlier, a discipline is distinguished by an esoteric point of view held by its corps of practitioners. Out of this, two basic characteristics develop: a recognizable body of knowledge, and a peculiar system of techniques and procedures for researching and storing that knowledge. Each of the school subjects is an outcome of deliberate efforts by educators to modify certain aspects of one or more of the scholarly disciplines to render them teachable to young children.

In order for the unsophisticated learner to gain initial insight into the fascinating intricacies of a particular discipline, some adjustment in the meticulous regimen of that field of knowledge must, of genuine necessity, be allowed. But a disturbing question is posed: *Just how much should a discipline be modified for the sake of the learner?* This is the point at which opinions begin to separate. And there are valid arguments leading to both extremes.

The Subject or the Child?

On the one hand, a highly disciplinary frame of reference more nearly approximates the scholar's own precise confrontation with knowledge. According to this view, the intellectual probity of dealing forthrightly with facts, principles, and concepts in an authentic relationship yields important satisfactions for the learner and contributes significantly to a systematic convergence upon key elements in the knowledge structure. Proponents of this line of reasoning tend to regard curriculum as an arrangement whereby pertinent knowledge is presented honestly and attractively—even proudly —in a sequence and at a rate that can be handled by the child. That the learner, with his obvious lack of experiential background, must make a considerable effort to project himself into incumbency with the necessary level of abstractness is accepted as a calculated risk. The alternative, it is felt, would neutralize the content and dissolve the structure. Consistent with these considerations are high priority for the intellectual function of the school and a working philosophy supporting a subject-centered cur-riculum.

In almost diametrical opposition is an equally strong conviction that, in curriculum matters, the nature of the child is· of infinitely greater mo-ment than the nature of knowledge. Thus, mastering knowledge is not so much a matter of responding to a bill of specifications for the material to be learned as an advent in the growth and development of the individual. According to this viewpoint, school learning experiences should be con-templated more in terms of satisfying intellectual wants of the learner than in relation to the particulars of the knowledge to be achieved. Curriculum planning is mainly a matter of determining specific educational needs of the individual pupil and attending to these needs through the provision of suitable learning opportunities. This approach, which fundamentally calls for marshalling subject matter to meet learner demand, sharply contrasts with the assumption that the learner be expected to conform to the pecu-liar conditions of subject matter. While some inevitable deterioration of knowledge content and structure will result from the change of focus, the more zealous advocates firmly believe that the few hazards are overshad-owed by the several benefits in other respects. Clearly, the impetus sug-gested is toward a learning-oriented, psychologically responsive program. Philosophically, this position favors a child-centered curriculum.

Thus, in essence, we have two extreme points of view. Each has been challenged and cross-examined on numerous occasions in repeated efforts to resolve the issue satisfactorily. The major difficulty in uniting these widely separated positions has not come from any particular weakness in the evidence presented on either side. Rather, the dilemma has been in the very fact that *both* arguments have been consistently strong and valid in their basic assumptions. In plumping for a logical plan of curriculum to preserve the integrity of knowledge—a plan just slightly removed from the "respectability" of the scholarly disciplines—the advocates of subject-centeredness have been on solid footing. But the proponents of a psychologically based, learning-oriented approach have been equally well grounded in pointing out genuine merit in "beginning where the child is." Despite the clear indication, however, that each of the opposing theories —in its own special way—has been fundamentally sound, generally a compromised, less-than-dynamic elementary curriculum has been maintained intermittently at various points along a continuum between the two. As yet, there has not been any wholly satisfactory resolution.

No Compromise

Compromising between a subject-directed, logically plotted departure and a child-centered, learning-focused development may not actually constitute the most intelligent approach to curriculum. In fact, it may be something akin to debating whether an automobile needs both an engine and a full set of wheels. The nature of the child and the nature of knowledge are *both* vital considerations in building an effective education program. Scholarship requires simultaneously a fair mastery of pertinent knowledge and a ready facility to use that knowledge voluntarily in ways that are personally satisfying and individually enhancing. A middle-of-the-road compromise between child-centered and knowledge-centered approaches is fundamentally weak and ineffective because it is an honest representation of neither. Such a two-way concession, being basically subject matter oriented, is limited in the degree to which it can be adapted to the individual learner. And, since it is considerably watered down from the original disciplinary substantiveness, it does not provide a sharp insight into subject matter.

The underlying thesis of this book is that there ought not be any compromise between the stringent requirements of substantial subject matter and the felt needs of a growing child. Both points are valid, and both must be retained—somehow—as legitimate guidelines in the elementary curriculum. Therefore, a dual approach is recommended: first, from a psychological or child-centered reference; second, from a logical or disciplinary direction. These two avenues should not be compromised, but rather maintained as separate and discrete. The significance of the relation-ship between the two will be realized by the child himself—in his own way and in his own good time.

Rationale for a Dual Approach
to Elementary Curriculum

The philosophy of a dual approach to elementary curriculum has virtually nothing in common with the idea of compromise. In a compromise, the truly distinguishing aspects are flattened into a neutral blend that neither excites nor really satisfies. Quite conversely, however, a dual approach deliberately accents contrasts and peculiarities. The unique and distinctive advantages inherent in each of the principal orientations are boldly fea-tured—without apology or compensation.

Advantages of a Disciplinary Approach

Of the several valid reasons for establishing a strong disciplinary base in dealing with curriculum development, perhaps the most impelling is that a child is *entitled* to the benefits of such an approach. The accumulated knowledge of the race is a part of the inheritance of every person. And, by virtue of membership in the human corporation, each child is autho-rized a realistic confrontation with this birthright. As he achieves the necessary readiness, it becomes his undisputed right to have access to those organized and systematized caches of knowledge that are contained within the disciplines.

Other good reasons may be cited for operating from a formalized reference. For example, there are definite economies in a straightforward introduction to organized knowledge. Obviously, the learner cannot re-structure every principle and every concept from scratch. Many of the sophisticated abstractions must be made easily available or the individual will be unduly hampered in his efforts. A knowledge-oriented emphasis may contribute to efficiency in learning.

Such an approach provides a clear view of a disciplinary area in its relatively unadulterated form. While a very young child probably cannot achieve a working relationship with a discipline in its absolutely pure state, he can at least become familiar with a modified, minimally-distorted ver-sion. Since mastery of knowledge is one of the respectable outcomes of learning activities, it is helpful if the child develops a pleasant face-to-face acquaintanceship with a knowledge field at an early age.

Also—and, again, rather early in his lifelong career of becoming educated—the young learner should have opportunity to develop understanding and appreciation of the unique content and structure of various academic disciplines. If he works with subject matter that still retains much of the original flavor and distinctive characteristics of the disciplinary areas from which it was derived, he may quite possibly be better equipped to relate one scholarly field to another and to realize the shadings in techniques of research and details of classifying and recording. Knowing something of the fascination and beauty of each of the disciplines is often one of the keys to intellectual achievement and scholarly behavior.

As stated in the preceding chapter, every elementary pupil will, hopefully, have opportunity to develop a solid foundation of genuine scholarship. An essential part of this achievement is a level of knowledgeableness in at least one area to enable the child to *use* that knowledge toward self-selected ends and in ways that are personally satisfying. An additional benefit of a disciplinary approach, therefore, is that it may contribute toward a degree of mastery in a particular field of knowledge to enhance its acceptability as an object of scholarly behavior.

These are some of the important arguments for including a disciplinary approach as one of the two major orientations in elementary curriculum. Further substantiation, no doubt, could be arrayed to bolster the case, but the five reasons given may be sufficient:

1.   A child is *entitled* to an honest confrontation with knowledge.

2.   A straightforward introduction to organized knowledge contributes to efficiency in learning.

3.   Such an approach provides a clear view of a disciplinary area in its relatively unadulterated form.

4.   A knowledge-based reference leads to understanding and appreciation of the unique content and structure of each of various academic disciplines.

5.   A disciplinary approach contributes to mastery of knowledge in a particular field to make it acceptable as an object of scholarly behavior.

Advantages of a Child-Centered
and Learning-Oriented Approach

Some aspects of elementary curriculum plainly call for a candid alignment with actualities of the learning process and other psychological considerations. In a child-centered approach, the ultimate value of a particular learning experience lies in the quality of that learning experience per se as it relates directly to the felt needs and personal satisfactions of the learner. Strictly in terms of a learning-oriented reference, accrual of knowledge as such may be considered only a byproduct of the endeavor. Activities in such an uncompromised approach are planned, therefore, not in regard to what a given experience will do for a child, but rather according to *what the child will likely do with that specific learning experience.*

There are several very sound reasons for developing elementary curriculum from this direction. Appropriately heading the list is the oft-demonstrated essentiality of self-esteem. Of all the success determiners, none is more basic or more significant than having respect for, and confidence in, oneself. It is a quiet, but genuine, compliment to the individual to focus upon matters that he himself deems important—a recognition that his ideas are deserving. And it follows—more or less subconsciously—that, if his ideas are good, then he *as a person* must also be worthwhile. The ultimate perquisite is that he will aspire to a commensurate level of personal behavior and achievement. Helping the child to feel good about himself is a vital part of curriculum strategy.

A particularly fascinating aspect of maturity is the growth from selfishness to selflessness—an essential part of effective social living at all echelons. Far too often, however, an unnecessarily weak tack is employed to cajole or coerce a child into a rather nonenunciative selflessness. On occasion, for example, he is urged to "do for others" and to "share." Or perhaps he is admonished not to be greedy or stingy. Certainly, these are marks of maturity. But, to a noticeable extent, they are invoked negatively. They tend more to impinge upon the individual's natural expression than to foster it. Furthermore, such attributes are highly abstract, requiring almost exclusively an intellectual process of assimilation. Fortunately, the elementary school is in an almost ideal situation to contribute toward the development of selflessness in the young child—and in a thoroughly concrete way. During most of every school day, the child is in the physical presence of his peers, each of whom has his own unique demands and offerings to be considered and either accepted or rejected by the group. From a learning-oriented curriculum stance, easy communication among the children may be encouraged, and the insight of each into the potential strength of the commonality may be sharpened, thereby creating the essential opportunity for every child to relate his own individual needs and satisfactions with those of his classmates. Thus, he may be privileged to mature into an outgoing selflessness that emerges gradually out of a growing self-realization that giving of oneself to one's group brings personal satisfaction—a second realistic argument for a child-centered focus upon curriculum.

A third good reason for a learning-oriented approach is that it affords occasion for relating nonschool experiences with school experiences. Actually, a child is *out* of school during a typical calendar year about seven times as many total hours as he is *in* school. In view of this, the importance of relating inschool activities in a realistic and meaningful way with out-of-school experiences becomes clearly significant. For, while it is by no means a *cross section* of life, schooling most certainly is a special part of life that must be viewed with respect to all other aspects of daily living. Otherwise, education loses all relevance. Deliberately building inschool learning experiences around considerations that pertain equally to the child's ongoing out-of-school affairs helps him to perceive formal education in true perspective. Thus, rather than regarding school as being separate—even insulated—from the rest of life, the individual tends more to assume that it is an environment of specially arranged opportunities that render all of his experiences, both in and out of school, more worthwhile and more satisfying. A learning-oriented approach ties in the nonschool aspects of life more closely with the purposes of school, and relates the curriculum of the school more realistically with the purposes of life.

Centering curriculum upon the nature of the child also enables the learner to identify areas of immediate personal concern. This becomes increasingly important as the ultimate significance of formal education becomes greater. The lengthening period of years of school attendance and the growing complexity of the world to which the individual must relate are indicative of the evolving difficulty of coming personally to grips with real issues at an early age. Of course, as the child gains in maturity, he is better able to postpone active involvement in matters of keen interest and concern. And many aspects of education do necessitate the putting off of confrontation until some later time. But a child's entire education need not be premised upon waiting. Some ventures ought to be undertaken immediately. The gusto of being fully committed personally to something genuine and important cannot be simulated. There simply is no substitute for the real and the now.

Engaging regularly in truly satisfying learning experiences ought to be a standard feature of every pupil's agenda. And every reasonable effort should be made to increase the likelihood that the most favorable condition will prevail. Certainly, a child-centered approach constitutes a necessary part of that effort. In concentrating freely upon felt needs of the individual, and in striving creatively for the means whereby such needs might best be attended, such an approach is deliberate and to the point. Providing genuinely satisfying learning experiences for every child is one more sound reason for a basically psychological consideration of curriculum.

Possibly last, but certainly not least, of the advantages of a child-centered and learning-oriented curriculum posture is the development of an abiding love of learning as an end in itself. As suggested earlier, the two essentials of true scholarship are a certain level of knowledgeableness and a love of learning for its own sake—a nice summation of the full rationale for a dual approach to elementary curriculum. Subject matter study is, of course, expected to provide the necessary command of knowledge. But the other half of the sine qua non of scholarship lies deep in the *feelings* of the learner toward learning *as such*—toward learning as an activity that is worthwhile *in and of itself.* It is principally an emotional, rather than an intellectual, development. In terms of real, lifelong scholarship, the intensity of this predisposition to love of learning is a considerable factor. Just *tolerating* learning efforts or mildly *enjoying* learning as an activity will not suffice; it must be a passionate love of learning. And, since it is mainly emotional, it must be developed as any other aspect of emotional growth: subtly, consistently, and unhurriedly. A strong and lasting love of learning results not from one or two satisfying learning efforts, but rather from a great many personally gratifying experiences over an extended period of time. A curriculum should be deliberately designed to produce a preponderance of self-fulfillment. An uncompromised child-focused, learning-for-the-sake-of-learning reference is called for.

To complement the arguments supporting a disciplinary point of view, and further to demonstrate the potentialities of a dual approach to elementary curriculum, six distinct advantages of a child-centered and learning-oriented approach can be identified:

1. Developing self-esteem is essential to personality and behavioral growth.

2. Each child must be helped to relate his own needs and satisfactions with those of his group.

3. Every child must be enabled to relate nonschool experiences with school experiences.

4. There must be opportunity for every child to identify areas of immediate, personal concern.

5. Engaging in genuinely satisfying learning experiences is a necessary part of every child's education.

6. Developing an abiding love of learning as an end in itself is basic to scholarship.

Achieving Purposes of Elementary Education Through Subject Matter

The intent at this point is not to suggest a detailed, foolproof scheme for presenting elementary school subjects, but to demonstrate that neither child nor subject need be sacrificed or compromised. Both disciplinary and child orientations may be realistically implemented.

In a dual approach to elementary curriculum, the clear emphasis of subject matter ought to be focused upon mastery of knowledge as a desirable and worthwhile end. To the extent that it is feasible, therefore, the selection and organization of content should harmonize with the structure of those particular disciplines from which it is drawn. Scope and sequence must be determined from a logical reference; and, although other legitimate aims should not be overlooked, educational purpose may be stated mainly in terms of intellectual development.

Ideally, the child's early encounters with the preciseness and rigor of formalized knowledge ought to approximate as closely as possible the scholar's own positive, yet reverent, occupation with the peculiar fascination of his respective discipline. This suggests a regard for subject matter that clearly transcends practical application. The much more profound implication is for an unequivocal valuing of knowledge, nor merely for its usefulness, but *purely for its own sake.* To effect this considerable attainment, a subject must be undertaken in some "respectable" depth and at a pace that permits the savoring of what is being experienced. Too great an emphasis upon the "tool" function of content, or a hurried, superficial attack that reflects overconcern for some intermediate objective, such as "covering the material," cannot possibly yield the desired results. Rather, a child must be helped to look for structure as well as content, and to view the intriguing interrelationships of the matter as he would the intricacies of an exciting new game. It is also highly important that essential process and product aspects of knowledge be kept in good balance at all levels of learning.

These criteria for effective subject matter indicate a need for programs that are a far cry from the generally shortsighted approaches of traditional curricula, with their typically narrow preoccupation with content in its applied, or "practical," form. It is indeed fortunate, therefore, that many of the newer school subject reforms that are now in the innovative stage nationally have been designed deliberately to promote these important ends. While certain subject reforms have been overstated in terms of *total* educational benefits, certainly many of the programs show real merit in regard specifically to knowledge mastery and intellectual achievement.

Some modification from the pure disciplines is basic to rendering organized knowledge teachable, but a firm caution against going too far in the direction of accommodating the psychological considerations is definitely called for. Substantial, logically ordered subject matter must be made available to every child as an integral part of his curriculum.

Achieving Purposes of Elementary Education Through Case-Action Learning

A basic condition of curriculum development is that achievement of educational aims requires a suitable vehicle by which good intentions may be transferred systematically to actual learning experiences. Since a dual approach is a forthright attempt to give uncompromised support to each of two distinctively different curriculum references, it reasonably follows that each of the widely separated viewpoints necessitates its own particular means of providing this service. While school subjects may be used effectively in bringing about the proper degree of substantiality in terms of a knowledge-based consideration, a medium of singular design is needed to carry the unique expectations of child-centered and learning-oriented aspects of curriculum to fruition. Just as a logical grounding and an outright veneration of knowledge are fully consistent with the special function of subject matter, so must a psychological foundation and a frank emphasis upon personally gratifying experiences be seen to apply in the second instance. Specifically, the demand is for a workable, manageable, and effective way of deliberately planning school-based learning activities around the felt needs and personal satisfactions of each child. Thus, a distinctive curriculum approach definitely calls for a distinctive means of implementation. The recommended answer that will be discussed at length in this book is termed *case-action learning.*

Characteristics of Case-Action Learning

Case-action learning, as the term suggests, is a significant learning experience that grows naturally out of a "case" which is taken on voluntarily by a group of children and then developed and ultimately closed as a direct result of the concerted action of the learners themselves.

Case-action learning is a *total* response to challenge that is neither confined to, nor restricted by, subject matter lines in any way. Although it definitely belongs to none of the subject areas, it may, in a given situation, include content from any or all of the various subject matter fields. In this particular respect, it bears a striking, but superficial, resemblance to what some curriculum planners have called "unified" learning activities. The philosophical predication, however, is quite different. The intent of unified experiences is to draw together certain useful elements of knowledge from two or more subject matter areas by way of making them more personally meaningful to the child. Thus, unified study is fundamentally subject-oriented with a generous overture to the more obvious attributes of child-centeredness. In fact, the very word "unified" connotes a bringing together of entities or considerations that are basically discrete. Case-action learning, by sharp contrast, is developed completely apart from any concern for subject matter or logical ordering of content.

Case-action learning is derived carefully, but without apology or concealment, from the child's own purposes—including some of his deepest concerns and most heartfelt intentions. If the individual is in this way provided with opportunity to engage in a genuine pursuit of his own interests, it is immaterial whether such purposes are school-related or otherwise. As a matter of fact, at least some of these concerns (or cases) will, hopefully, have an obvious out-of-school origin of which the individual may have become aware through the normal, day-to-day business of growing up in his home and community. The delicate matter of curriculum relevance may be considerably enhanced through the bringing of child-identified, basically nonschool issues into the classroom in a straightforward manner. However, the particular needs and satisfactions that figure in the planning must *in actuality* be those of the child and not something contrived or simulated. To allow any tinge of deception is a surefire method of destroying the potential value of the learning experience. Much of the essence of case-action learning is its fidelity to the child's own point of view.

Another important observation about case-action learning is that children do the work. The significance of this becomes increasingly clear as one considers the degree to which a child is by nature a doer—a normal, healthy child really likes to work. He genuinely enjoys keeping busy— provided, of course, that the nature of the work harmonizes with his own particular interests. It is virtually impossible to resolve the fascinating question as to the place of work in children's free, unsupervised activity: do children work in order to achieve certain objectives that they consider important, or do they create projects in order to provide a legitimate excuse to engage in work? To a great extent, it is through work, especially work of his own choosing, that the individual is able to achieve self-identity and self-realization. Meeting the challenge of personally meaningful work helps him to recognize himself at his best. Making it possible for a child to work at jobs that he deems important also constitutes an excellent means of helping him to appreciate the value of work in general. It is, therefore, especially vital in case-action learning that—within reason, of course—all of the work be done by the children themselves. Furthermore, the children should be encouraged to perform the work in their own peculiar way, inefficient though it may be. Likewise, they need to make their own decisions as an integral aspect of the work, despite the strong likelihood that some of the decisions may be poor ones. It becomes the teacher's role to serve as consultant, guide, and resource person.

Another characteristic of case-action learning is that each venture is planned and executed as a complete package. Each case is a fairly inclusive undertaking; it has a definite beginning and a definite ending; and it is begun and ended within a period of relatively high interest on the part of the children who are participating in it. A given case must include neither too much nor too little; it must be commensurate with the capacity of the learners. There must be enough of substance to satisfy, but not to glut.

Other things being equal, the duration of a case planned for older and more mature pupils may be proportionately greater than one designed for younger children. At the kindergarten level, for example, a given case might typically be carried on with good interest for several days, while the considerably greater maturity of a group at the grade five or grade six level might make it profitable to continue for as long as five or six weeks. The crucial point is that the whole endeavor must be carried through from start to finish while enthusiasm is high. There must be no attitude of indifference or feeling of going on indefinitely with something; the end must be clearly in sight. In essence, then, a design for case-action learning calls for a group of children to identify a mutual concern, become interested enough to do something definite about that concern, and enjoy the sense of satisfaction that results from the effort and the completion of a specific undertaking.

The educational value of case-action learning—in diametric opposition to subject matter study—is determined almost exclusively by the quality of the learning experience *as such,* not necessarily by the worth of the content that is learned in the process. Almost inevitably valuable knowledge will be gained, even incidentally, through this approach, just as enjoyable and satisfying learning experiences might be achieved through efforts to master subject matter. However, accrual of knowledge is really a *by-product* of case-action learning, not an ultimate end. Precisely the opposite emphases, of course, obtain in the instance of subject matter study—a really critical point of differentiation between case-action learning and subject matter study, and a fine distinction that should be clearly understood.

A final observation to round out a working definition of case-action learning concerns objectives of typical undertakings. A particular case may be a work project, a problem-solving effort, an attempt to get information, or any combination of these.

The work project type of case may be most like some of the unsupervised activities of children in a residential neighborhood: clearing a vacant lot for a ball field, building a clubhouse, putting on a backyard circus, or staging a puppet show. The work project corresponds closely to the sort of endeavors customarily undertaken by the community at large in response to identified public needs: planning and building a civic center, constructing a new freeway, carrying out a citywide cleanup campaign, or coordinating a united fund drive. Quite similarly, a work project instigated by a group of elementary children brings about some definite accomplishment that the children themselves have set as a worthwhile objective. A case might be developed, for example, in response to a genuine desire to collect clothing to be sent to children in an overseas "adopted" school, to beautify the school grounds, or to raise money for the purchase of a black leopard for the local zoo. The work project is fundamentally a matter of identifying something concrete that needs to be done, then doing it.

Problem solving (despite frequent references in the literature as to its supposedly universal appropriateness) actually presents fewer really feasible opportunities than does the work project type of case. While problem solving techniques are vital to effective living, human activity is by no means a solid round of solving problems. Most aspects of living, both in and out of school, are handled rather routinely. In a sense, actually, it is the very infrequency of demand that renders a given situation a problem. The point here is not to depreciate the problem solving case, but rather to indicate the futility of forcing a problem where, in fact, none may exist. In the event, however, of an actual problem—which directly affects the children—that can be identified by the group and a solution attempted, a truly outstanding learning experience may result.

Not too surprisingly, most ventures in case-action learning will undoubtedly continue to develop around attempts to obtain specific kinds of information. The likelihood of this is underscored significantly when one considers the ratio of vicarious learning to firsthand experience, not merely in school, but in all aspects of daily living. Basically, the information getting case is a systematic encouragement of the incessant question asking that seems to be such an inherent trait of early childhood. But older children also have genuine need to ask questions. The apparently insatiable curiosity of children would seem to insure an endless list of ideas that children want to explore and things that they want to "find out about." It should be expected, therefore, that most case-action designs will be focused either upon information getting or possibly upon a combination of information getting and work project or problem solving.

Summary of Characteristics

Thus case-action learning can be defined and further identified by the following characteristics:

1.   Case-action learning is a *total* response to challenge that is not confined to, or restricted by, subject matter lines. It belongs to no subject matter area, but may include content from any or all subject matter fields.

2.   Case-action learning is derived from children's own purposes.

3.   In case-action learning, children do the work. They do it in their own way. They make their own decisions. The teacher is consultant, guide, and resource person.

4.   Each undertaking in case-action learning is planned and executed as a complete package. That is, it is a fairly inclusive learning experience with a definite beginning and a definite ending. It is begun and ended within a

period of relatively high interest on the part of the children. It must include neither too much nor too little.

5.   The educational value of case-action learning—in diametric opposition to subject matter study—is determined by the quality of the learning experience *as such*, not necessarily by the content that is learned. In case-action learning, accrual of knowledge is a *by-product*, not an end.

6.   A particular case may be a work project, a problem solving effort, an attempt to get information, or a combination of any of these.

Relating Case-Action Learning and Subject Matter

Case-action learning and subject matter study ought to be precisely complementary. Between them, most of the identified purposes of elementary education may be attained in the curriculum. The ultimate benefits of a dual approach are realized in the degree to which the distinctive characteristics of each of these basic orientations are fully integrated into the behavioral growth of the individual child. The essential relationship between case-action learning and subject matter study must be developed by the learner himself on the basis of his personal efforts in each of the major curriculum aspects. The two approaches are mutually supportive: success in the one serves as incentive for greater effort in the other. While personally gratifying experiences in case-action learning whet the intellectual appetite for further knowledge, achievement in subject matter provides needed enrichment to enhance the quality of child-centered activities. The end result, of course, is the building in every child of that true scholarship that comes inevitably through the delicate articulation of mastery of pertinent knowledge and a frank and honest love of learning for its own sake. It is vital, therefore, that both approaches be featured boldly—yet in proper balance.

It is difficult to indicate with any exactness just what might constitute a proper balance of case-action learning and subject matter study in the curriculum of a particular elementary school. In fact, probably every situation is unique; numerous variables render a pat formula unworkable in specific circumstances. Pending a more accurate method of determining an effective ratio of case-action learning to subject matter in a given instance, the considered judgment of the respective faculty and supervisory staff will have to suffice. There are, however, certain helpful generalizations that may be made:

1.   Every elementary pupil, to some degree, needs both case-action learning and subject matter study. It follows, therefore, that every elementary school ought to feature to some extent both approaches in every section and at every level.

2.   In general, younger and less mature children have greater need for case-action learning than do those who are older and more mature.

3.   Conversely, older and more mature pupils have a proportionately higher capacity for subject matter study than do younger and less mature children.

4.   As a rule, children with culturally poor backgrounds are particularly in need of the compensatory benefits of case-action learning experiences.

5.   Children from culturally rich backgrounds are, on the whole, better able to confront the rigors of subject matter study than are culturally deprived youngsters.

6.   While a carefully determined proportioning of the two approaches is highly desirable, the actual amount of school time devoted to case-action learning and the particular pattern of scheduling it are not, in themselves, especially crucial. Varying circumstances may result in greater or lesser amounts of time being available. Absolutely vital, however, is the utter frankness and the complete honesty of whatever is undertaken, whether it be much or little.

Summary

Opposing arguments as to the relative merits of subject-centeredness versus child-centeredness remain largely unresolved in most elementary school curricula. Since knowledge in its pure state is not easily assimilated by the immature learner, some adjustment in the formalized regimen of each knowledge field must be allowed. The question is: Just how much should a discipline be modified for the sake of the learner? There are strong and valid arguments for approaching elementary curriculum according to both the nature of the child and the nature of knowledge. As yet, the two extremes have not been resolved wholly satisfactorily. Rather, a compromised, less-than-dynamic elementary curriculum has been maintained somewhere between the opposing views.

The underlying thesis of this book is that there ought not be any compromise between the requirements of substantial subject matter and the felt needs of a growing child. Both points are valid, and both must be retained. Therefore, a dual approach is recommended: first, from a psychological or child-centered reference; and, second, from a logical or disciplinary direction. The two approaches, rather than being compromised, should be maintained separately and discretely. Five distinct advantages of a disciplinary approach and six advantages of a child-centered and learning-oriented approach have been presented in this chapter.

In a dual approach to curriculum, the clear emphasis of subject matter ought to be focused upon mastery of knowledge as a desirable and worthwhile end. Knowledge is valued, not merely for its usefulness, but also purely for its own sake. The child must be helped to look for structure as well as content, and to consider both process and product aspects. These criteria suggest that traditional subject matter curricula have been short-sighted and narrow. It is fortunate, therefore, that many of the school subject reforms now in the innovative stage have been designed to promote these important ends. Substantial, logically ordered subject matter must be made available to every child as an integral part of his curriculum.

While school subjects may be used effectively in bringing about the proper degree of substantiality in terms of a knowledge-focused consideration, a medium of singular design is needed to carry the unique expectations of child-centered and learning-oriented aspects of curriculum to fruition. Specifically, what is required is a workable, manageable, and effective way of deliberately planning school-based learning activities around the felt needs and personal satisfactions of each child. The recommended answer is termed case-action learning; a significant learning experience that grows naturally out of a "case" which is taken on voluntarily by a group of children, developed, and ultimately closed as a direct result of the concerted action of the learners themselves.

Case-action learning and subject matter study ought to be precisely complementary. The essential relationship between the two approaches must be developed by the learner himself, the end result being the building of true scholarship. Both approaches, therefore, should be featured boldly and in proper balance.

Part TWO

A Design
for
Case-Action Learning

Love of learning is a mutual affair.

Chapter Three

Group Action
by the Case

Case-action learning can be advantageous to any group of children whose love for research, study, and hard work is less fervent than it might be. And, at one time or another, this might apply to most of the school population. Participating enthusiastically in an interesting case can also provide occasion and incentive for a child to develop more functional human relations and specific social skills. Struggling together with several classmates in lively pursuit of a mutually identified objective can do much for an individual's self-respect and his regard for others.

While some young persons may seem to have a more crucial requirement than others for the special dividends of pupil-centered group endeavors, virtually all of them can profit from at least occasional learning-oriented undertakings. Emotionally or socially immature children, of course, have particular need for the nonthreatening growth opportunities afforded by such ventures. The same approach, however, can be equally helpful for those well adjusted, but chronologically young, pupils who have not as yet formed a viable personal relationship with subject matter. Low achievers who have become conditioned to repeated failure, as well as high achievers whose intellectual curiosity has been jaded by too steady a diet of the three Rs, can find renewed inspiration in a change of curriculum thrust. Case-action learning can be of significant relief both to young people from the upper-middle-class neighborhoods who have been shielded too well from hardship and difficulty and to products of the central city who genuinely need to experience inner security and widened horizons. Likewise, children residing in small towns and rural areas, as well as those living in a metropolitan environment, may benefit accordingly.

It should be understood and appreciated that each group action case is truly unique: developed exclusively for and with a definitely identified group of children at a particular time, and never repeated in just the same way with any other group at any other time. Only in a broad sense, therefore, is it proper to refer to any specific case as "typical." However, to the extent that certain elements of various instances of case action are similarly applied, it may be helpful to consider a few undertakings as fairly representative.

The Case of the Foldaway Playhouse

At least five months after the particular case had been closed, most of the children in Mr. Ortega's classroom continued to regard their venture in playhouse building as one of the most satisfying experiences that they had ever had—in school or out. At the time that the job was undertaken, however, it really didn't seem like such a "big thing."

Denton Elementary School was housed in one of the newer and more attractive buildings in the city. Five years earlier, it had been completely rebuilt—from the blueprints up—on the site of the charred rubble of the original plant. The new school was a splendid improvement in the neighborhood and an obvious source of pride among the residents.

The enrollment was drawn from a thin rectangle of houses and apartments that constituted a fairly representative cross section of the city's population, for the school sat precisely on a not-quite-invisible line that separated a typical slice of the central-city environment from the comparative affluence of substantial middle-class homes. Full integration in Denton Elementary School had been achieved quite naturally.

Other facets of integration had also been attempted with some success at Denton. Although organized on a self-contained-classroom pattern, a simple form of nongrading had been practiced since the opening of the new building. In registering a given child in a particular section, the matter of academic achievement was not necessarily the chief concern, since the faculty accommodated to such individual differences *within* the classroom. Rather, the priority factor in assigning a pupil was that of making sure that he would be placed in a group, and with a teacher, who would make him want to do his best—socially, emotionally, *and* intellectually. As a result of this philosophy, every classroom above kindergarten fostered a clutch of girls and boys of various colors, creeds, ages, sizes, and abilities. And, while the classrooms constituted a series of levels that ranged from "little kids" to "big kids," the net differences between adjacent levels were virtually indistinguishable.

Mr. Ortega viewed it as his pleasure to work with one of the more mature of the eighteen groups comprising the school's population. He sincerely liked children, and he enjoyed the daily challenge of teaching. The easy example that he set was inspiring without being preachy; he believed in working hard and playing hard. It was a comfortable relationship in the section—pupil-to-pupil and pupil-to-teacher.

It was in this favorable setting about the first week of November that the notion of building a playhouse came about quite naturally and utterly without fanfare. None of the group could later recall who first had actually said, "Let's build it"; but they did remember that what apparently constituted the original germ of the idea had been carried into the classroom by one of the girls who had visited the kindergarten area where her younger brother was a pupil. She had observed several of his classmates playing house in a space crudely delineated by a bookcase and the back of the piano; and, upon returning to her own group, she had mentioned the incident to several others, commenting something to the effect that "those little kids are so cute."

Sometime later, another child ruminated over the scene that had been reported and wondered aloud why the kindergarten didn't have a "real playhouse." It was then, at Mr. Ortega's suggestion, that three of the group went to Miss Warren, the teacher of the kindergarten in question, and asked her. Her reply was that the school's budget for such things was always limited, and it had been necessary to choose between a playhouse and some other items that the children also enjoyed. She added that a very old playhouse that had been in the room two years earlier had been discarded because it was so badly splintered that the pupils sometimes tore their clothing on it. "However," she sighed, "it would be very nice to have one again."

That was approximately the way it started. One thing led to another as additional members of the group responded in some slight way. Before long playhouses seemed to have a strange fascination even among those whose personal concern for small children was only nominal. During the first few days, no doubt, many of the youngsters would have been astonished at their own show of interest in the matter if they could have viewed themselves in perspective. But the more they mused about it, the more appealing the thought of a playhouse became. Eventually, they could observe the situation coolly and objectively, and declare with complete candor that they wanted to do whatever they could to get a playhouse for the kindergarten children.

Of course, Mr. Ortega was not sitting back during all of this. Basic to his belief in and understanding of children was a personal conviction that doing for others is fundamental to human happiness. He was therefore constantly tuned in on the slightest opportunity for his pupils to make themselves helpful to someone else. The moment that the group showed apparent concern for a playhouse for Miss Warren's class he began—with utmost tenuousness, of course—to encourage them. An "innocuous" remark of his, for instance, led the children to discover that Mrs. Anderson's kindergarten was also without a playhouse. Another of his well-timed hints prompted someone to look through a stack of old magazines for pictures of small children at play to work into a bulletin board display. Also, he arranged for two pupils to visit briefly at a nearby school in which there was known to be a most attractive playhouse in one of the kindergarten rooms. But perhaps the most productive inducement that he subtly cultivated was simply that of permitting the normal course of conversation to continue unabated whenever the playhouse idea came up.

Despite all of the reconnoitering and preliminary probing, it was a bit startling for the children to realize that they had actually committed themselves to the proposition that the kindergarten children ought to have a playhouse. They knew that they were, as of that moment, deeply involved. But just *how* deeply they would not discover until later.

The first plan was that of obtaining a large cardboard box, such as a refrigerator or home freezer carton, cutting a door and windows, and painting the box inside and out. A delegation carried this proposal to Miss Warren and Mrs. Anderson. The children's eagerness made it difficult for the teachers to let them down easily. Certainly, the shipping carton playhouse would be both useful and attractive; but, unfortunately, neither kindergarten room was spacious enough to accommodate the playhouse during periods of nonuse. Would it be possible to cut the box so that it might be folded up between times? The children were not sure. But it was obvious that they had been deflated, even though the two teachers had made a deliberate effort not to cause any hurt feelings.

The best advice discouraged any consideration of cutting up a shipping carton. Several people who claimed to have tried it pointed out that a cardboard box loses much of its strength when the surfaces are separated. But just what to do was a problem. The children inquired, discussed, looked in toy stores for possible answers, and talked to anyone who would listen. But, perhaps surprisingly, the solution came right out of their own group: they would construct the playhouse out of light plywood!

Knowing that Mr. Ortega, in his youth, had worked as a carpenter's helper undoubtedly encouraged the children as they regarded their decision. Miss Warren and Mrs. Anderson were quickly convinced; and they gave the project their unqualified blessing, promising to keep the secret from the kindergarten children so that the finished product could be presented as a surprise gift. The students felt that they were finally on the right track.

Having decided upon a definite course, the children next confronted the necessity of getting themselves properly organized to handle the essential work. Some jobs definitely called for specific skills. Building a plywood playhouse would, quite obviously, be an undertaking in carpentry; and activities of sawing, hammering, and painting came readily to mind. But there would, also, be other exacting responsibilities. The construction design had to be drawn carefully to scale. And, since the group had no funds, they would face difficulty in procuring—at least by honest means—the required materials, including the hardware, paint, and lumber. Also, in view of the requirement that the playhouse be taken apart and put back together, it would be helpful to have a simple set of directions so that the children could assemble it. By general agreement, three committees were appointed: one would proceed with the design, another would begin to procure materials, and the third would assume the task of writing the directions for assembly. Naturally, the committees would need to maintain liaison. Actual construction and painting activities would be handled, when the time came, by all of the children on an availability basis. It was further agreed that, while some school time would be allotted for the work, as much as possible would be taken care of outside of school hours.

Every child had his own task. The committees fell to work without delay. Despite great ability differences within the membership of each subgroup, the efforts were coordinated well. The materials committee began to explore the possibility of finding suitable pieces of wood in the custodian's workshop in the school basement; when this proved to be a false lead, they turned to other likely sources. Members of the design committee had a lot of fun in their initial attempts at architecture, but soon settled down to more serious aspects of the job. Since it was not feasible for the group responsible for the assembly directions to get immediately at the actual writing, they visited the kindergarten rooms, where they acquainted themselves with some of the possible difficulties of communicating with small children.

The work pulsed forward. Each committee developed its own peculiar style, and available periods of time were used efficiently. By the time the basic elements of a suitable design had been blocked out and presented to the class for approval, the "lumber scroungers," had succeeded. Ultimately, their foraging had led them to several lumber yards and a woodworking mill—and at the mill they finally hit their bonanza. The manager had listened to the children's ambitious plans before suggesting that he could probably find "a few scraps." The group returned with an impressive stack of materials loaded on two borrowed wheelbarrows. Obviously, some of the "scraps" were sizable sections of plywood sheets that could well have been sold. Their visit to the mill had been profitable in another respect: one of the employees had directed them to a building contractor who agreed to let some of the boys—but no girls, please—bring their hand tools to a job site the following Saturday morning and retrieve some used hinges and other pieces of hardware from a wooden structure that was being torn down.

Details of the design were soon completed, and assembly directions were being written. The group had received permission from the custodian to use one end of his basement workshop for the construction; sounds of sawing, hammering, and drilling could soon be heard throughout the school. A sign-up sheet had been posted just inside the classroom door; and, whenever a pupil had a few minutes to devote to the project, he simply wrote his name and noted the time of departure and expected return. Good scheduling of available PTA volunteers made it *almost* possible for Mr. Ortega to be "in two places at once" as he made countless trips up and down the basement stairway to keep in touch with both work areas.

Although the Thanksgiving holiday resulted in some delay, by the end of the first week in December, the second coat of paint was being applied. An easily understood set of directions for assembly had been prepared, and a copy was being laminated in plastic for permanent mounting on one of the plywood surfaces.

The design had turned out even better than anticipated; the kindergarten children themselves would be able to fit everything together with a minimum of teacher direction. Each of the sections was light enough to be handled by two children working together. Color-coding of joints eliminated any inherent puzzle characteristics: assembly was strictly a matter of red-to-red, green-to-green, blue-to-blue, and yellow-to-yellow. (It was to be *hoped* that color blindness would not cause a problem.) Securing the joints required slipping in two drop-bolts at each corner and at the eaves. Furthermore, the bolts were tethered on heavy cords. Thus, in addition to the enjoyment of playing *in* the house, the kindergartners would have the great satisfaction of "building" it as well.

Miss Warren and Mrs. Anderson were planning to hold Christmas parties for both their morning and afternoon sections the day prior to the winter vacation break. It had been agreed that Mr. Ortega's pupils would make the surprise presentation of the new playhouse at that time. Therefore, as the finishing touches were being applied, the youngsters were mindful of the calendar. Everyone was excitedly looking forward to the big day, for it would be a marvelous Christmas present for the younger children.

The kindergarten children had a nice party; they sang songs, danced, and performed appropriately for those parents who were able to attend. In the midst of the festivities older children invaded the party, rolling something on a large rack that was fitted with casters. When they had the rack in the center of the room, they asked a few of the kindergartners to help them unload it. There were squeals of delight as the sections slipped quickly together. Suddenly, there it was: a beautiful playhouse that had grown miraculously right before their eyes! Mr. Ortega's group stayed for the remainder of the party, playing with the smaller children and enjoying the refreshments. Miss Warren and Mrs. Anderson each made a sincere speech of gratitude on behalf of their pupils. The looks on the faces of the kindergarten children would be remembered for many months.

Back in their own classroom, the older children felt compelled to talk about their accomplishment. They had worked hard—in fact, much harder than they had bargained for. But they had succeeded beyond their earlier expectations. There was a certain satisfaction in reviewing the various aspects of the project, and the discussion went on for several minutes. At length, one of the girls popped up with a query that left everyone looking suddenly blank.

"Say!" she demanded, "how did we ever get into this in the first place?" No one seemed to have an answer. And Mr. Ortega just smiled.

The Case of the Classroom Pets

When her lively group of first graders arrived at the momentous decision to obtain a pet for their classroom, Mrs. Martin was ready for them. More than three months earlier she had started gathering the specific kinds of information and materials that would be needed if—and when—the idea should arise. She was prepared even for eventualities that didn't occur! And *that,* she later reflected, was a significant factor in her own fascination with the children's project: she could afford to bend with their spontaneity.

Actually, the notion didn't strike the group suddenly. There were quite a few indications—for anyone able and willing to read the signs—

of what was coming, and Mrs. Martin had recognized most of them. The youngsters had especially enjoyed a unit on animals that they had recently completed in their science program. Also, they were inevitably thrilled at the sight of a bird or a squirrel that they chanced to encounter on any of the class walks about the neighborhood. Too, their pleasure in browsing through the animal books at the free reading table and in the school library further evidenced their continued interest in this aspect of their natural environment.

It had been Mrs. Martin's general practice to keep some living creature—perhaps some goldfish or a parakeet—in her schoolroom to brighten the atmosphere. But shortly before the opening of the present term her latest zoological investment had died of old age, and she had postponed finding a suitable replacement. She thought that the children might find satisfaction in participating in the selection.

Possibly the unexpected incident that triggered the chain of mushrooming interest in the matter of pets was a child's bringing a just weaned kitten to school one morning to give to a classmate. The softly mewing ball of delight naturally did not go unnoticed by the other children; everyone was eager to lift the tiny bundle of animation from its cardboard box and stroke the silky fur. It was no surprise to their teacher that, for the next few days, pupils undertook to stock the classroom with a homegrown circus of life-size specimens. But the children willingly adhered to an informal schedule of assigned days for bringing pets to school.

Being especially careful not to push the idea beyond what the group could take in easy stride, Mrs. Martin worked patiently to whet the interest that had begun to form. There were private conversations and full-group discussions about the advantages and disadvantages of different kinds of animals for pets. Experience charts vividly recorded the impressions made by different pets that had visited the classroom. Bulletin boards displayed both domesticated animals and wildlife. Children listened attentively to stories that their teacher had selected. On one occasion, four pupils dramatized one of the stories for their classmates. A film about household pets was shown one day. Another time, a filmstrip on birds was enjoyed. The group played such games as "Doggy, Doggy, Where's Your Bone?" and "Guess What Animal I Am." Creative dancing was done to the accompaniment of a recording of "Noah's Ark." During a free play session, a child pretended that he was the pet dog of the "family." During exercise time, the youngsters sometimes imagined that they were different kinds of animals, and, in cadence with the piano, they jumped, flew, ran, butted, swam, or pounced. Library time focused on books about pets or other animals. Even the mathematics lessons, with examples featuring pets, contributed to the overall effect.

Considering the foundation that had been laid, it seemed little more than the next obvious step when someone suggested one day that the classroom ought to have its own pet. Indeed, it would probably have seemed strange had there been any response *other* than unanimous endorsement by the other children. The decision came more or less automatically: there was no debate, and no one thought it necessary to call for a vote. Rather, there was generally a tacit assumption that obtaining a pet was simply the reasonable and expected course of action.

One very important aspect of the decision, however, was not at all clear: what *kind* of pet were they to obtain? The grand menagerie that had been hilariously phased through the classroom earlier had served to demonstrate that virtually anything that swims, runs, flies, crawls, bites, or makes a noise may be regarded by someone as a legitimate pet. The range of possibilities, it was quite apparent, would have to be sharply reduced. And, so, there were more discussions as to the relative merits of potential nominations. Those special requirements for a pet that would be maintained in a school classroom had been deliberately emphasized in the talks. These and other vital considerations were kept firmly in mind as the children consulted parents and families about the care and feeding of certain prospects. Would a given animal stay indoors or out? How would its cage or sleeping box be kept clean? How could it be kept from getting too cold or too warm? Where does it go to the bathroom? Would it have babies? How long would it live? Would it smell bad? How would it be cared for on vacations or weekends? Would it bark or make other disturbing noises? The children labored diligently to get the necessary information.

In the light of their research findings and other pertinent factors, the youngsters narrowed the field to three acceptable categories: small birds, tropical fish, and gerbils. It was agreed that a pet selected from these possibilities would meet the basic standards that had been established, and that the final choice would be principally a matter of preference. Once again, the pupils began to gather information, this time with much more specific questions in mind. If they were to choose a bird, what kind should it be? How much would it cost? Where could they obtain a cage? What would it eat? Should they get a male or a female—or maybe a pair? Similar kinds of questions were posed with respect to a possible choice of fish or gerbils. Integral to this stage of the investigation were a walking trip to a nearby pet store and a ride on a school bus to two others located somewhat farther away. The group was going about its business in an objective, methodical way.

After due consideration, the children made their selection: a handsome pair of gerbils! The proprietor of the pet store agreed to take care of them until all of the necessary preparations had been made for their proper introduction into the classroom. Each child had already contributed a small sum of money to purchase the animals and a supply of food. A cage was brought from the supply room; and, although it appeared to be clean enough, the youngsters administered another going-over with soap and water—just to be sure.

It had now been nearly two weeks since a tiny kitten had unceremoniously entered the classroom in a cardboard box. An assortment of unique ideas had flitted through the children's minds in the brief period. They had wondered; they had inquired; and they had concluded. The excitement of anticipating the arrival of the gerbils on the following afternoon pressed for an outlet, and there were impulsive cheers when someone proposed that they hold a housewarming for the new pets.

"Mr. and Mrs. Happy," as the two gerbils were to be known, were the guests of honor at the party. Another group of first-grade pupils had been invited to share the fun and greet the new residents as they got acquainted with their future home. And, just to make absolutely certain that the tiny animals would feel wanted, a large banner had been draped across one end of the room to proclaim: "WELCOME HOME, MR. AND MRS. HAPPY!" The sequence of experience charts that had been developed over the two-weeks period, as well as the children's drawings, depicted the whole story, including the succession of family pets through the classroom, the busy research efforts and field trips, and the final selection of the gerbil couple. Throughout the undertaking, Mrs. Martin had used her 35mm camera to good advantage, and now she was able to show a number of delightful color slides of the youngsters at work on the project. They sang several of the animal songs. When someone suggested that the class keep a diary for "Mr. and Mrs. Happy," the idea met with instant and enthusiastic approval. And, then, refreshments were served. The gerbils munched on the special meal from the pet store. But the girls and boys had fruit punch and gingerbread animal cookies.

The Case of the Congested Playground

When, after extensive remodeling and enlarging, the old James Whitcomb Riley Elementary School was reopened in early September, at least two major differences quickly became apparent. First, as a result of more children having been brought in to fill the additional classrooms, the total enrollment had suddenly shot from fewer than three hundred pupils to more than eight hundred. And, second, the handsome new wings had bitten a sizable chunk out of the already meager play area. Consequently, playtime became noticeably complicated by the fact that nearly three times as many children were now attempting to use an area that had been only barely adequate originally. Carefully scheduled physical education sessions were difficult enough, but before-school times and recess periods were chaotic. Soccer balls thudded without warning onto hopscotch grids. Softball fielders in hot pursuit of fly balls tripped over jump ropes or trampled exposed fingers in the marble rings. Runners collided painfully in midcourse. Carefree enjoyment seemed at best only an occasional thing. Angry words, tears, and—literally—even bloodshed became almost routine.

The situation easily qualified as the major item of business at an early meeting of the school faculty. While everyone present readily concurred as to the seriousness of the matter, no one had an automatic recommendation. As one person wryly punned, it was another instance of "putting two and two together—too many kids and too little playground." After several minutes of circular discussion, Mrs. Carlson, one of the sixth-grade teachers, suddenly said, "Let my class take it on as a special project."

Momentary reactions of the other twenty-eight teachers included mingled admiration and disbelief. But, even before the open mouths could be restored to a semblance of composure, Mrs. Carlson continued.

"So many of the children in my class," she explained, "need an honest-to-goodness challenge. Not just a chance to do better in their regular work or encouragement to be 'good citizens'—whatever that may be—but something personal and realistic. I think they need to get themselves genuinely involved. And right here is a problem that actually affects them directly. Furthermore, it's a problem that not even the teachers can solve—at least at the moment. In fact, maybe there is no solution. But I have a feeling my kids would consider it a compliment to be asked to try. And—who knows—they might even succeed."

Mrs. Carlson paused. A number of the group made probing observations or suggestions. Several saw some merit in the idea of letting the children try, even if they should fail in the attempt. After all Mrs. Carlson had been teaching with better than average success for some fourteen years, and there was no doubt that she had gained some pretty good insights into children's likes and dislikes, as well as their capabilities.

But there were also a few serious doubts. For example, the question was raised as to whether it is fair to children to let them plunge into something beyond their depth. And it was pointed out that although children need to experience more success, there actually didn't seem to be much hope for success in this particular consideration. The first of these comments drew an overly quick retort about the even greater unfairness of consistently underrating youngsters. The observation about children's need for success was countered—but rather more gently—with an expression of concern for the "fundamental right of children to fail at something occasionally." But, then, came the potentially most disparaging remark of all: "What if your children don't want to do it?"

"In that case," said Mrs. Carlson simply, "I'd have to respect their wishes."

For some moments Mr. Richards, another sixth-grade teacher, had been sitting quietly. The last question, coupled with Mrs. Carlson's brief reply, seemed to be his cue. "And in that case," he called out suddenly, "I think I'd see whether my gang would like to take a crack at it."

It was Mrs. Carlson's turn to look surprised. "Well! Why don't we both work on it?"

It was quickly agreed that the problem would be turned over, at least tentatively, to Mrs. Carlson and Mr. Richards to place before their respective groups of sixth-grade pupils.

That evening the two volunteers conferred by telephone. Mr. Richards was particularly concerned as to the best way to bring up the problem with the children. "It would be nice if they could feel that it's their own idea," he thought.

"And it *can* be their idea," Mrs. Carlson replied. "This is certainly their problem as much as ours. And, if we can just be ready to provide support when they declare war on it, I think we'll have good enthusiasm."

The very next morning Fred, one of Mrs. Carlson's pupils, was called out of class to take his little sister home. It developed that she had been playing on one of the swings when she was struck by a stray ball, and, in the resulting fall, she had received some bruises and abrasions. By the time Fred had returned to school and was reporting how upset his mother was about his sister's injuries, another playground incident had involved two children in Mr. Richards' room. In neither instance was there lack of precedent, for some variation had occurred nearly every day since the opening of school. On this particular day, however, concern and indignation seemed at the bursting point. Perhaps it was because both teachers were especially alert to the children's compulsion to talk about the problem, or possibly it was that these most recent misfortunes on the jammed playground simply constituted the last straw. Whatever the ultimate incentive, it seemed that the children simply had to talk; and steamy discussions in both classrooms vented abruptly from the feelings of frustration that had been building up.

In the normal course of lunchtime conversation, it came somewhat as a reassuring surprise to pupils in each of the two sections that similar discussion sessions had taken place in both classrooms that morning. The realization that other people were equally stirred up about the inadequacy and the actual danger of the play areas seemed to add authenticity to the complaint and further to stimulate the mutual concern—and this led to the idea of checking with the respective teachers about "conducting an investigation." Then it occurred to several pupils that it would also be a very good idea to talk with Mr. James, the principal, about the whole situation. An ad hoc committee was agreed upon, and an appointment was arranged for the following morning before school.

Mrs. Carlson and Mr. Richards met briefly by chance as they checked their mailboxes in the faculty room. Mrs. Carlson was curious about what had gone on in the other section. She inquired with a twinkle, "Will you be able to get their attention on the playground problem?"

Mr. Richards shook his head in slight puzzlement. "There's no question about attention; they're already fired up to the point that they actually want to, as they say, 'hold an investigation.' " His face suddenly took on a more sober look. "Of course," he continued, "they may be onto something entirely different before the day's out."

"No, I don't think so," Mrs. Carlson reasoned. "This thing is really their problem; and, if we can just help them keep up their confidence, I think they'll want to pursue it. Of course, they'll need help. And maybe you and I had better get our heads together for a little planning after school to see what we can do."

In the middle of the afternoon, three girls approached Mrs. Carlson and asked if they might remain after school to work up a bulletin board that would focus on the predicament. "Would you have time to help us just a little bit?" one of them added.

In Mr. Richards' room, four people were planning a little dramatization and brainstorming some ideas that would season the seriousness of the matter with a bit of humor. Meanwhile, another cluster of youngsters was considering a more down-to-earth suggestion: inviting the Supervisor of Physical Education to the school to inspect the playground with a representative pupil delegation. Other children were still going over some of the comments made during the morning discussions. The playground problem, it was apparent, had caught the imagination of children in both classrooms to a degree that clearly surpassed the expectations of either teacher.

It was quite natural, of course, that Nancy, the daughter of a professional photographer and fairly skilled with a camera herself, should explore the possibility of photographic documentation. She was obviously pleased to receive permission to check out the school's only polaroid camera for the purpose of shooting some of the familiar scenes of congestion on the playground. It was her own idea to ask a classmate—only partially in jest—to accompany her and warn of any unidentified flying objects that might jeopardize the mission.

Jerry hit upon the notion of comparing the number and seriousness of playground accidents at the James Whitcomb Riley School with those of other elementary schools in the district. He was encouraged to call the

Director of Pupil Personnel for an after-school appointment to get the necessary data. He planned first to pick up his father's cassette tape recorder to facilitate the interview and insure his getting all of the facts straight. He was confident that he could report his findings to his class-mates on the following day.

When the bell rang to mark the end of the school day, somewhat more than the usual number of children appeared to be in no hurry to leave the premises. Some of those who regularly commuted by school bus almost missed their rides. In some respects, it seemed as if the day were just beginning.

The girls who had suggested making a bulletin board had, in the meanwhile, recruited another girl and two boys and were now considering two boards rather than one. They talked excitedly as they began to block out their messages tentatively in chalk. Mrs. Carlson helped them select their materials, then informed them that she would check back in a few minutes. Then she sat down with Mr. Richards to plan.

As the pupils entered the classrooms the following morning, their eyes were drawn to one or the other of two attractive bulletin boards that were mounted prominently in the hallways. Each layout included detail that was simple, colorful, and to the point. The message of one declared, "WE HAVE A PROBLEM," while the other asked, "WHAT CAN WE DO?"

The dramatic skit that was the slightly premature brainchild of the previous afternoon's four excited collaborators had somehow been writ-ten, rehearsed, and was now ready for staging with cardboard costumes. To be sure, it wasn't polished, and the dialogue was a bit uncertain; nevertheless, it was quite clever, and the casually formed audience was most appreciative. The theme centered around the tribulations of a kinder-garten teacher who had to help her children put on their steel armor before going out on the playground which was overrun by enemy troops. The fact that the production had been cast exclusively from the membership of the sixth grade and some of the "kindergartners," therefore, were taller than their "teacher" added an extra touch of humor to the basically serious theme.

In company with her faithful "bodyguard," Nancy had completed her photographic reconnaissance just before the nine o'clock bell—in fact, one of her most remarkable shots had been made *during* the actual ringing. She had beautifully captured the mood of the situation: a wild tangle of legs, arms, and play equipment, and what appeared to be a free-floating body soaring blissfully above it all. Someone quickly dubbed it "the popu-lation explosion."

In response to his teacher's inquiry, Jerry said that he had had an interesting conversation with the Director of Pupil Personnel, and that he would be glad to report his findings later in the day or whenever the group wished. The children who had telephoned the Supervisor of Physical Education reported that he would visit the school in two days.

Membership of the ad hoc committee that had met earlier that morning with the principal included children from both classrooms. They reported that Mr. James had suggested that the two sections select a steering committee that would include representation from each room. He had further suggested that such a committee could meet regularly with Mrs. Carlson and Mr. Richards to coordinate the plans of the two rooms. The response of the pupils to this notion was overwhelmingly supportive.

The joint steering committee named by the children included four members: one girl and one boy from each room. (Whether such a precise balancing of the sexes in the selection process had been intentional or simply chance was not clear to either of the teachers.) Each of the four was generally respected for individual maturity and consideration for others. The new committee convened briefly during the lunch period and set up a tentative schedule for meeting regularly.

Both Mrs. Carlson and Mr. Richards held as closely as they reasonably could to the regular routine of school work; but, understandably, they found it necessary to make some allowances and postpone some things in order to work in the essential opportunities for the children to continue with their declared "investigation." Jobs involving only one or two persons were squeezed into spare moments. For instance, Nancy found time between her different subject matter assignments to arrange her pictures of the playground in an effective display, complete with captions. And, neatly lettered at the top was the suggestion that "OUTDOOR PLAY IS HEALTHFUL—SOMETIMES."

But some activities had to be handled more deliberately. For example, Jerry had to report separately to each classroom. Since most of his interview with the Director of Pupil Personnel had been tape recorded, he played back some of the especially interesting portions for the benefit of the two audiences. He had also prepared a chart of the facts that he had collected. For one thing, he was able to show that the accident rate at James Whitcomb Riley School since the beginning of the term had been four times that of either the Burnside or the Meadow Gate School, both of which were situated in similar neighborhoods and with approximately equivalent enrollments, but, in both instances, with plenty of good play areas.

Another priority item, of course, was getting the first report from the steering committee. While there was some similarity in the activities of the respective classrooms that afternoon, the proceedings were by no means identical. In Mr. Richards' room, Susan and Mark brought their classmates up to date on the committee's joint planning. Susan concluded her comments with a recommendation that the children in each section get busy and determine what aspects of the playground situation should be pursued. "Yesterday," she reminded them, "several people were saying that we ought to have an investigation of the playground. So what we ought to do now is decide just what it is that we're going to investigate."

Susan's point was eagerly accepted by the whole group. Mr. Richards suggested that, if a general discussion were desired, perhaps someone would volunteer to serve as recorder so that none of the suggestions would be forgotten. He looked agreeable when someone pointed out that, as a double precaution, the classroom tape recorder could be switched on as well.

"Claudia," one of the boys volunteered her, "is a good secretary." Claudia seemed pleased to accept, although she probably would not have offered her services if she had not been asked. But she was confident that she could handle the assignment. Her handwriting was both quick and legible, and she had a good facility for remembering a statement long enough to get it down on paper with remarkable accuracy. She picked up her notebook and pencil and moved to a table at the front of the group where she would be able to hear without difficulty.

There was a short pause for reflection; then the comments began. Mr. Richards moved comfortably around the sides and rear of the classroom. Now and then he sat in their midst; and his presence, even though only momentary, lent quiet support without distracting from the group purpose. Generally, the children did not raise their hands for permission to speak, but simply took turns offering suggestions. Occasionally, Mr. Richards subtly encouraged one of the more shy pupils. At first, most of the expressions were offered as statements of fact or opinion; and a few of these were disputed by other members of the group. As the discussion warmed up, though, the comments came more and more in the form of questions; and, as might have been expected, the levels of astuteness seemed to run the full range. But, to try to discern any reflection of comparative judgment in the teacher's face, one might have concluded that he regarded all of the questions as good—and equally so.

"Why do we have so many accidents on the playground?" asked a child.

"How many people have been hurt?" was the next question.

Fred asked, "Why don't they take out the swings so the kids can't fall off of them?" Such a question was not unusual for Fred, but it constituted the very sort of expression that more than once had prompted Ralph to pronounce Fred stupid. Fortunately in this instance, Mr. Richards chanced to be standing right beside Ralph, and a light touch on the outspoken youngster's shoulder reduced the automatically blurted epithet to no more than a snort. Fred's question had been accepted.

Another child spoke. "Could the kindergarten teachers watch the little kids better?"

"How come we can't have a hardball field?"

"Where did Burnside School get all of their jungle gyms and stuff?"

"Maybe the school board could buy more land so we could have a bigger play yard."

Claudia wrote furiously. The children's concerns bubbled out like ginger ale from a well-shaken bottle. With each statement or question, Mr. Richards nodded, smiled, or looked thoughtful, giving the definite impression that the comment had been heard and accepted at face value. His manner made it comfortable for the children to be quite open.

Bert waved his hand for attention. "Why don't we make some picket signs," he sang out gleefully, "and march on city hall?"

An explosion of laughter rattled through the room, followed by a ripple of giggling and desk slapping. But Mr. Richards was unruffled. Claudia looked at him helplessly, wondering whether to record Bert's question—or joke or whatever it was intended to be. Mr. Richards assured her that it was a legitimate question. Then, when things had settled down a bit more, he spoke again. "You know," he said thoughtfully, "some of our ideas that may sound a little strange or surprising sometimes turn out to be very useful. So we should all feel free to say whatever comes to our minds. Right now we need all of the ideas that we can get. We can decide later what is most appropriate."

The discussion went on. By the time that the pupils had finally exhausted themselves, they had formulated a total of twenty-seven statements and questions bearing more or less directly upon the playground situation. The tape recorder had been turned off. Claudia was alternately shaking her right hand and rubbing her knuckles.

Although a slightly different procedure had been followed in Mrs. Carlson's room, the outcome was very much the same. Rather than conducting a large-group discussion, her children had first separated into clusters of three or four to identify the individual concerns, then had gotten together as a whole class to make a composite list. The resulting total included twenty-two items, mostly in the form of questions.

It was the decision in both classrooms that the four-member joint steering committee would be the logical agent to take on the responsibility of reviewing the two discussion records and editing them into a single, manageable list. The committee members agreed to remain after school to get at the assignment immediately, with the expectation of having the job completed for further consideration the following morning by pupils of both sections. Mrs. Carlson said that she would be happy to work with them in such capacity as they wished.

After school the four students and Mrs. Carlson got together in Mrs. Carlson's room. By that time, the two lists, representing the individual concerns of both classroom groups, had been copied for each committee member. The children read each item. Even Bert's startling call for action didn't seem quite so preposterous neatly recorded in Claudia's handwriting. The two inventories contained some duplication. Some notions that had been arrived at independently in the two discussions only seemed to emphasize the basic soundness. "These are really good questions," one of the children observed.

The editing took more than an hour, and everyone was tired—but elated—when it was finally completed. With a minimum of help from Mrs. Carlson, the four youngsters had carefully gone over all of the points that had been specified, eliminating duplicates and combining nearly identical concerns. Since all of the items had been taken down verbatim during the classroom sessions, some of them were awkwardly expressed; these were rewritten more effectively. The two lists with which the committee had started had included a grand total of forty-nine statements and questions. At the close of the busy work period, the substance of all of this had been compacted into a single, crisp document with a final total of twenty-one items, all uniformly phrased as questions.

But the outcome of the afternoon's work was more than just a trimmed-down list of questions. Rather, the effort produced a neatly compartmented action-guide in the form of a question outline. There were five major categories consisting of from three to six questions each. Included were the following:

> "*Category A:* Inventory of Existing Play Equipment and Survey of Play Areas." (Three questions.)
>
> "*Category B:* Exploration of Possibilities of Getting Additional Equipment and/or Enlarging Play Areas." (Five questions.)
>
> "*Category C:* Recommended Standards for Playground Equipment and Play Areas." (Three questions.)
>
> "*Category D:* Catalog of Outdoor Games and Activities Preferred by Children in James Whitcomb Riley School." (Six questions.)
>
> "*Category E:* Survey of Outdoor Equipment and Play Areas of Other Schools." (Four questions.)

Mrs. Carlson complimented the four children on their dedication and good judgment. A bit embarrassed, but obviously pleased, they acknowledged her observation and thanked her for her advice. The second day of what the children had earnestly proclaimed as their "investigation" had finally come to a satisfying, if belated, close. But not for the two teachers; they still had serious planning to do. Later that evening, they conferred at length by telephone.

In the course of that conversation, they considered various aspects of the undertaking. Both frankly admitted to being impressed by the still accelerating show of enthusiasm on the part of the children. Mrs. Carlson related the highlights of the afternoon's editing session.

Both teachers felt that it was definitely time for the children to organize more formally so that they could move ahead with greater independence. Also, the work would have to be conducted in such a way as not to disrupt the normal routine of subject matter activity.

They agreed that both sections would devote approximately an hour the next morning to consider the newly developed question outline and try to arrive at some appropriate organizational plan. Mr. Richards expressed some surprise that the separate groups had, thus far, seemed to move almost in parallel paths, despite a minimum of actual direction by either teacher. "And now," he marveled, "we think we can predict what they're going to be ready to do in the morning! Somehow, I had the idea that kids were unpredictable."

Mrs. Carlson said that she shared the feeling. "As a matter of fact," she continued, "I don't think that children *can* be predicted—not really. But I'm convinced that they want whatever seems to make good sense— at least to them. So, maybe what we as teachers have to do is to reconstruct our thinking and see things more from their point of view."

Both teachers were ready the next morning when the two groups of children indicated that they were anxious to get on with the business that now ranked uppermost in their minds. A transparency of the question outline was projected onto the screen in each room in turn as the respective sections met. Both groups of children greeted the steering committee's effort with enthusiasm. The only change that was suggested was the addition of one further question. Everyone agreed that it was a good idea to find out whether the playground was equally congested at all hours of the day or if certain times were worse than others. The insertion was noted on the transparency in grease pencil.

Attention then focused upon the matter of organization. The jobs to be done were clearly listed on the screen. And the available work force obviously consisted exclusively of the fifty-six children in the two sections. Some other aspects, of course, were not quite so apparent. Various suggestions were considered, then discarded, modified, or accepted in full. Before lunchtime, each group had completed its separate planning. It would be up to the steering committee to dovetail the two versions that afternoon.

About that time, word came that the Supervisor of Physical Education had postponed his inspection of the play areas until the following day. This proved to be welcome news, inasmuch as there appeared to be greater likelihood that the children would be ready to take full advantage of his resources at a later time.

The two teachers conferred briefly at lunch. Although both groups had already taken more than the one hour that had been allotted for the whole day, they decided that another thirty or forty minutes on the playground problem might, in the long run, be a good investment. The first item of business that afternoon would be to convene the steering committee, with Mr. Richards sitting in on the meeting.

There were several differences in the organizational plans that had been recommended by the separate sections, but there were enough similarities that the committee had no unusual difficulty in resolving the two schemes into a reasonable proposal. The resulting pattern that was adopted less than an hour later by the combined membership was remarkably simple.

Most basic to the plan as finally adopted was the formation of a separate committee appointed at large to assume responsibility for the work specified under each of the five categories in the question outline. Committee membership was to be selected more or less by consensus, taking into consideration, primarily, the specific talents or skills that were considered essential to the functioning of the committee, and secondarily, the personal preferences expressed by the children. Internal organization of each committee would be left to the discretion of the membership of that particular committee. The committees were to begin functioning immediately upon formation, with a substantial progress report due in one week. The joint steering committee, with the possible appointment of two extra members, would continue in its present role and, in addition, would compile a written record of the complete "investigation." A photography committee was to supplement the written record with a pictorial history of all facets of the undertaking. One hour per day was to be set aside for work on the playground problem; anything that could not be taken care of during this time would be done after school or on weekends. Each individual would accept responsibility for his own mature behavior. And, finally, Mrs. Carlson and Mr. Richards were to serve as general consultants and—if necessary—arbiters.

In the few minutes of the school day that remained, the children worked briskly to catalog the different work skills that were considered

most important to each of the five committee functions. Next, they methodically sifted through the class rosters in a deliberate effort to identify
objectively those individuals possessing the specified qualities. The idea,
of course, was to make sure that each committee would receive its fair
share of people who were known to be especially good in such activities
as reading, writing, drawing, interviewing, figuring, and even performing
physical labor. Then, just before the closing bell, each child wrote his name
on a card and marked his own first and second choice for committee
assignment. All of this information was gathered up and turned over to the
joint steering committee, which looked forward with perhaps more a sense
of duty than delight to another after-school work session. But everyone
felt good in the knowledge that the next day would be their opportunity
to get at the problem more directly.

When school began Friday, virtually three full days had elapsed since
Fred had been called out of class to take his injured sister home. But time,
somehow, had lost much of its relevance; the three busy days had not
separated cleanly into easy units of measure. Looking back, it was hard to
remember when the children had *not* been fired up over the inadequacy
of the play areas.

The steering committee had done its work well the previous afternoon. Once again, the four members had approached their task seriously,
and, with the guidance of both teachers, they had weighed all of the factors
with care. In line with the group decision, first priority had been accorded
the matter of providing each of the designated committees with an effective team of able workers. To the extent commensurate with this, however,
the personal preferences of the children were followed.

The list of recommended assignments had been neatly duplicated,
and a copy was handed to each child. Each of the fifty-six names had been
included under one or another of the committees. There were mingled
responses of delight or quiet acceptance as the assignments were considered. A member of the steering committee reminded everyone that the list
as distributed constituted merely a recommendation, and that a full-group
endorsement would be necessary to make it final. It was quickly agreed,
however, that the assignments had been handled objectively and fairly,
and the list was accepted without change.

There was, in fact, only one specific criticism, and that was offered
purely as a low-key jest. "I don't much like the idea of being on Committee
D," teased a boy, "because that's probably the grade we'll get—a 'D'." He
continued to smile even as Mr. Richards assured him that, at least on this
undertaking, there would be no necessity of any report card grades for
anyone. This comment set off a verifying exchange of glances around the
room; it seemed nice, for a change, not to be thinking about grades.

The available manpower of the two sections had been budgeted in such a way as to cover each committee function with an adequate number of workers having the essential skills. The overall equitability became even more noticeable as the children fanned out to designated areas to set up the internal organization of each of the respective committees and to consider operating procedures.

Eleven people, including girls and boys from both classrooms, had been assigned to Committee A, which had been charged with the responsibility of surveying the school's playground equipment and play areas. The moment that the members had seated themselves in a reasonable facsimile of a circle, someone asked—almost automatically—who was going to be the chairman. Others were not so sure that having a chairman was really essential. They decided to ask Mrs. Carlson for her opinion. She listened to the different arguments, then offered her advice, emphasizing that it was to be taken strictly as advice and nothing more.

"Whether a committee needs a chairman," she suggested, "depends upon several factors, such as the number of people involved, the complexity of function, just how much coordination is actually needed, and—especially—how the members themselves feel about the advantages and disadvantages. Some committees get along very nicely without a chairman; not having one makes for greater informality, as a rule. It's really something for you people to decide according to your own expectations."

For just a moment, all eleven were noticeably quiet. Then, abruptly, they were back where they had left off. After some brief consideration, they concluded that they would prefer a co-chairmanship to coordinate the various activities. Two agreeable candidates were selected more or less by acclamation. During the next several minutes, they made good progress in reviewing the four items in the question outline that comprised their own specific charge.

Committee B was to explore any possibilities of the school's obtaining additional playground equipment or of increasing the size of the play areas. The eight pupils assigned to this task force appeared to be full of imaginative ideas as they began their first meeting.

Committee C had also been allotted a membership of eight. The people in this group had been given the responsibility of securing an up-to-date set of recommended standards for playground equipment and play areas.

The fact that Committee D had been authorized the greatest number of workers was a direct reflection of the general assumption that its job would be the most time-consuming. The twelve children who had been named to this group were to take on the cataloging of all of the outdoor games and activities in which the eight hundred youngsters of the James Whitcomb Riley School engaged. As might have been expected, the internal structure of this particular committee turned out to be quite formal. A chairman, a vice-chairman, and a secretary were selected.

Eight pupils had been assigned to Committee E, which was to find what kinds and amounts of playground equipment and play areas were available to children in other schools in the district.

When the steering committee met again, its membership had been strengthened by two additional persons specifically chosen for their writing ability. Besides the general coordinating function that it had already undertaken, the now-augmented committee was further charged with maintaining an appropriate written record of the whole endeavor.

With only three members, the photography committee understandably had a minimum of difficulty in getting organized. Certainly, there was no call for a chairman in this little team. And, just as everyone had fully expected in consideration of the excellent photography earlier in the week, Nancy was one of the three.

With the exception, then, of the original four members of the steering committee, this brief session constituted the initial meeting of each of the various committees, and the purpose was largely to agree upon some organizational plan. Despite the fact, however, that only a few minutes could be spared, most of the committees succeeded in going somewhat beyond the minimum expectation. Some individual assignments, for example, had been handed out, and, in some instances, limited committee activity had been planned for the weekend.

Mrs. Carlson and Mr. Richards were obviously pleased with the way in which the children had seized the opportunity to move out on their own. The youngsters, too, felt much the same, although perhaps less inclined to take any special note of what very definitely was a departure from routine. And, when—shortly after ten-thirty—the teachers suggested that they turn their full attention back to the pursuit of subject matter for the remainder of the day, no one objected.

The single exception that was made to the return to formal content study was to excuse one member of each of the seven committees for about thirty minutes that afternoon to accompany the Supervisor of Physical Education on his scheduled inspection of the playground.

Enthusiasm remained high as the children returned to school on Monday morning to confront the busy week ahead. The deadline of committee reports that had been scheduled for the following Friday morning was a constant reminder that there was no time to waste.

The weekend had enabled some people to get together in twos or threes or to exchange ideas by telephone. Several pupils had made a special point of discussing the situation with their parents and families, and had received some useful suggestions. Two members of Committee C had gone through a number of books and other materials at the public library to gain a better knowledge of certain items of playground equipment, some of which had been completely unknown to them. Three youngsters from Committee E had ridden their bicycles to four other elementary schools located within a reasonable radius of their homes to observe the general layout of play areas and stationary equipment. Realizing that it would be extremely difficult to survey the outdoor areas of their own school during a regular school day, Committee A had detailed five of its members to take advantage of the abandoned grounds on Saturday morning. With a borrowed surveyor's tape, they had obtained accurate measurements of all dimensions of the play areas. In their own ways, both Committee B and Committee D had made equally good progress on their respective assignments. Although members of the steering committee had not found it convenient to meet for deliberation on their most recent responsibility, a few telephone conversations had sufficed as the next best thing. And, on Sunday afternoon, the three members of the photography committee had gathered at Nancy's home, where her father had given them some helpful pointers.

As the work of the separate committees proceeded during the next two days, there was some tendency on the part of the children to want to extend the one hour per day that had been allotted; there just didn't seem to be enough time in sixty minutes to take care of all of the jobs that had to be completed. But both Mrs. Carlson and Mr. Richards remained firm in holding to the time limit as agreed. Naturally, this led to more tasks being handled before and after school. Then, as efficiency increased and priorities were observed, it seemed that the daily hour might actually be adequate. It appeared that the committee reports would be ready on schedule—and they were.

When the appointed time came at ten o'clock on Friday morning, it had been only ten days since the children had first manifested a keen interest in what they had since termed their "investigation." And the committees that were now ready to report had been functioning just a little less than a week. Extra chairs had been moved into Mr. Richards' room so that the two sections could meet together.

Committee B was first to report. Speakers explained briefly the way in which the group had organized and its method of procedure. Their research had included interviews with a number of persons, among others, the principal, the custodian, and one of the city commissioners. Their most accurate and most complete information, however, had resulted from a visit to the Office of Buildings and Grounds of the school district. Here, the children had learned that definite plans had already been made by the Board of Education to obtain approximately six acres of adjacent property for the purpose of enlarging the grounds of the James Whitcomb Riley School. Unfortunately, a court action was pending to clear up some question of ownership of one of the lots under consideration. It was quite definite, therefore, that, despite good reason for long-range optimism, there was little likelihood that the school grounds could be expanded within the next year or two. As to the possibility of getting additional playground equipment, there was no direct difficulty. In fact, several permanent-type items had already been purchased and were now in storage until space could be made available for their installation. All in all, the committee concluded, the facts that it had managed to dig up were not especially cheering; but, at least, they were the real facts.

The report of Committee C was especially visible, inasmuch as the children had almost all of their information prepared on large charts that were displayed at the front of the classroom. Their chief resource had been the Supervisor of Physical Education. He had answered some of their questions at the time of his visit to the school the previous week, then on Tuesday, in a thirty-minute conference in his office, he had provided copies of the pertinent information and had explained certain aspects of the standards. The committee had tape-recorded the entire conversation, and played back selected portions at this time to supplement the charts. Undoubtedly, the most noticeable impact that the report seemed to have upon the children was the extent to which it verified their already strong suspicion that, even in comparison with the *minimum* level of recommendations, the playground facilities of their own school were significantly below standard.

A total of seven other elementary schools in the district had been checked out by members of Committee E. And, since they had been accompanied on three of the visits by a member of the photography committee, their report was sharpened by the inclusion of visual illustrations. Pictures of equipment and play activities at the other schools were thrown onto a screen by an opaque projector. The contrast of playground facilities did not require pointing out.

The chief feature of the report of Committee A was a true-scale map of the school, which the children had constructed with obvious precision. They had first plotted a large graph by carefully joining two heavy sheets of chart paper and spacing in the grid lines so as to effect an easily managed ratio with the actual measurements of the school plant. Over this, they had drawn in the exact overall outline of the building. Then, with different colors, they had identified lawn areas, plantings, asphalted surfaces, and cemented areas such as walks, curbs, and driveways. But, rather than drawing the outline of standing equipment and playing courts directly onto the map, they had prepared these on separate cutouts that could be shifted about the map as desired. The result, of course, was more than just an accurate graphic representation of the existing playground: it was also a useful tool for planning any future changes in the playground design.

There was little doubt that the job that had been taken on by Committee D was the most ambitious of all. While this had been pretty much anticipated at the time the various assignments had been made a week earlier, the realization became even more pointed as the report was presented in an astonishing volume of detail. Fortunately, the seeming top-heaviness of internal organization—chairman, vice-chairman, and secretary—that had been adopted at its first meeting had apparently not slowed the committee in any way; quite obviously, it had functioned with efficiency. In a sense, this might have been considered its second report, the first having been a particularly self-critical committee meeting in which the members had reviewed their tentative findings and had decided to add an item to the questionnaire that they had already begun to administer throughout the school. The opinion of every child in the James Whitcomb Riley School had been solicited in compiling a catalog of all of the outdoor games and activities that were enjoyed by various groups. These had then been classified as to whether they were principally boys' or girls' activities, according to grade levels, and with respect to the seasons of the year. In addition, each child had been asked to indicate a ranking of his various preferences.

At the conclusion of the reports, Mr. Richards complimented the children on the fine job that they had done. Mrs. Carlson concurred, saying that she was sincerely proud of the imaginative ways in which they had handled the different committee assignments. Then came the question of what the next step ought to be. Certainly, some of the avenues that had earlier been regarded as at least remote possibilities now appeared definitely closed. It occurred to the teachers that the children might respond more creatively after a rest. And, when one of the children suggested something much akin to this notion, most of the others gave it quick endorsement. "I think we're probably all too tired to decide about the next step right now," a girl had offered. "Maybe if we all think about it over the weekend, we can meet in our committees Monday morning and figure out what to do."

Mrs. Carlson's children, returning to their classroom, appeared quite content to concentrate upon their regular school subjects for the remainder of the day.

As hoped, the two-day respite proved quite salutary. The facts and figures that, on Friday morning, had scudded through the children's heads like mental dust storms had nicely settled during the interim. The youngsters were now alert and ready for the challenges of another Monday. The six members of the steering committee had come to school a few minutes early in order to meet with Mr. Richards for one or two quick decisions. Everything was comfortably under control as the committees met separately to study possibilities for the next development.

It had been agreed that the committee sessions would continue for twenty-five minutes, then a general meeting would be called for the full membership of both classroom sections. The pupils had found that, by working in this way—first in the smaller groups and then in the larger—they were better able to look at each of the individually-offered suggestions or proposals, and yet have time to weigh quite carefully the two or three ideas that were sifted out for further consideration.

The discussions proceeded briskly; even before the allotted hour had run out, the children had firmly settled upon the direction that they would take. They were fully in accord as to the futility, under the circumstances, of waiting for an official solution to be handed down to dispose of the overcrowded playground problem permanently. Although they were convinced that it would be only a matter of a year or two before the "Louisiana Purchase"—as a member of Committee B had dubbed the proposed six-acre addition—would effectively relieve the situation, they had decided not to wait. Instead, they would move ahead as though the responsibility were solely theirs.

Definitely, a turning point had been reached. It was obvious to everyone that the fact-finding stage of the undertaking—that which the youngsters had designated their "investigation"—had come to an end. Each of the specified committees had completed its particular inquiry. What remained was a requirement for action. But, while action frequently calls for a different organizational framework than what might be appropriate for research, it was agreed that the presently constituted committees would continue to function in the new assignments in order to avoid the delays of reorganization.

The proposed scheme that the two groups of sixth graders determined to implement would be basically a matter of resolution between supply and demand, the available playground facilities of the school constituting the supply, and the priority-ranked preferences that more than eight hundred elementary children had listed for various outdoor games and activities comprising the demand. Data that would be fed into the necessary compromise would be selected largely out of the combined findings of Committee A and Committee D, with some possible modifications stemming from the three other reports. The pupils felt good about the commitment that they had made, for they honestly regarded their decision as the best possible course. Nevertheless, they had no illusions about the job still ahead, and they were counting upon a great deal of trial and error, good luck, and hard work.

The five research committees had reconstituted themselves into work squads, and, operating more directly now under the coordination of the steering committee, each team had taken on a given portion of the overall task. Also, within each of the subgroups, there had been a further redelegating of specific jobs on an ad hoc basis to individuals or details of two or three persons. The informality of the arrangement permitted the pupils to engage in the activity during any free moments throughout the day, making it convenient to have some aspects of the work in progress almost continuously.

The frustration level was touched on several occasions, for the challenge seemed to have some of the characteristics of a four-dimensional jigsaw puzzle. Interrelated factors of space, time, motion, and change had to be delicately balanced to meet a variety of heavy demands upon the playground throughout the school year. And, as a given element in the jumble was adjusted, another became inevitably displaced. At times the children felt certain that it was a job that only a computer could handle. But, by fits and starts, piece by piece, something was slowly and painfully taking form. And, on Wednesday afternoon, it finally all came together.

Most of Mrs. Carlson's pupils were quietly absorbed in a social studies assignment when the three children who were working on the playground enigma at that particular moment suddenly realized that the final piece of the puzzle had fallen—almost automatically—into place. In retrospect, the solution seemed so direct and so obvious as to depreciate the seeming near-impossibility prior to the breakthrough. In essence, the answer lay simply in staggered play periods combined with a rotating "off limits" for specified activities during the most severely crowded times. But, at the moment, the event was greeted as a major discovery.

Startled children spilled from their seats and surged toward the chart that had been the focal point of the three-day struggle. Someone asked for permission to take the happy news to Mr. Richard's class. Then, in a matter of seconds, all fifty-six gesticulating and chattering girls and boys were crowded around the design that had finally evolved out of their combined effort. Neither teacher made any move to dampen the impromptu celebration.

The emotion-charged scene lasted for just a few minutes. Then, as the pressure of high feelings subsided, there were scattered inquiries as to the next development. So a completely unplanned plenary session was convened on the spot; and, in less than ten minutes, the immediate steps had been outlined. The steering committee, it was agreed, would remain after school, and, with the assistance of three volunteers to handle the necessary art work, the precious chart that represented the children's proposed playground schedule and design would be attractively and durably reproduced so that it might safely be displayed at various points throughout the building on the following morning. Permission of the principal would be sought to allow representatives to carry one of the new charts to each classroom for the purpose of explaining the plan to each group of pupils and getting their frank responses. Should the proposal merit the general endorsement of a substantial majority of the over eight hundred children, it would then—with whatever modifications might seem warranted—be submitted to the faculty for still further consideration.

Except for the steering committee and seven who declined the assignment, every member of both sections was involved Thursday morning in making the rounds of all of the classrooms in the James Whitcomb Riley School to explain various details of the playground proposal. Casually teamed in twos or threes, and in a few instances accompanied by a member of the photography committee, they made their presentations and answered questions. Several teachers in the visited classrooms later reported that the youngsters had performed commendably, and that the explanations were lucid and to the point. Even the kindergartners, it was happily noted, seemed to understand not only the proposal itself, but even the supporting rationale.

A special faculty meeting was held immediately after school that afternoon, and two members of the steering committee were asked to attend for the purpose of responding to any questions or comments that the teachers might have. The few minor changes that had been suggested in the course of meeting with each of the pupil groups were, for the most part, helpful. And, as the faculty members again examined the chart and listened to the knowledgeable responses of the children, they were visibly impressed by the amount and quality of work that had gone into the proposal. A telephone call from the principal to the Director of Buildings and Grounds was the final stamp of approval for putting the plan into effect.

On Friday morning, there was another meeting of all of the children from both sections. Unlike the impromptu session of Wednesday afternoon, however, this one had been carefully planned, and an agenda had been prepared in advance. The steering committee had gotten together for about half an hour before school and had thought through the situation, thus providing a good basis for the full membership to view things and lay out the work yet to be done. Discussion moved briskly. The same committees, which had functioned so well to this point, would definitely be continued through the next round, it was agreed. Various jobs that would have to be completed had been identified and listed on the chalkboard; and the list was impressive enough to make it clear that no one would be idle for the next few days.

Several items required immediate attention. One of these was a conference in the office of the Director of Buildings and Grounds. Three people were delegated to accompany Mr. James, the principal, to the district headquarters for a comparison of the children's playground design with blueprints that showed the location of underground cables and pipelines. Also, there was the matter of requesting that a maintenance crew come in with power machinery to move some swings and other play equipment that had been anchored down with concrete. Enroute back to the school, Mr. James picked up several buckets of yellow lining paint and some brushes at the district warehouse.

It would, of course, be an exaggeration to say that the work went forward without a hitch, although, relatively speaking, things did proceed smoothly. By this time, each of the committees had developed an easy internal relationship that contributed to the general efficiency. And, now that the operation had advanced well beyond the talking stage, and most of the effort was being applied directly to the playground itself, the apparent increase in momentum was most heartening.

As the fourth week of the undertaking began, both classrooms continued to budget an hour each day for the project that still gripped the imagination of the youngsters, even though virtually nothing remained in the way of problem solving activity. The period was mainly devoted to checking out and clarifying the time schedules and the staggered play periods that had been adopted. Most of the outdoor work, for obvious reasons, had to be taken care of during hours when school was not in session. It was largely for this reason that everyone had tried to be on hand on Saturday.

The children were shooting optimistically for the grand opening and dedication ceremony that had been scheduled for the coming Friday afternoon. Written invitations had already gone out to the homes of all of the school patrons, as well as to the Director of Buildings and Grounds and the Supervisor of Physical Education. And, naturally, all of the children, faculty, and staff members of the James Whitcomb Riley Elementary School had been asked to help celebrate.

A work order for the maintenance crew had gone through promptly; and, shortly after lunch on Tuesday, three men drove onto the playground in a truck fitted with a block-and-tackle hoist and carrying a variety of tools and supplies. Children were delegated two at a time to go out on forty-minute shifts and "observe," which meant keeping their eyes open for any possible mistake but not interfering in any way. The first item of play equipment that was removed from its concrete moorings was a large and rickety swings standard which was being replaced by one of the new slides from the warehouse. Everything else that had been listed for relocation, however, seemed to be in satisfactory condition. The crew, working through the afternoon, moved everything that had been requested. Whatever remained to be done on the playground could be completed by the children.

Throughout the week, as the proposed playground schedules were firmed up and the actual physical changes were effected on the play areas, attention turned increasingly toward the celebration that would commemorate the project's completion. Mrs. Carlson and Mr. Richards noted with satisfaction that the same enthusiasm and pride that had enlivened the work during the earlier stages were still very much in evidence as the children planned the upcoming observance. A guided tour of the playground itself would be the major highlight of the afternoon. Additional displays and posters were being prepared. An interesting program would include two or three live presentations, as well as appropriate visuals which would graphically depict the problem that the children had faced and the ways in which they had confronted it. The humorous dramatic skit about the kindergarten teacher and her armor-plated pupils was rewritten with a happy ending. A photographic summary of the four weeks would be mounted on large cork boards and placed on easels in the main hallway. And the written record of the whole enterprise that was being prepared by the steering committee would be duplicated for general distribution. But the most recent bit of good news was Mr. James's unsolicited offer of petty cash to cover the cost of light refreshments.

Time, however, was rushing by, and there were many loose ends to gather up. On both Wednesday and Thursday, evening work sessions were added to bolster a final sprint for the finish line.

The Director of Buildings and Grounds and the Supervisor of Physical Education were both present for a portion of the celebration Friday afternoon. Also in attendance were more than one hundred and fifty parents—mostly mothers, but also several fathers. The children were gracious hosts and hostesses. The guests had been permitted some leeway in timing their visits to tour the grounds either before or following the formal program, which had been scheduled from two-thirty until three o'clock with refreshments immediately afterward.

A guide was assigned to direct each of the various groups of children and their teachers through the newly designed play areas and point out again the way in which the limited-movement, quiet activities had been located close to the building, with the noisier, running games positioned at the outer extremes of the areas. Yellow lines had been stenciled onto the asphalted surfaces to designate hopscotch grids and playing courts. New lawns not yet ready for constant traffic had been sectioned off so that the older, tougher grassed areas could be used without concern. Relocating some of the standing play equipment had realized better space utilization; in fact, it had made possible the installation of additional pieces that had been in storage. The kindergarten play corral now had its own slide, seesaw, swing, and several portable devices. But perhaps the particular aspect of the whole scheme in which the two groups of sixth graders took the greatest pride was the new staggered-period play schedule that they had worked out so meticulously. A chart showing the times and available play areas noted for each classroom group had been placed near each entrance for ready reference.

The formal exercises were held in the multipurpose room; and the program proved to be delightful. The short speech of welcome was followed by the other oral presentations and, in turn, by the dramatic skit. The visuals were thoroughly appreciated for their accuracy and perspicuousness. Copies of the written report were distributed as the audience filed out of the room. And, of course, the refreshments seemed to make the day complete. The inevitable cleanup chores were undertaken as several guests lingered to admire the playground alterations or view the displays in the hallways. Fifty-six children were on the verge of that empty feeling that is standard in the completion of a tough job. But the honest compliments of departing guests served to sustain them a bit longer.

Mrs. Carlson and Mr. Richards had deliberately tried to remain as inconspicuous as possible during the festivities; but people sought them out to offer praise for the children's work.

Mr. James moved around complimenting the pupils, letting them know that their work had been genuinely appreciated by the entire school.

By the time that the children had returned to school after the weekend, that vacant feeling had been dissipated; and, in its place, was a lovely afterglow. Both Mrs. Carlson and Mr. Richards let them take a few minutes to bask in the good feelings that remained. For thirty minutes, they relived the pain and the triumph of the intense experience. In the relaxed atmosphere, they were beginning to realize that a sense of self-confidence and mutual respect had been forming during these weeks. There was unmistakable pride in their voices as they reflected on rediscovered qualities of persistence in their own behavior. "Sometimes it's fun to sweat," a boy said thoughtfully.

The regular faculty meeting was scheduled after school that afternoon. It had been a full four weeks since the problem of the congested playground had been introduced. And, as the teachers thought about the outdoor activities throughout the day, they felt that a reasonable solution had been achieved—at least a solution that would suffice until the six-acre addition could become a reality in probably another eighteen months. Mr.

James was lavish in his praise of the hard-working children and, more particularly, of their inspiring teachers.

Summary

Case-action learning can be advantageous to virtually any group of children. Each undertaking is truly unique in that it is developed exclusively for and with a certain group of children at a particular time and never repeated in exactly the same way. Strictly speaking, therefore, no specific case may be regarded as really typical; to the extent, however, that some elements of the approach are similarly applied in various instances, it is appropriate to consider some fairly representative examples.

Chapter Four

Achieving Group
Spontaneity by Design

Stated in its most starkly simple terms, a teacher's job in planning case-action learning may seem an impossible incongruity: achieving spontaneous group action through deliberate design. By nature, children are impulsive activists. But in school, where—for administrative reasons— they are placed more or less arbitrarily in fairly large groups with an attendant requirement of at least some degree of formality, their natural bent seems destined for frequent curtailment. The striving for individual expression on the one hand and the constraint of reasonable group limitations on the other inevitably clash to press counterdemands upon the curriculum that are not always conducive to effective study. Indeed, it may often appear that academic achievement is gained in *spite* of, rather than because of, such mutually opposing circumstances. Against this uneasy setting, it is the unique challenge of planning in case-action learning to design educational experiences that take intentional advantage of each of these significant factors. Case-action learning at its best is a joyful phenomenon in purposeful group spontaneity.

Group Spontaneity with Purpose

A clear understanding of the relative roles of pupil and teacher is basic to incorporating spontaneous group action purposefully into elementary curriculum. Any stereotype of a highly active teacher cleverly motivating essentially passive learners must be dispelled at the outset. Fundamental to the approach is that children be frankly encouraged to lead out vigorously in directions suggested by their innermost feelings and drives. And, though cleverness on the part of a teacher remains a virtue, there must be no manipulating of youngsters' whims. Rather, that cleverness must be focused imaginatively upon an accurate and continuous "reading" of children's barely perceptible needs and desires as they evolve out of experience and personality development. The job of a teacher is not a matter of concocting something interesting and useful out of whole cloth; instead, it is one of being especially alert to the subtle manifestations of need for children to respond to one another and to their shared environment as they interact openly and freely. It is for a teacher to anticipate and seize upon that precise moment when children are most keen for positive movement, but may not quite yet be fully aware as to their own readiness. The fostering of purposeful group spontaneity calls simultaneously for children to engage in the natural thing and for a teacher to make it feasible for the natural thing to be also the proper thing.

Getting Rid of the Guilty Feeling

It is essential that a teacher actually feel good—really good—about an honest child-centered approach. But, while most elementary teachers openly encourage their children occasionally in spontaneous group behavior, too often they may regard such unpredictable activity more as a departure from legitimate school purpose than as a worthwhile educational venture. For many teachers, therefore, the first big step toward designing group spontaneity deliberately into the curriculum is that of getting rid of whatever guilty feeling may accompany any intentional condoning of freedom in the classroom. And this feeling is not at all surprising when curriculum is narrowly viewed from the limited perspective of a long tradition of an exclusively knowledge-based approach. Even subconsciously, a teacher may be plagued by a gnawing concern that he is doing no more than standing idly by while youngsters "goof off" and waste valuable time. Therefore, if he cannot specifically document in the official course of study an identified need for some child-instigated pursuit, he may feel torn between a very human desire to allow children to discover themselves and a professional ethic to insist that everyone buckle down to the business at hand without delay. Such a teacher, undoubtedly, will need to recondition himself emotionally, as well as intellectually, to seek a more equitable balance between uncompromised subject matter and a genuine child-centered focus. For, rather than sensing any reflex of guilt, he needs to respond with a clear tingle of delight to the youthful release. A timid or halfhearted acceptance of the notion that, more and more, children ought to point their own directions and satisfy their own desires will not suffice; the enthusiasm must be positive and unmistakable. A teacher's commitment must be both genuine and deep.

Helping Children to Be Themselves

To respond adequately, every child must feel that he can relax in the classroom without threat or loss of status, despite an occasional mistake. Conversely, his self-esteem requires a quiet, but constant, assurance that his presence in, and contribution to, the group are genuinely sought and appreciated. Certainly, the need to be needed is a powerful thrust in personality development. How a teacher may seek to bring about the most effective condition in a school setting may seem to stem more from art than science. There is no doubt that a teacher's own convictions as to the essentiality of each child's role is an important attribute.

The behavioral traits of children that are most essential to case-action learning are not so much developed or strengthened in school as acquired during the normal, day-to-day process of growing up in a friendly, stimulating environment. Confidence, enthusiasm, and an unquenchable curiosity are basic. An inborn drive to *do* is, of course, the ultimate taproot. Promoting appropriate pupil activity, therefore, is principally a matter of encouraging youngsters to respond to a given situation with absolutely no concern for any possible judgment as to the performance. Simply and honestly helping children in every way to be themselves constitutes a teacher's most useful function in this particular regard.

Anticipating the Unpredictable

Freedom and spontaneity are, of course, at the heart of any really honest child-centered undertaking. The underlying philosophy of case-action learning, in particular, is predicated squarely upon this notion. Equally basic, however, are firm purpose and deliberate planning. The proper role for a teacher in this approach can be neither one of making children's choices for them nor one of merely tagging passively behind in the manner of a cleanup detail following a parade. The job definitely calls for thoughtful and meticulous advance planning, but—at the same time—conscientiously avoiding any teacher-commitment of children to that resulting plan. The situation may seem almost dilemmatic. Certainly, the task is not easy; but for a teacher to settle for a less scrupulous function must be regarded as unthinkable.

Seriously attempting to foresee just what a given group of emotionally healthy children, free from any pressure and of their own volition, will choose to do at a particular time is inevitably an experience in futility and frustration. Quite clearly, impulsive youthful behavior cannot be predicted; yet, if any venture is to prove satisfying and rewarding, much of the groundwork must be laid well ahead of the actual moment of requirement. Obviously, a high degree of flexibility on the part of a teacher is fundamental if both spontaneity and purpose are to be retained in the activity.

Ultimately, it becomes a matter of imaginative anticipation, calculated guessing, and relentless overplanning. "Thinking big" is an important part of the answer, because it tends to keep a teacher psychologically attuned to the most outlandish ideas that children may suggest. And this, in turn, supplies youngsters with a constant encouragement to override their inhibitions. But a teacher need not operate entirely from ignorance —he does know a great deal about the individuals in his group. And it is this kind of information, coupled with imagination and good judgment, that enables him to narrow the possibilities to a more reasonable range. Then, by intentional overplanning, that is, preparing for more options than can possibly be picked up, it actually becomes feasible to accommodate group spontaneity without sacrificing essential long-range planning.

Consulting, Guiding, and Being Resourceful

In defining his own role in the development of a case, it will be helpful for a teacher to determine just what he, personally, ought to do and what he ought not to do. It has been suggested that he serve as consultant, guide, and resource person. As such, much of his work will go unnoticed— especially if he does it well.

A major part of a teacher's effort will have been expended in preliminary planning before the youngsters ever become involved; the moment that they begin to get into the act, he ought to be quietly getting out. As soon as they have identified their area of concern and have delineated it to what can be reasonably handled, he can safely permit himself to be gently absorbed into the background where he will remain readily available, but never obvious. A teacher will tend to function more effectively if he views himself as moving usefully, but patiently, at the periphery of the action.

Without doubt, the most trying aspect of a teacher's role in case-action learning is the self-imposed restriction against participating directly in the fascinating and exciting things that are going on while children muddle through with noticeably less efficiency. But it is an irritation that he must tolerate in good grace. Also, it may chafe a bit that his own considerable contribution to the group endeavor is scarcely recognized as such by the chief beneficiaries themselves. Nevertheless, the arrangement does constitute a significant factor in throwing the greater emphasis of the undertaking upon learning rather than upon teaching. And, especially in the light of more positive attitudes toward learning activities and increased self-confidence, it may seem, in perspective, a small price to pay.

Briefly, a teacher must do nothing for any individual or group that the children can do for themselves. But, lest the "don'ts" seem to outnumber and outweigh the "do's," it may be a welcome inclusion here to specify a few tasks that quite legitimately belong to a teacher. For example, he provides constant encouragement and a quiet show of enthusiasm for the work in progress. And, since the level of social skills is not likely to be well developed in young pupils, it is an important responsibility of the adult representative to assist in bringing members of the group together in a functional situation and to promote opportunities for leadership to emerge naturally from the group as the occasion may warrant.

If a teacher sees himself as serving offstage rather than in the spotlight, it is also likely that he will regard the duty more as that of a stage manager than as director of the show. Several jobs are plainly logistical and custodial. Necessary liaison with sources outside the classroom, for instance, may sometimes require an adult's assistance or intervention. Procurement of materials and equipment often necessitates a teacher's direct participation. And, of course, a teacher will probably want to share with children the responsibility of keeping an eye on deadlines and schedules, and making sure that any items borrowed from outside the classroom are properly cared for and returned promptly. In the final analysis, a teacher will have no difficulty in keeping busy, although the children will handle the most interesting tasks.

Case-Action Unlimited

One of the most consistent attributes of case-action learning is the virtually unlimited range of matters that may become the substance of a worthwhile and satisfying venture. An effective case is often "where you find it"; and some of the most consequential group-identified struggles have been undertaken perhaps as much by chance as by choice. For instance, children have sometimes responded with amazing energy in the amelioration of some school-related dissatisfaction. Possibly the nearness and immediacy connoted in such a cause may almost suggest to a youngster that he has been tapped by fate. The examples described in Chapter Three are representative in that each case evolved spontaneously and naturally from a child-oriented approach. But a multitude of diverse concerns that might similarly be pursued from a school-based operation could well be listed. Whatever can become of genuine importance to a group of children may be viewed as potential grist.

A Few Cases in Point

Endeavors in youthful philanthropy, if handled with imagination and discretion, can be especially rewarding. Particular caution must be exercised, however, lest children sense that they are merely being used to promote someone's do-gooding. This, quite understandably, they will resent. Nevertheless, there are numerous instances of legitimate opportunity. A fifth-grade class found particular satisfaction in an attempt at play production, in the course of which they adapted an interesting story for puppetry dramatization and presented it to youngsters confined in a crippled children's hospital. They even made an outright gift—at the end of the show—of the brightly costumed puppets and the miniature stage that they had designed. Another group of pupils worked hard for more than three weeks prior to the Christmas vacation in order to sponsor a qualified family in a communitywide "Sub-for-Santa" campaign.

Occasionally, an expression of beneficence may be of such magnitude as to challenge the combined effort of several classroom sections—or even an entire school. One such joint enterprise was a gift to the local zoo of a rare specimen purchased with funds produced through the activity of over seven hundred pupils in cooperation with the school's PTA chapter. In another impressive example of sustained coordination, the total memberships of three neighboring schools entered into an agreement through a recognized international committee, and labored at a variety of fundraising schemes. The hard-earned proceeds, consisting of nearly three thousand dollars, were sufficient to underwrite the construction of a simple, two-room school in a rural African village.

Children in less affluent communities may sometimes find renewed confidence in their own resources as a welcome concomitant of the struggle to establish themselves in an actual, ongoing economic activity. An unusually brilliant example of self-help was that of some of the older children in a small elementary school located in a run-down agricultural community. The outcome of their inspired effort was the beginning of a modest, but successful, poultry business which the group set up—and operated at a profit—on rented property near the school. The income thus produced was used by the pupils to cover certain "luxury" expenses which otherwise would have been beyond their means. While the incidence of such splendid enterprise among elementary school children is admittedly limited, there have been many somewhat less ambitious attempts that are equally worthy of serious consideration.

People of all ages frequently want to learn about a certain commercial or industrial enterprise that relates directly to the financial well-being of a given community. In fact, the standard grand tour for visitors from out of town is likely to include a guided inspection of "the plant" or some other visible evidence of economic growth. Most children normally have an equally healthy curiosity for this aspect of daily life in their own home towns. To some extent, of course, limited study of these foci of local pride may be included in many elementary schools within the scope of one or more areas of the regular subject matter curriculum. A modest amount of such direct exploration, without doubt, is essential to concept development in most formal content fields. But this is no reason to curtail the vigorous development of a child-centered, group-identified quest. The unrestricted free agency of the children themselves, as they consider a potential case for group action, will suffice to keep things in balance.

Most large corporations have efficient public relations departments that are prepared to honor requests for information of various kinds. Less widely known, perhaps, is the increased attention that many small businesses have given the matter. Such an arrangement provides a definite and convenient procedure for acquiring a fair understanding of a particular operation and organization, and has an obvious advantage for a group of children wanting to acquaint themselves with the functioning of a certain manufacturing or commercial enterprise.

Whether a particular business or industry might be more appropriately investigated by younger or older children hinges mainly upon the degree of sophistication and desired depth of inquiry. Given favorable circumstances, either kindergartners or sixth graders might consider the operation of a fish cannery or a tractor factory with equal satisfaction. As a general rule, children's capacity for research and the normal extent of their curiosity will nicely determine the commensurate profundity of their study. The more mature the group, naturally, the greater is the fascination in probing more deeply. For example, while a second-grade class found it worthwhile to learn more about the telephone, both as a means of communication and as a business, an older group would undoubtedly have thought it necessary to explore with sharper specificity. Fourth-grade children in a coal town had notable success in researching several facets of the local mining industry. The study of radio and television broadcasting was enthusiastically undertaken by some third-grade children. Regardless of their maturity, a group of youngsters may deem it important at times to inquire into agricultural pursuits, oil refining, or newspaper publishing.

These and many other concerns potentially interesting to children are possibilities for case-action learning.

Some pupils have regarded it as especially challenging to take on a case that leads purposefully to the inception of a valuable activity which is intended as a permanent adjunct to the classroom—or school—repertoire. For example, an intermediate-level group undertook the founding of a school newspaper. The youngsters devoted themselves unselfishly to the project for approximately five weeks, and celebrated their success with the first issue of an excellent publication which continued to function in the school as the official periodical, thus providing opportunity for journalistic expression for pupils at every grade level for years to come.

Another excellent case resulted in the formation of an outstanding camera club in which every member of a fifth-grade section proudly claimed charter membership. Fortunately for the children and their burgeoning wonder, their teacher was a confirmed camera bug and was quite capable of providing any technical advice essential to the endeavor. Interest in photography had noticeably quickened among the pupils during the Christmas vacation when a number of the group had tried out the new cameras that they had received as gifts. The resulting six-week campaign enabled the pupils to gain useful information and develop skills in the care and operation of a camera, selection of film, creative picture making, and —for a few children—producing their own prints.

Another example that might be cited is that of pupils in a desert location who enjoyed a vigorous plunge into the esoterica of rockhounding, several of them laying the foundation of a lasting hobby as they sampled the special delights of amateur petrology. As with the case that led to the birth of a school newspaper and the concerted effort that terminated in the establishment of a camera club, the outcome in this instance was, likewise, the beginning of an ongoing activity.

Some elements of a cultural consideration may occasionally provide the impetus for a valuable learning experience. Various commemorative dates, such as centennials or other milestones of progress or tradition in local or national life, often connote a significance that children are reluctant to forego. If a group's interest in such an event is particularly keen, an unusually good case may develop out of the enthusiasm. A loyal group of children in a small town were sufficiently motivated at the approaching advent of the community's seventy-fifth anniversary to research and write an impressive "diamond jubilee history" of their town. Several weeks of on-the-spot probing, searching through courthouse records, perusing old newspaper files, and the direct interviewing of several loquacious old-timers ultimately resulted in a single, large volume that was sturdily bound in a sheet of locally tanned leather and presented with deserved pride in a fitting ceremony to the school library.

Depending upon the particular set of circumstances, a successful case may sometimes be built around a crucial need that has been identified by the children involved. Second-grade pupils were both sympathetic toward a classmate and concerned for their own safety when they were informed that she had been hospitalized with a serious injury following a street-crossing accident. Understandably, their teacher had no difficulty in getting them interested in a definitely-pointed safety campaign. Similarly, an apartment fire in the neighborhood prompted a kindergarten group to spend a week of rather concentrated study to consider both the benefits and the hazards of fire. And some third-grade children in a mountainous area shortly before the autumn hunting season trained themselves deliberately in the fundamentals of survival in the unfortunate event that they should become lost in the forest.

A topic in the news or a matter of public concern has often spurred a particular quest by a group of youngsters. For instance, some intermediate-level pupils, prompted by public concern for a current national problem, initiated an objective study of drug abuse in their own county. An upcoming Apollo moon voyage, for another example, was the focus of an uncommonly fine study by a sixth-grade class. Happily, the event coincided to some extent with work that the children had recently completed in their science program, and they were thereby encouraged to go more deeply into some of the technical aspects of the event. Through a combination of foresight on the part of their teacher and hard work on the part of the pupils, they were able to complete their study on the precise day of the actual splashdown. And, in a Western state, children became incensed over the reported wholesale shooting of eagles in certain sheep-raising areas. Ensuing claims and counterclaims of stockmen and conservationists left a gnawing doubt in the minds of the pupils that led to their own unbiased research into the matter.

Although many of these briefly identified examples seem ultimately to have been ignited by some externally generated spark, it does not follow that the inception of a worthwhile undertaking in case-action learning is necessarily contingent upon circumstances beyond the deliberate influence of the participants. Indeed, a number of child-oriented group endeavors seem to have been elicited mainly from a healthy curiosity and a robust self-confidence. Clearly, some cases are manifestations of raw challenge or out-and-out pursuits of information solely for the exhilaration of the pursuit. An adventuresome group who actually produced an 8mm motion picture film, complete with plot, casting, and a tape-recorded "sound track," were probably responding more to an inner urge to *do* than to any necessity to conform to an outer persuasion. The seeming nonobjectiveness of such an effort is by no means grounds for depreciating the struggle; rather, it should be recognized for what it is: a legitimate enterprise in learning for its own sake.

Some Pointers in Any Case

Even at the risk of redundancy, it ought to be stressed that there is one characteristic common to all youngsters that is fundamental to case-action learning: *children like to work.* This is a major premise; if it can be accepted, the rest will follow. At the heart of any worthwhile case is the notion that children be *allowed* to work—to throw their full energy into that which they feel at the moment to be most important, to act immediately, to do whatever must be done, and to do it in their own way. Impulsiveness, exuberance, challenge, and frustration are all within the fabric of a group-identified undertaking. Moments of failure and success are the spice of all-out pupil activity. Nothing is guaranteed but the opportunity to try.

Taking on a case connotes a great deal more for pupils than merely following instructions. Certainly, youngsters need constant encouragement from their teacher—but not direct supervision at every turn. Children must accept the option of assuming charge of a situation, and, with it, a thorough understanding that decision making is a vital aspect of the responsibility. They must come to view leadership as a bright facet of group function, rather than a rare personality trait or a privilege of authority; and this will obtain only if the burden of control and management is genuine.

When children lead out in the development of a case, there must be no mental reservation as to the actuality of the relationship. They are not playing make-believe; within specified limits, they are running things. The candor of whatever agreement exists between pupils and teacher must not be compromised. That which is duly apportioned for the group's responsibility should be given and received in good faith. A useful parallel in principle may be seen in a child's weekly spending allowance. Whatever the parent grants is assumed to be freely given, and without strings attached, for the youngster to spend as he wishes and to learn from the experience. In the event that a child is too young, or otherwise too immature, to spend wisely and learn commensurately, then he may get a correspondingly smaller amount. And so it ought to be in turning over a share of the classroom opportunity for children to manage: whatever the amount, it should be assigned freely and without strings.

An important part of the self-determination so essential to case-action learning is the very decision by a group to take on a case at the outset. With virtually an infinite number of possibilities, whatever is undertaken ought to reflect the free choice of the participants themselves. Irrespective of any preparations that a teacher may have made, or regardless of what he may consider more appropriate, the group itself must arrive —without pressure or coercion—at its own decision. Finally, it must be presumed that the pupils hold the ultimate power of veto over any proposed case that may be suggested for group action.

The fact that a case is premised upon group action may seem to make evident the importance of the group to each child. But the relationship is much too consequential to be taken for granted. A teacher can, in many ways, subtly point up the mutuality of group and individual. Naturally, every effort ought to be made to enable each child to enjoy and appreciate his classmates. The group itself must be viewed as a definite asset.

In general, children are quite reasonable in asking for concessions from the total school program with respect to the development of a case. While they do appreciate being met halfway in terms of school time and facilities, they usually have not been averse to handling a significant portion of the work during out-of-school hours and through their own resources. Such an arrangement, of course, contributes to a favorable curriculum balance by moderating any tendency to cut dangerously into regular subject matter programs.

A teacher's obvious enthusiasm for a case can often be an important factor in the success of a group venture. But in his circumspection against too direct personal involvement in the ongoing work, he runs some risk that his reserve may be construed as indifference. Most children feel strongly about things that they regard as significant. And since they want to believe that their own concern is shared with equal intensity by their adult member, a teacher should let his emotions show a bit.

Ultimately, every case must be closed. At the moment that children take on a major job, their firm intention is to develop it effectively and carry it forward to a satisfactory completion. But the advent of bringing everything together after an extended period of hard work must not go unnoticed. A case must be closed properly. The occasion must be fittingly commemorated. Such a celebration would generally include a review or summarization of the accomplishments and an acknowledgment of any failures. Also, there should be appropriate recognition of the efforts of the participants. And, naturally, at the closing of every case, there should be a reasonable semblance of a party, complete with refreshments of some sort.

With a few exceptions, it may be expected that all of the children in a typical, graded, self-contained classroom will be able to agree on a case that is fully acceptable to every pupil in the section. Individuals of widely different interests and abilities can generally identify unique, personal opportunities in the overall challenge of a proposed undertaking. An alert and imaginative teacher can usually help children to see a greater range of possibilities than may have been immediately apparent. The voluntary aspect of the individual commitment, however, is basic; under no circumstance should any child ever be drafted or pressured into a group-identified cause. There is no solid reason, as a matter of fact, why two—or even three —separate groups within a classroom could not each identify and pursue its own peculiar concern to a satisfactory conclusion, although the arrangement would obviously call for increased flexibility on the part of a teacher as he attempted to maintain liaison with each group. With a school organization based upon some pattern of team teaching, of course, the inherent difficulties in attending simultaneously to several case-action undertakings are substantially mitigated.

While it remains extremely doubtful whether any long-range benefit has ever resulted from the traditional marking, or grading, of children even on their subject matter assignments, it certainly ought to go without saying that there is no legitimate call for the practice in case-action learning. The very notion that one person should sit in judgment over the honest effort of another is utterly foreign to the underlying philosophy of a child-oriented approach to curriculum. There is a simple answer to the question of marking individual children for their work on a group action case: forget it.

For any teacher who has had encouraging success with case-action learning, there is, sooner or later, a temptation to impress the design upon some school-related activity that does not genuinely qualify as a child-oriented, group-identified undertaking. For example, it might seem that a certain requirement in a subject matter area would be more enjoyable if studied as though it were a case that had been proposed and accepted for group action. The utter spuriousness of this may be recognized in the very fact that, inasmuch as the particular study *is required,* the children definitely *do not* in this instance hold the veto prerogative. At best, any pupil decision could be no more than a Hobson's choice. And, even though the short-term gain might appear favorable, the eventual reaction of the children as they ultimately realized that they had been duped, would surely be one of resentment. The beneficial effect of case-action learning, though powerful when handled properly, is too fragile for such deliberate mistreatment. It is earnestly recommended, therefore, that any opportune thought of bastardizing the design of case-action learning be quickly and firmly rejected.

Another point to be considered is the possibility of failure. No group of children is guaranteed success in taking on a case. But, while repeated failures most certainly would have a debilitating effect, there is no reason to assume that anything less than one hundred percent success is intolerable. Children *can* absorb an occasional failure in good grace—provided, of course, that no particular stigma attaches to the incident. Actually, it is not so much the failure per se that hurts as the signs of depreciation that sometimes accompany it. Therefore, rather than attempting to shield children from every remote possibility of failure, it makes better sense for a teacher to do his utmost to help a group to succeed, but not to be overly upset if things don't always work out to complete perfection. It might behoove a teacher to go a bit heavier on the planning, but lighter on the fussing and stewing.

Design for Case-Action Learning

There exists, undoubtedly, at least a remote possibility that a child-oriented group undertaking might be identified and carried to a satisfactory completion without benefit of a definite pattern to guide the teacher's necessary preparations. But such a haphazard arrangement is certainly not to be recommended. By adhering to a workable, precise design, a teacher may simplify the matter of planning, and significantly increase the chance of a successful venture.

The planning of worthwhile learning experiences demands intelligence, creativity, and a remarkable sensitivity to the needs and feelings of children. Inasmuch as case-action learning is regarded from a psychological, rather than a logical, reference, a much higher degree of flexibility is necessary than is required in subject matter planning. Because a child is a dynamic and growing organism, his needs and satisfactions are constantly changing. And, since case-action learning relates directly to the nature of children and the characteristics of their behavioral growth, effective planning calls for anticipating that which is not predictable.

Case-Action Learning as Seen by Children

It is particularly enlightening to view case-action learning through the eyes of the children who participate. From their collective viewpoint, the whole undertaking may be an unbroken continuum that is carried through from beginning to end without any real awareness of system or precedence. For the children it is, in the very finest sense, a happening—spontaneous and inevitable. Somehow they have identified a mutual concern that has caught the fancy of the group. And, as they become more alert to certain aspects of this particular concern, their interest and enthusiasm increase to the point of their wanting to pursue it actively. So they consider the possibilities, agree upon one or more definite objectives, organize for serious work, and set themselves to the task. Then, upon achieving their declared intentions, they reflect with considerable satisfaction upon what they have accomplished. For the children, this constitutes a fairly accurate description of a case. From the teacher's point of view, however, it is quite an oversimplification.

A Teacher's View of Case-Action Learning

A thoughtful teacher is inclined to see a happening more as being caused than as totally spontaneous. He will not take a convergence of related circumstances for granted. He knows from experience that designing a successful group action case is hard work. But he is cheered by the realization that the reward justifies the effort.

Pupil-Teacher Planning

Although children are definitely expected to participate actively in every step of a case, it is quite unlikely that they would benefit from viewing the design, as does a teacher, as a series of steps. It is more probable that children will simply regard the entire undertaking, with all of its ramifications, as an intensely fascinating, total effort in which they are happily involved. The sequence of planning steps that is suggested may constitute a systematic procedure, therefore, only from a teacher's vantage. Thus, while children may be thinking of a case as a happening, their teacher ought to be very much concerned with the interrelationships of several overlapping steps in a deliberately designed planning sequence.

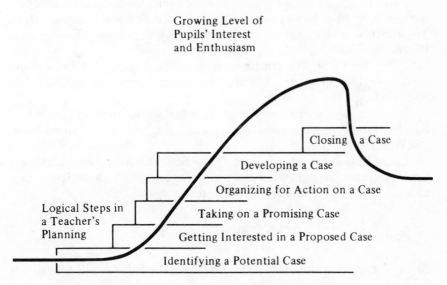

Figure 1. *Distinction between perspectives of pupils (curved line) and teacher (series of steps) as they contemplate the development of a case.*

Figure 1 illustrates the basic distinction between the perspective of a group of pupils and that of their teacher as they contemplate the development of a case from their respective viewpoints. The accelerating sweep of the curved line reflects the gradually increasing tempo of the children's undifferentiated enthusiasm for the undertaking—a sharp contrast with the logical relationship indicated in the definite series of steps as regarded in the cool deliberation of the teacher.

Elements of Design

A recommended design for case-action learning is comprised of six logically sequenced, overlapping steps. And, although a teacher, at any given moment in his planning, will probably be involved simultaneously in two, three, or more of these developmental stages, each step will be considered in detail in its sequential order in a separate chapter.

In preparing a case for group action, a teacher will want to make very sure that it will be appropriate, under a definite set of circumstances, for those particular children who are expected to participate. And this is the focus of Chapter Five, "Identifying a Potential Case."

Chapter Six, "Getting Interested in a Proposed Case," is directed toward the matter of drawing attention to an area of concern and laying the groundwork for the following stage in a group undertaking.

After children have become genuinely interested in some facet of a suggested venture, they need to define their direction and intended effort. The function of this step is discussed in Chapter Seven, "Taking on a Promising Case."

Chapter Eight, "Organizing for Action on a Case," takes up the matter of children getting effectively organized for participation in an undertaking.

Facilitating the performance of the actual work, study, or research in which children engage as they develop a case is the focus of Chapter Nine, "Developing a Case."

And, rounding out Part Two of the book, Chapter Ten, "Closing a Case," includes recommended procedures for bringing a group action case to a successful and memorable conclusion.

Summary

Achieving spontaneous group action by design calls for pupils to lead out boldly in consonance with their own feelings and drives. Freedom and spontaneity are basic to case-action learning, but firm purpose and systematic planning are equally essential. Since impulsive youthful behavior cannot be predicted, a teacher must anticipate and seize upon the exact moment when children are ready for action but may not yet perceive their own need.

A high degree of flexibility on the part of a teacher is fundamental; this is attained through imaginative anticipation, calculated guessing, and relentless overplanning. Much of a teacher's work, if he does it well, goes unnoticed; in the main, he functions unobtrusively as consultant, guide, and resource person.

The range of matters that may come within the focus of a child-oriented endeavor is virtually unlimited. Any concern whatsoever, provided that it is of genuine importance to children, may blossom spontaneously and naturally into a group action case. Among the examples offered were instances of impulsive response to school-related concerns, philanthropic opportunity, self-help enterprise, study of certain aspects of community life, development of new skills and activities, cultural consideration, confrontation of crucial situations, response to topics in the news, and even of clear challenge or voluntary pursuit of information.

Fundamental to case-action learning is the assumption that children genuinely desire to work and that they should be allowed to work in their own way toward their own purposes. In taking on a case, therefore, they must assume charge of a given situation and all that goes with it. Pupil choices, including even the ultimate prerogative of the veto over any proposal, must be freely made and utterly without pressure.

Other points of consequence include matters such as the essentiality of group action on a case, the importance of not intruding upon subject matter study time, and the beneficial effect of teacher enthusiasm. The extent to which the overall success of any effort is contingent upon closing a case properly should also be fully appreciated. The voluntary aspect of individual commitment should be regarded as absolute; there must be no exception to the prohibition against pressuring a child into a group endeavor. Since the notion of personal judgment is not consonant with the philosophy of a child-oriented approach, it is strongly recommended that there be no marking or grading of individual children for their work on a group effort. A serious potential hazard is the possibility that the design for case-action learning might be misused in applying it crassly or spuriously to subject matter study or other school activity that does not fully qualify.

Since the planning of case-action learning demands intelligence, creativity, and sensitivity to the needs and feelings of children, haphazard procedures must be eschewed. A teacher may simplify matters and greatly increase the chances for a successful case by carefully observing a dependable pattern in his preparations. A recommended design for case-action learning is discussed in appropriate detail in the six chapters immediately following.

Chapter Five

Identifying
a Potential Case

Identifying a specific matter as a possibility for case-action learning is clearly within the rightful domain of the pupils directly concerned. But, in most instances, long before children ever become involved in a decision to take on a case, a teacher will already have spent many hours earnestly contemplating their ultimate choice. Although the final selection, it is hoped, will reflect the enthusiastic consensus of the full group, a teacher's long-range planning compels him to confront the circumstances as candidly as if he alone bore the entire burden.

Possible learning situations in which children might engage are infinite. When a teacher considers a potential group endeavor for children, he is, in a very real sense, functioning as an investment broker—dealing, as it were, in children's futures. A teacher is under professional and moral obligation to approach the matter with a genuine assumption of personal responsibility.

Basic Criteria for Selecting a Case

The basic consideration in selecting a case for group action is its authenticity and appropriateness in every way. Specifically, the proposed undertaking must be worthwhile, learnable, and interesting.

Is the Case Worthwhile?

Whatever becomes the focus of children's learning activities must be deemed *worth* learning. The understandings, concepts, appreciations, facts, and skills that are intended as outcomes of the work ought to be of significant and permanent value to the individual child and to his group; otherwise, a youngster may later conclude that his time was wasted. In some instances, an objective measurement of value may be applied; in others, a teacher may have to rely upon his own best judgment. In every selection decision that he ponders, a teacher ought to pose for himself this question: "Is what I am suggesting for these children actually *worth* their very best efforts?"

Is the Case Learnable?

Key to a successful venture in case-action learning is the quality of the learning experience as such. "Learning how to learn" may be achieved to the extent that a child develops confidence in himself as an independent learner, a sense of respect for that which he is to learn, and deep joy and profound satisfaction in the agony and ecstasy of the effort itself. A child's learning experiences must be genuinely challenging, but rarely frustrating. His objectives should be achieved, but not without real effort. Success should come after an honest struggle. Briefly, the work must be neither too difficult nor too easy. The criterion of learnability should enter into every selection decision. Two appropriate questions would be: first, "Am I helping each child to succeed as an independent learner?" and, second, "Am I helping him to develop an honest *love* of learning?"

Is the Case Interesting?

A necessary ingredient of real scholarship is the emotional feeling of delight with which the true scholar approaches his work—the keen expectation of pleasure that will accompany the intense effort. A young child, being inexperienced in intensified learning activities, and with a relatively short attention span, will require careful guidance if he is to develop the attitude of the true scholar: that learning is a delightful experience. A child may sometimes feel that there is little in many of his school lessons about which to be delighted. Special effort must be made to accentuate the delightful aspects of learning. To circumvent the possibility of a less than positive attitude on the part of each child, a teacher will strive to identify a concern in which his pupils *already* have an actual or potential interest. Learning ventures built around such immediately meaningful considerations may, if carefully planned and executed, result in consistently pleasurable experiences for the youngster. Thus, intense learning efforts may gradually become associated with expectations of pleasure. A teacher's question in regard to a possible selection could well be: "Is this undertaking of actual or potential interest to this child?"

Other Criteria for Selecting a Case

In addition to these basic criteria for selecting a case, further considerations ought to be taken into account. Among these are the need to coordinate present effort with other learning experiences, and the practical matter of making sure that a particular idea is feasible.

Coordinating Present Effort with Other Learning Experiences

An important responsibility not to be overlooked in any selection decision is that of coordinating present effort with past and future experiences of a group of children. Such experiences include not only other group action cases that have been completed or planned, but also subject matter study that may be going on concurrently.

A child's elementary school career ought to be a meaningful sequence of learning experiences that are skillfully interwoven into a consistent pattern of behavioral growth. It should include elements of contrast, of complement, and of counterpoint. There must be provision for both variety and continuity. An elementary school program must be more than a disjointed series of unrelated learning experiences—however valuable they may be judged independently. Each of the years that he is under the care and direction of the elementary school must be an integral part of this phase of a child's total education. An entire faculty ought to accept the mutual responsibility of ensuring that each child's six- or seven-year program will, when viewed as a whole, represent a balanced and harmonious plan, rather than a random patchwork.

When a teacher considers a possible choice for a given group of children, one of his criteria must be that of the relationship of the suggestion to other learning experiences that the child has had in previous months and years, and also to that which he is likely to study in the future. There must be an effort to provide a proper degree of variety along with a meaningful relatedness of learning experiences. There may be circumstances that would warrant a new case growing out of one being completed —or occasions in which the choice will reflect a rather clean break with the work that has immediately preceded it. Sometimes it may be appropriate for a group of children to undertake, at an intermediate grade level, a case that is perhaps more complex, but otherwise rather similar to, an area of consideration that was the focus of their concerted effort two or three years earlier.

A case ought to be selected not only for its own value, but also for the way in which it fits into the total pattern of elementary school experiences. A series of endeavors should provide for ever increasing learning opportunities through the gradual widening of interests, enlarging of concepts, and deepening of understandings and appreciations. Care must be exercised in the selection of a group action case that it will dovetail nicely with those that have preceded it and with others to follow. In addition, a teacher must be ever mindful of the relationship of case-action learning to subject-matter study, and be alert to opportunities for enriching learning experiences. During the development of a case, children may identify a need for a particular fact or skill that may be most effectively taught in a subject matter lesson. Opportunities for such mutual enhancement of case-action learning and subject matter study should not be overlooked.

Feasibility of a Selection

Another general question that must be faced in the selection of a case concerns the practical matter of whether it actually is possible to carry out the objectives of the undertaking after they have been established. The criterion of feasibility might appear almost too apparent to warrant even bringing up, but sometimes it may not be easily determined. What may seem at first to be an excellent choice may later prove to be quite unworkable. A concern that has been the focus of delightful and worthwhile learning experiences in a previous situation may fall flat under different circumstances.

A somber note of realism in the selection of a case is strongly recommended. Are there conditions that might preclude the successful completion of the work undertaken? Is there adequate time? Are the necessary supplies and equipment available? Might certain aspects of the work interfere with the routine of other classroom groups in the building? Is the consideration timely? Is it the proper season of the year? Are geographic and climatic conditions favorable? Can essential field trips be arranged? Is it possible to conduct certain experiments or demonstrations that may be basic to the development? These are but a few of the questions that may enter into the criterion of feasibility.

A Teacher's Responsibility in Selecting a Case

That children will make the ultimate decision to take on a given case in no wise mitigates the gravity of a teacher's role in identifying the "right" case. In some ways, it might even be viewed as further call for thoroughness and integrity on his part. However awesome this responsibility, a teacher may, nevertheless, approach it with enthusiasm and confidence. Such a realistic response to duty is certainly a far cry from the lackadaisical approach of "letting the children do what they want," or the opposite extreme of religiously "following orders to the letter"—if not necessarily to the spirit. A teacher is a professional, and perhaps no other teaching job requires more of his professional sincerity and know-how than that of the intelligent selection of such an undertaking for children. The following suggestions indicate some of the directions from which a teacher may approach this important work.

Official Courses of Study

Official courses of study might very well be the first reference to be consulted. Depending upon state and local practices, these documents may include official guides that have been developed by school offices at the state, county, city, or district level. Sometimes one may be regarded as *the* "curriculum bible" for a particular school. Rarely will there be any serious conflict between any two guides at the various administrative levels. Occasionally a guide may offer only a bare outline of suggestion or proscription. More often, however, at least one of the above mentioned courses of study will have been developed in considerable detail. As a rule, such detail should serve to widen the opportunities that are open rather than to limit a teacher's freedom.

It is good to be reminded that a properly developed curriculum guide represents a workable combination of theory and practice. It often presents a locally oriented theory built upon successful practices of inservice teachers. Of course, there is no guarantee that a particular theory that has been developed out of past practices will work equally well in a new undertaking. But it can be encouraging to know that some ideas proved sound under certain circumstances, and, to the degree that new conditions are similar, the results may be equally rewarding.

One helpful feature of a good curriculum guide is a grade-by-grade overview, which enables a teacher to examine expected outcomes of his own teaching at a given grade level with that of the entire school program. Such an overview is essential in coordinating present learning activities with previous and future experiences of a group of children. And it can help a teacher to see additional ways of relating case-action learning to subject matter study that may be going on more or less concurrently. Through the instrument of a curriculum guide the teacher may see his own work in the larger perspective.

Some courses of study may attempt to allocate particular group action topics to certain grade levels in much the same way that progression of subject matter study may be suggested. Although these may appear to be arbitrarily selected for no other purpose than that of insuring at least a modicum of variety in a child's curriculum from year to year, some group endeavors may also be reserved for specified grade levels with the idea of maintaining an effective balance of areas of concern within each grade. Should certain possibilities be recommended for particular levels, there will generally be included more suggestions than actually can be undertaken during the period indicated. A teacher needs to be flexible and imaginative in his planning, and to adjust work to the unique needs and abilities of a particular group of children.

A curriculum guide may also offer certain detailed helps. For example, it may include useful annotated bibliographies both for teacher use and for pupil reference. Films, filmstrips, and recordings may be suggested. Recommended field trips suitable for children of various levels may indicate how community resources may be tapped. Names and addresses of institutions, business firms, and public and private offices that have previously indicated a willingness or desire to provide information or free or inexpensive materials will facilitate a teacher's efforts to enrich learning experiences. Centrally stored school equipment and materials may be listed, as well as games, songs, and a variety of useful ideas.

Seeking the Cooperation of School Principal and Supervisors

Faculty relationships in many elementary schools are such that enlisting the principal's help is no problem. Most elementary school faculties are small enough to permit a degree of informal cooperation and face-to-face handling of much of the work. Under such circumstances, it becomes an easy and natural thing for a teacher to discuss plans with his principal—without a special appointment or a formal proposal or request. More often than not, it can simply be a matter of two colleagues "thinking out loud" as they informally share ideas.

In discussing tentative plans for a group action undertaking, it should be kept in mind that the responsibility remains with a teacher rather than the principal. A teacher must not be reticent to assume his professional obligation as a qualified decision maker. And, while indications of mutual respect are in order, there certainly should be no show of deference because of any real or imagined status differential in the school hierarchy.

A school principal can bring some unique assets to a planning conference. In the first place, he can assist in locating and obtaining necessary supplies and equipment, and in arranging field trips and special scheduling. Because of his central position in the school, he is able to help a teacher see more of the larger picture and to appreciate better how various elements of the whole program fit together. A principal frequently will be aware of certain situations or conditions that may contribute either to the benefit or to the jeopardy of a proposed activity. And he may be able to make suggestions based upon previous experiences of other teachers in the school.

Perhaps the most valuable help that a principal may give in an informal planning conference is to assume the very natural role of an interested, intelligent, and objective listener. In this capacity he may give genuine and enthusiastic encouragement to the creative efforts of a teacher.

School supervisors working out of the central office of a school district, despite increasing demands upon their time, may also offer assistance to an individual teacher when circumstances warrant. A supervisor must serve hundreds of teachers in a typical school system; and, in order to achieve optimum efficiency, he generally will want to work with selected faculty groups or with inservice committees. But he may also find time somehow to consider the special problem of just one teacher. For example, a supervisor will usually make a special effort to be available to a new teacher who may be unfamiliar with local practices. Likewise, he will likely be pleased at an opportunity to consult with a veteran teacher who may be interested in a particular curriculum innovation or in a bit of informal research in his own classroom. Many supervisors recognize that improvements often have a grass roots beginning; and, for this reason, they may respond favorably to an individual teacher's request.

A supervisor can help a teacher to enlarge his horizons and thereby visualize additional opportunities for good learning experiences for his own group of children. And he may be able to suggest additional learning resources. Occasionally, he may arrange for an interschool visit for a teacher who is eager to observe the work of an outstanding individual in another section of the district. These are but a few examples of the countless ways in which an interested supervisor may be of real help.

Coordinating with Other Teachers

The process of selecting a case for group action ought to include some provision for planning together with other teachers who are working in the same building. Children profit most from a school program that reflects effective team work and enthusiastic cooperation on the part of an entire teaching staff. Essential to that effort is the matter of checking one's long-range plans with other members of a school faculty.

Those teachers who are responsible for the various sections of a particular grade level will often have developed a habit of working together rather closely and informally. And, while the mutual sharing of problems and plans may seem casual and unorganized, it nevertheless constitutes an important facet of the kind of team work that may produce a well coordinated educational program for each child. Since much of the work of these teachers is similar, they share a common background that fits them ideally for reacting to a problem identified by one of their number. Not infrequently they may engage in a brief, but vigorous brainstorming session during which a teacher whose particular plan is under scrutiny at the moment may receive far more suggestions than he can possibly use. This same group may also help in pointing up some of the possible difficulties and the not-so-obvious hazards that must be faced. Occasionally, the work of one teacher may directly relate to that of another. For example, the children of two or more classrooms may sometimes be committed to a joint undertaking. In such a circumstance, the teachers involved will likely form a temporary teaching team.

Even though a school may be organized on a self-contained plan, it may have certain subject specialists such as a teacher of music, or science, or physical education. If a school faculty does include one or more teachers of special subjects, it may be quite appropriate for a teacher who is in the process of selecting a case for group action to consult with these people who likely will be eager to relate their own work, insofar as may be practical, to certain aspects of a proposal. In this way, the work of both the classroom teacher and the special subject teacher may be mutually benefitted.

There are other teachers with whom there might well be some contact in the matter of case selection. Former teachers of children in a given group may have some valuable suggestions to make. And, in some instances, teachers at higher grade levels may contribute.

There are, of course, several valid reasons for a teacher to discuss a potential case with other interested members of a faculty. If a child's elementary education is to be truly outstanding, it undoubtedly will result from cooperative efforts of excellent teachers working smoothly as a team. Coordinating with others in the selection of a group action undertaking is an important aspect of that essential team spirit.

Capability of a Particular Group of Children

Always a crucial point in making a selection for case-action learning is the capability of the particular group of children who will be engaged in the work. This matter may sometimes have been resolved to a degree, perhaps in the allocating of certain topics by grade level in the official course of study. However, this can be considered at best only a rough screening.

To the extent that a given group of children is like all others at the same grade level, the unique capability of one particular group may not seem an issue. But differences among children are as significant as the likenesses. For example, in a typical group of age mates, every measure of growth other than that of chronological age will show a distribution range of from four to six years—not including occasional instances of the extremely high or the unusually low. And, as the complex patterns of individual traits show up in marked differences between one child and another, classroom groups may present combinations of these complexities which may tend both to iron out and further to emphasize individual likenesses and differences—thus, the phenomenon to which teachers sometimes refer as "group personality" or "group capability." Suffice it to say, there *are* actual differences in capability of one particular group of children as compared with another group.

To speak of the capability of a group is not to be concerned with that of the most capable or the least capable child, or even the average capability of all of the children. Group capability has to do with the amount and quality and kind of work that can be satisfactorily accomplished through the concerted effort of all of the children in the group. This is especially true as regards the designing of case-action learning.

Included in the pertinent aspects of group capability is reading ability. It may almost go without saying that a group of children undertaking a case will of necessity be engaged in a considerable amount of reading in the process of carrying out the intentions of the group. While it may not be necessary for *all* of the children to read rapidly, to read difficult material, and to have facility in the use of standard references, it usually will be essential that *some* of the children have these important skills. Quite likely, the reading and library research that must be accomplished by the group as a whole will somehow be parceled out in appropriate assignments to different children of varying degrees of competency in reading and related research skills. There probably will be some division of labor to handle any required reading in much the same way that different position assignments may be given to the various members of a baseball or football team. And, just as one might consider the capability of a ball team in terms of the combined expertise of the whole team, so might the capability of a classroom group of children in reading be properly thought of in terms of the collective competency of the whole group.

Depending upon the circumstances and the nature of the undertaking, several other vital aspects of group capability ought to be weighed. Physical growth sometimes may be a consideration. Will there be required some basic level of physical strength or endurance on the part of all or some of the children? Will the proposed handling of certain delicate equipment or fragile materials necessitate a degree of coordination and dexterity that some children may not have yet developed?

Perhaps the work will involve communicating with potential resource persons either orally or in writing. If so, a teacher should be sure that at least a few of the children, with a reasonable amount of guidance, can perform these functions satisfactorily.

Are there children in the group who, with appropriate supervision, can do the necessary construction jobs? If accurate maps or charts must be planned and drawn to scale, are there at least a few children who can qualify for such assignments? Are there members of the group who will be able to perform any necessary calculations in mathematics? Can the children follow directions? Are they sufficiently mature to work with some degree of independence and self-direction?

The nature of some cases may necessitate a great deal of committee work. Several skills are incorporated into effective committee behavior, and these skills generally will have been developed over a period of several years. A teacher cannot take it for granted that a given group of children is ready for committee work simply by virtue of being enrolled at a certain grade level.

A teacher who wishes to exercise judgment in the selection of a case for group action will give careful consideration to the question of capability.

Special Needs and Interests of a Particular Group of Children

Inasmuch as there are far more possibilities for case-action learning than can possibly be squeezed into a child's elementary school program, it is good sense to make every effort to insure that those relatively few considerations that can be included be chosen with great care. Each selection criterion, as it is applied in its turn, represents in essence a finer and finer screening. On occasion the matter of providing for special needs and interests of a particular group of children will be a prime consideration.

Being concerned about the total educational welfare of each child, a teacher will strive to maintain a good balance as to types of learning experiences. For this reason, as well as others, he will constantly be looking for opportunities to encourage each child to develop new and varied interests.

Other things being equal, it generally is best for children to be engaged in learning activities in which they manifest genuine interests. Sometimes, however, a teacher may deliberately—albeit subtly—arrange a situation that may not immediately be to the personal liking of a child. If discreetly handled and not attempted too often, this may constitute one way to help children develop new interests. But the teacher must exercise caution, for there is considerable risk of souring the child's attitude toward trying anything that may be new or different. In getting children to attempt the new or the unfamiliar, patience may be as great a virtue as motivation.

Frequently a teacher will feel that a child ought to be applying himself not to a task which he may perform very well, but rather to one at which he is relatively unskilled. For example, a certain child may not be a good reader, yet his teacher, quite understandably, may be convinced that additional opportunities to do more and more reading for various purposes may satisfy a genuinely personal need. Or perhaps a child may be seen as needing legitimate opportunities for self expression in the form of oral discussion or written reports. Again, a teacher may identify in his group of children a need for physical activities or handicrafts. Perhaps further experiences in informal group work or committee assignments may be seen as a real need for several children. A teacher may recognize a need for leadership development, or a need for certain children to learn to be more tolerant. In a typical classroom group of children, an alert teacher may single out a variety of different needs that quite properly may enter into his considerations.

Some of these important individual needs may not be accompanied by correspondingly strong manifested interests on the part of the children concerned. This may present somewhat of a problem for a conscientious teacher, for he will sense the need to resolve two pertinent factors: first, that of including in his design the kinds of learning activities that are calculated to satisfy the individual needs that have been identified, and, second, that of making sure that each child will be genuinely interested in the work that is contemplated. Meeting special needs and interests of a particular group of children in the selection of a group action case is certainly not a simple matter, but it is a very important one.

Permanent Value of a Learning Experience

Early in the chapter, discussion focused upon certain basic criteria for the selection of a group action case. One such criterion was that of the *worth* of a particular undertaking. A teacher cannot always easily determine the degree to which a given concern qualifies, for there are no absolutes. It would be extremely difficult to show a particular suggestion as being either completely worthwhile or totally useless. Judgment will necessarily be in terms of relative values. Certainly a teacher will wish to make sure that whatever is being learned in his classroom is actually worth learning.

A major purpose of case-action learning is to provide meaningful experiences in "learning how to learn." The unique contribution of this approach to curriculum consists largely in the deliberate and conscious effort that children make to identify a problem or an area of concern within their experiential awareness, to organize and plan, and to work systematically toward a solution of that problem or the accomplishment of their objective. Case-action learning, of course, is focused principally upon the learning experience as such; *what* is to be learned assumes an ancillary importance. Valuable though the selected bits of knowledge may be, the specific facts, understandings, appreciations, and skills that are gleaned by a child through his participation in a given undertaking are secondary to the central purpose of case-action learning. The quality of the learning experience itself ranks first.

This is not to say, however, that it makes no difference what facts, understandings, appreciations, and skills the children acquire. For at least two reasons a teacher should be very much concerned about what children learn in a particular endeavor. In the first place, since the available choices are practically infinite, and, inasmuch as the children in any event are going to be expending precious time and energy in a learning effort, one might reasonably argue that they might just as well obtain some useful bits of knowledge in the process—more or less of a bonus, as it were. In the second place, and of much greater importance, the quality of the learning experience is enhanced by the significance of the product of that learning. *What* is to be learned and *how* it is to be learned are inextricably bound up together. Process cannot be entirely separated from product. In the selection of an undertaking for case-action learning, therefore, an important factor is that of permanent value.

Timeliness or Cruciality of a Case

Another of the several considerations that must be taken into account in the selection of a case is that of effective timing. The developmental readiness of children to undertake a certain learning activity is, of course, part of this. But also, a given concern must be introduced at the most opportune moment. The full impact of a particular case may be better realized in some instances by "striking while the iron is hot." The timeliness or cruciality of a concern, especially in regard to the season or a special occasion, may constitute a pertinent selection factor.

There are, of course, many possibilities that seem to be "good anytime." Provided that a consideration is within the capability range of a group of children, it may make no particular difference whether a given case is scheduled for autumn, winter, or spring. An occasional highly durable undertaking that happens to meet the special needs and interests of a definite classroom group may even seem to have a perennial quality that makes it appropriate year after year.

Other ideas may be more perishable. The season of the year may be a rather rigid determining factor in some instances. Considerations requiring more study of animal or plant life than may be accommodated in classroom cages or window boxes may necessarily be confined within a limited period during the autumn or spring. Observation of natural phenomena such as freezing and thawing, evaporation, erosion, soil composition, and rock formations may have to be arranged with some thought for cooperative weather. Certainly, field trips for various purposes may often be accomplished in greater comfort and with more efficient learning if scheduled at a time when the children can keep reasonably warm and dry.

Legal and traditional holidays and public celebrations may suggest the planning of certain efforts to coincide with an appropriate date on the calendar.

Other cases may be planned around a "one time only" event. A teacher will frequently be able to adjust his long-range plans in order to take advantage of the natural motivation provided by developments and occurrences reported in the daily news. Political, industrial, and cultural affairs are of potential interest to children. The construction of a new public building, the opening of an airport, or the dedication of a bridge or dam may possibly be incorporated into an interesting and worthwhile group endeavor. Even a disaster such as an earthquake or a flood, if handled so as to avoid over-emphasizing the bizarre and the morbid, may help to provide effective challenges for a group of children. If employed judiciously, events in the news can contribute much to make case-action learning a dynamic and ever-changing aspect of elementary curriculum.

Availability of Essential Materials and Equipment

Last, but perhaps not least, among the several factors entering into a teacher's decision regarding the selection of a group action case is the thoroughly mundane question of availability of essential materials and equipment. Planning ahead to insure that the necessary items will be on hand at the proper time and in the proper place may frequently spell the difference between a case that comes off smoothly and on schedule, and one that is marred by delays, interruptions, and confusion.

It is a mistake for a teacher to assume, simply because he has occasionally seen the desired materials or equipment in the building, or perhaps has used them himself in his own classroom, that the required items will be at his disposal on a moment's notice. A more realistic practice is to take nothing for granted, but rather to look ahead and place orders well in advance.

Supplies of consumable goods have been known to run out at a most inconvenient moment. Requirements should be anticipated, therefore, even for such classroom supplies as chart paper, stencils, crayons, butcher paper, colored chalk, paste, scissors, paint, string, masking tape, and thumb tacks. In some instances, purchase requisitions may need to be forwarded through the principal's office.

Orders for films, film strips, and recordings generally should be placed several weeks—even months—in advance to avoid later disappointment. Use of special equipment maintained by a district media center may require tight scheduling. Equipment regularly stored within the building may not present such a rigid requirement; nevertheless, requests for such items as projectors, recorders, microscopes, carpenter's tools, miscellaneous science equipment, animal cages, planters, aquariums, musical instruments, and sports equipment should be submitted in advance.

Supplementary books, miscellaneous reference materials, pictures, charts, and maps may need to be checked out or reserved at either the school library or a public library.

Occasionally, shortages may be disguised blessings. Learning to improvise, providing it is not overly time consuming or does not distract too greatly from the primary purpose of the undertaking, may be an important part of a child's education. An austere school budget may make it necessary to substitute old newspapers for the lavish use of something more costly. Simple equipment may have to be constructed out of available materials by the children under the teacher's guidance. Some items may have to be repaired or borrowed. Again, a teacher must exercise judgment. If the children are getting valuable learning experiences through such improvisation, it may be all to the good. However, if their time is not being well spent, or if the overall development of a case is being sacrificed, then such makeshift arrangements should not be condoned.

A teacher's responsibility in the selection of a group undertaking for case-action learning cannot be lightly dismissed. Determining the availability of essential materials and equipment requires imagination, foresight, and judgment.

Role of the Children in Selecting a Case

Since the ultimate decision to take on a case is a prerogative of the group directly concerned, it is important that children be actively engaged in the matter of identifying a suitable undertaking.

Making Sure that a Potential Case Holds Interest for Children

An undertaking must be of interest or potential interest to all of the children who will participate. It has been established that interest is essential to the development of a positive attitude toward learning and the building of scholarship in each child. The children's full involvement in the selection helps to assure that a suggestion does indeed have an immediate or a potential interest for every member of the classroom group.

Giving Children Experience in Decision Making

A second excellent reason for children to have a major role in the selection is that it provides them with valuable experience in cooperatively making decisions within their ability. Working together as a group to arrive at a reasonable decision that is satisfactory to all concerned is an important aspect of "learning how to learn."

Whatever may be the role in decision making that children assume, it must be realistic and *within their ability.* To turn over to children a decision which is clearly beyond their comprehension or level of responsibility serves only to make a mockery of the selection process. Children must feel that they are fully qualified to participate in selection proceedings by virtue of their maturity and demonstrated skill and sincerity in accepting responsibility. It is essential, therefore, that they be secure in the function they are undertaking. They must understand what they are doing and why.

Making intelligent decisions requires disciplined thinking. In working with a group of children, a teacher may plan the deliberations in such a way that children are encouraged to approach each of the available choices with an open mind, to weigh the pros and cons objectively, and to arrive at a decision with a sense of satisfaction and lively anticipation for the work ahead.

Two common hazards should be avoided in bringing children into any selection decision. Perhaps the more serious of the two is the practice of letting children vote before they have thoroughly considered all of the possibilities. A second weakness is that of going through the motions of permitting children to make a free choice, but, in reality, "talking them into" an option that has already been decided by the teacher. The first of these practices indicates a gross misunderstanding as to the educational value of learning to make sound decisions. The second practice is one of sheer dishonesty and, moreover, is insulting to the intelligence of children.

A teacher must recognize that a reasonable degree of meaningful participation by children in the task of selecting a group action case is a legitimate educational experience that yields both immediate and long-range benefits.

Giving Children a Sense of Commitment

An additional benefit of involving a classroom group in a selection is that it gives each child a sense of personal commitment for the success of the undertaking. When they genuinely have a voice in choosing what they will do, children are likely to feel a personal responsibility for achieving the objectives of a group-identified case.

An enthusiastic teacher can easily sway children into agreeing at the outset to almost any reasonable proposal. A dynamic personality and exuberant spirit can convince children that a given suggestion holds promise for a most delightful experience, and the class may be swept along purely on the excitement of the moment. But worthwhile group action cases are more than just fun and excitement; they also include much hard work. It takes sincere dedication to carry a group of children through the difficult days after they become occupied with the down-to-earth jobs that must be done. It makes good sense, therefore, to help children bolster their spirits for the less exciting experiences which they must face. The sense of commitment that they receive from participating actively in the selection of a case is well worth the effort.

Summary

Although it is clearly the prerogative of a group of pupils to identify and select an undertaking in case-action learning, a teacher must confront the situation long before children become involved. Since possibilities are infinite, the matter must be approached with candor and a sense of personal responsibility.

A case selected for group action must be genuine and appropriate in every way. Specifically, it must be worthwhile, learnable, and interesting. Additional considerations include coordinating present effort with other learning experiences and determining that a suggested selection is feasible.

Despite the seriousness of his own role in identifying a likely endeavor, a teacher may regard his task with enthusiasm and confidence. He may be guided by the following:

1. Official courses of study.
2. Cooperation of school principal and supervisors.
3. Coordination with other teachers.

4. Capability of a particular group of children.
5. Special needs and interests of a particular group of children.
6. Permanent value of a learning experience.
7. Timeliness or cruciality of a case.
8. Availability of essential materials and equipment.

Since the choice is ultimately that of the group concerned, it is important that pupils engage actively in identifying an appropriate case. Their involvement in a selection provides further assurance that a proposal has actual interest for children. A group's active role in a selection also provides valuable experience in cooperative decision making and gives each child a sense of personal commitment for the success of an undertaking.

Chapter Six

Getting Interested
in a Proposed Case

Spontaneity is of the essence in case-action learning, but getting interested in a specific undertaking is not generally an instantaneous happenstance. More often than not, interest gradually evolves from a fleeting moment of casual attention that somehow ignites and increases in tempo and intensity to a solid and lasting commitment. In preparing for this crucial step in the development of a case, therefore, careful consideration should be given to the full range of the transpiration. A variety of both planned and un-planned incidents and activities ought to be included as abeyant interest builders; and aspects both of initial attention calling and of subsequent, more earnest contemplation must be regarded as requisite.

Drawing Attention to a Potential Case

When a teacher believes that a potential group action case is appropriate and timely, he faces the challenge of helping children become initially interested. The identification process will not yet have been completed in every detail at this time, but will be continued to a noticeable extent even after a group has begun to show genuine interest in a proposal.

Purpose of Attention Calling

Attention getters in daily life may be as startling as the blast of an air horn or as subtle as the fragrance of a light perfume. Their function is to get immediate attention. A teacher thus plans ways and means of working with children to render the initial exposure of a likely endeavor as effective as possible. His purpose will be to draw attention to an area of concern, to arouse curiosity, to stimulate interest, to create wonder, and to encourage thinking.

Planned Techniques and Activities

A teacher knows from experience that various techniques, devices, incidents, and activities will be required in order to reach every child in a group and build initial interest in a possible undertaking. Since different children may be expected to react differently to a given inducement, he needs to plan a number of attention getters. While one child may respond to a visual suggestion, another may be motivated by a novel physical activity. A third may be intrigued by an intellectual challenge. Or an amusing incident may attract still another child. Actually, most children will react not just to one, but to several varied approaches. The key to effectiveness in developing spontaneous interest at this point is to avoid a heavy or overly serious feeling, but rather to keep the effect fairly casual and relatively brisk.

Unplanned Techniques and Activities

In addition to those well prepared and deliberately used attention getters that a teacher may arrange in advance, frequently totally unforeseen incidents may serve very well as instant motivators. While it is not possible to plan ahead in the usual sense to incorporate these unpredictable incidents or circumstances into the introductory stage of a group action case, some bits of realistic spontaneity may occasionally be included. For a teacher to be alert and ready to seize upon such an unexpected bonus opportunity is perhaps a result of "planning for the unplanned."

Considering Possibilities and Merits of a Proposed Case

Just as soon as children have shown initial keen interest, a teacher faces a second challenge—"striking while the iron is hot." In a teacher's planning, this aspect of interest building assumes a distinctive relationship within the step; but from a child's point of view, any ensuing activities will blend easily and naturally with those already having taken place. The transition from casual attention to sober contemplation should be so gentle that there will be no discernible change of pace or sharpening of emphasis. Whatever gradual quickening of development may be noticed should stem principally from the growing enthusiasm of the group itself.

Purpose of More Deliberate Consideration

A vital need then is to keep alive whatever interest has been indicated, and to build it into a genuine concern that will sustain the interest and enthusiasm of each and every child throughout the extended period of hard work that lies ahead. Procedures should be selected that will strengthen the determination of children to see an undertaking through to its satisfactory completion. In helping a group during this phase of becoming acquainted with a possible case, a teacher will likely express a more deliberate and positive feeling toward a proposal. The free and easy reaction that he manifested earlier will be gradually superseded by a more dynamic, purposeful response as he sets a favorable example for the pupils. A teacher's purpose at this time will be to exploit whatever motivation has been realized, to deepen the interest that has been stimulated, to help children become genuinely concerned about a proposal, to discover what may already be known about an area of consideration, to allow children to see a variety of possibilities in the ensuing action, and to personalize some aspect of the undertaking for each child.

Suggested Techniques and Activities

Suitable techniques and activities intended for later use as deliberate interest builders resemble those recommended for drawing attention initially to a possible group endeavor. Any actual difference is more in purpose than in form. In fact, because of the smooth escalation from the implementation of one purpose to that of another, children will likely make no distinction at all. A teacher ought to recognize, however, that the difference, though not clearly discernible, is significant. Whereas the requirement at the outset was to capture attention and get children momentarily interested, the need at this later point is to provide an effective orientation of a proposed undertaking, and to present opportunities for considerably more probing and exploring of an identified area of concern.

A comparison of activities during each of the two phases of the step will reveal definitely more seriousness at the subsequent level, both on the part of a teacher and by the pupils. Youngsters should become more deeply involved, both as individuals and as a group. Activities at this point will call for increasing pupil participation and, hopefully, will build a feeling of total commitment to a proposed case. By this time, a group of children will have progressed in expressions of interest well beyond that merely of "taking a fancy" to a concern; they will now—quite literally—be *doing something* about it.

Planning and Using Interest Builders Effectively

Imaginative overplanning is as basic to spontaneity in the matter of building interest as in any other facet of case-action design. A variegation of suitable techniques and activities must focus upon a proposal from several incentive vantages in order to present an objective view of the range of possibilities to each pupil. The ultimate list of motivational ideas that might be employed to good purpose by a highly creative teacher is perhaps endless. The following recommendations for selection, preparation, and use of some of the more common devices and tactics should therefore be regarded as suggestive rather than delineative.

Reading or Telling a Story

Most children enjoy hearing a good story. If selected with care, an interesting story can serve both as a bit of delightful entertainment and as a subtle means of directing a child's attention toward a possible consideration. Such a story may be either fictional or based on historical fact. It may be either read or told with equally good results. The presentation generally will be made by the classroom teacher, although occasionally it may be appropriate for one of the children to make a special preparation.

To be suitable, a story should be one that immediately appeals to a particular group of children. At the same time, it must somehow start them to thinking along the lines of some aspect of a case that has been tentatively identified. This may be accomplished through plot, setting, characterization, or perhaps a description of a given activity.

Children may not, however, react just as anticipated. In fact, it is quite possible that a story, chosen specifically for the purpose of directing children's attention in a desired direction, may backfire, diverting their thinking to something quite remote from that intended. But, if judiciously selected with regard to probable effect upon the class, and if presented skillfully, a story that is read or told to children can be effective.

Classroom Demonstration

A classroom demonstration has an advantage in that it is "live" action. It generally contains some element of uncertainty as to the outcome, and this serves to command attention. Any mechanical or chemical action or the demonstration of a scientific principle will often arouse curiosity on the part of the spectators, and, if handled skillfully, can create wonder and encourage children to try to reason it out. Likewise, a clever demonstration of a handicraft, a physical skill, or an artistic ability can be expected to stimulate interest.

Demonstrators may be a classroom teacher assisted by one or two children, a team of children who have volunteered for a special assignment, or perhaps a special guest who has been invited to perform. Children should be involved as much as possible, of course, since this personalizes the interest.

To be fully effective, a demonstration must be carefully planned in every detail and rehearsed so that it will be smoothly executed. Whatever materials or equipment will be needed should be at hand. Explanations and pertinent commentary should be clear, concise, and well timed. Also, the audience must be prepared. The effect of an otherwise good demonstration is occasionally spoiled because some children are unable to hear what is said or to see all that is going on. It is well, therefore, to arrange a "ring-side seat" for every child in the class. If the nature of a demonstration precludes staging so that everyone can see and hear, then it may be necessary to plan two or three replications with smaller groups.

It should be remembered, of course, that the purpose of a demonstration at this stage in a development is not to satisfy curiosity, but to promote interest. If used as an attention getter, a demonstration should raise more questions than it answers. The need is more to titillate than to teach.

Mounted Flat Pictures

A well-arranged display of mounted flat pictures can be an effective low-key device for getting attention and promoting interest in a new concern. If selected with thought and displayed tastefully, the pictures become, in effect, a part of the general decor of the classroom. Frequently, such pictures may be displayed two or three days before any actual class time is devoted to the introduction of a proposed case; and it may sometimes be appropriate to leave them up until after an undertaking is fairly well along. It may not even be necessary to make any mention of them, as their effectiveness is not dependent upon the concentrated attention of the whole group. It is quite enough if the display is quietly and casually viewed by individuals or clusters of two or three children at a time.

There are a number of possible sources of good pictures. Photographic prints, either black and white or in color, may be especially prepared to produce a desired effect. Calendar and magazine illustrations offer an almost inexhaustible supply in a wide variety of subjects. A good number of industrial and commercial corporations prepare free kits of informational materials, including attractive pictures. And, of course, it is possible to obtain good pictures for mounting from publishers and stationery shops. Many teachers habitually collect and file useful pictures, and thus have a convenient source immediately available when the need arises.

Pictures should be large enough to be seen easily from a distance of ten feet or more. As a rule, the minimum size ought to be approximately seven by ten inches, although a smaller one might be used occasionally if it is especially good. Color has an obvious advantage, but good quality black and white photographs can be attractively displayed. To be most effective, a display should be so arranged that the combination of several pictures presents a single theme relating to an area of consideration that is being introduced.

Display of Objects

Children entering a classroom on a given morning will quickly notice any strange object that has been given a prominent spot. Bringing in an object normally used outside of school can be a clever means of attracting attention and arousing curiosity. Even items which are regularly seen and possibly used by children in their daily lives may stimulate interest when displayed in a different setting. A household tool, a bird or animal, a piece of sports equipment, an item of furniture, a toy, perhaps a large growing plant all suggest possible objects, one of which might serve to attract attention to a potential case.

The effective use of objects depends to an extent upon the surprise element. Either a strange object or a familiar item that is not expected will prompt an immediate reaction. The manner in which the object is displayed will indicate a deliberate purpose, and the children will begin to look for a possible connection.

Whether class time is devoted to a discussion of the object being displayed is optional with the teacher. Of course, the item will constitute a ready conversation piece, which can spark a lively group discussion. Or perhaps the teacher will prefer to ignore the display while the children get more and more curious.

Objects as attention getters should be used with some restraint. Generally, the fewer the objects (one to three preferably), the more effective the reaction they stimulate. Each object should be selected for a definite relationship with some aspect of a concern that is being introduced. Unless care and judgment are exercised, the resulting effect, unfortunately, can be that of a jumble. Used with imagination and skill, however, an appropriate display of one or two objects in a classroom can significantly enhance the introduction of a case for consideration by a group of children.

Samples and Specimens

The peculiar nature of a proposed consideration occasionally suggests the use of samples or specimens as an additional means of stimulating initial interest. Especially useful in drawing attention to some aspect of the physical environment, such materials may make it possible to create wonder and gently encourage children to make inferences as they examine comparative samples of water or soil, or perhaps specimens of rock formation.

As with other attention getters, samples and specimens are most effective when exhibited with an eye toward showmanship. A display should be arranged so that children may examine materials with a minimum of teacher supervision. If any specimens are to be handled by children, labels may be attached to prevent confusion in identification. Or a glass case or transparent containers may effectively prevent undesired handling. A bit of foresight in this regard will reduce the risk of children being reprimanded as they manifest normal interest and enthusiasm.

Although most exhibits of specimens are intended for viewing with the unaided eye, occasionally microscopic slides may be prepared for use by more mature children, making it advisable for two or three pupils to be given advance instruction in the operation of a microscope so that they may assist other children.

Scale Models

While no device can be expected to prompt interest with absolute certainty, the use of certain motivators may *almost* guarantee success. High on the list of attention getters is the scale model, a three-dimensional representation of an object or a complex of objects. It usually is constructed as an exact-scale miniature of the original, although occasionally it may be life-sized or even an enlargement of the object represented. A model airplane, for example, is a miniature of the actual aircraft, while a scale model of a mosquito is more effective if rendered larger-than-life.

Models seem to have an almost universal attraction for both children and adults. If well made and carefully selected for a definite purpose, they can be highly effective in drawing attention to a suggested consideration and stimulating children's interest in the possibilities. A display may appropriately be arranged a day or two in advance of any classroom discussion focused on a new consideration. Perhaps the most serious drawback to the use of models as attention getters is the disproportionate demand upon the teacher's time and effort in their construction and display. Occasionally, however, it may be possible to incorporate miniature true-scale toys in an attractive and useful display.

Maps and Charts

An appropriate display of a map or chart during the early introductory stage of a development can have a beneficial effect in quietly directing the thinking of children along the general lines of the area of concern. Maps and charts can be either combined with other motivating devices, such as a story or a motion picture film or still pictures, or simply used as an element of the total room environment.

When used with another device, a map or chart should deliberately direct the immediate attention of an entire class to a consideration of what is shown and its relationship to a possible undertaking. Employed this way, a map or chart should usually be brought out only during the brief period suggested; it can be hung on a wall in a prominent place and taken down immediately after use.

It is also possible to blend a map or chart into the overall decor of the room in such a way that it serves as a low-key means of encouraging thinking over a more extended period of time. For this purpose, it is effective to arrange a well balanced display a day or two prior to any actual discussion of a proposal, allowing the children several days to observe individually and to react in their own way and in their own time.

An important characteristic of a map as a means of drawing attention and stimulating interest is its obvious value in locating an area of concern geographically. The type of map can be an additional factor: a political map will prompt a somewhat different reaction than will a physical relief map, a products map, a weather map, or a highway map.

A chart is designed to convey graphically a body of information in a clear and concise manner. It shows comparisons, rates of growth, and chronological development. Inasmuch as a chart presents its message in sharply abbreviated form, a certain degree of skill is required to read one meaningfully. Care must be exercised, therefore, to make sure that a given chart is not too complicated for the maturity level of the children.

As with several other motivating devices, maps and charts will be more effective if the total presentation is fairly light and casual. Clutter is certainly to be avoided. Whatever is displayed should be carefully featured or blended with a definite purpose in mind—the junkyard effect does not constitute a rich environment. A hodgepodge is not going to channel the thinking of children in a desired direction. Keys to effectiveness in getting children initially interested in a potential case are imagination, balance, taste, and restraint.

Posters

A poster is particularly useful in presenting a brief announcement in a forceful but impersonal manner to a number of persons within a limited period of time. It is not one of the more subtle persuaders; rather, it hammers home its message in a few quick, obvious blows. For this reason, the display should be limited to a few days. As soon as every child has observed it and reacted appropriately, or immediately following the announced event, the poster has served its purpose and should be taken down.

To be effective, a poster must be carefully planned, skillfully prepared, and attractively displayed. Lettering should be balanced and neatly applied. Any drawing or other illustration should be sharp and relatively simple. Colors must be judiciously chosen. A messy, unbalanced, carelessly-lettered poster is worse than none at all. But one that is well done and properly displayed at the right time can be well worth the effort.

Bulletin Boards

Particularly in a classroom in which a bulletin board is maintained as a year-round activity, the possibility of making excellent use of this device as a means of getting a class initially interested in a new endeavor is very bright. The most effective bulletin board is one that has become a routine part of the children's classroom behavior. A board that is kept up to date, either by complete changes of posted material at definite intervals or by continually fresh material and prompt removal of out-of-date items, is regarded in the classroom in much the same way that a daily newspaper is accepted in the home. Children habitually read a bulletin board because they have learned that it is a convenient source of interesting and pertinent information.

A classroom bulletin board should be placed in a well lighted, easily accessible location that is not in the line of heavy traffic. The appearance of the board is perhaps as important as the appropriateness of the material posted thereon. A neat, attractive arrangement of notices, clippings, and illustrations makes it possible for a child to scan the material very quickly and identify that which is of special interest to him. A messy, haphazard look, on the other hand, is not at all inviting; and, furthermore, it tends to camouflage whatever may be worthwhile. Maintaining a bulletin board properly does not demand a great deal of effort, but it does require regular attention. The degree to which a teacher may delegate the job of keeping up a bulletin board will depend upon the maturity of the children and their willingness to accept responsibility.

An effective bulletin board is not a passing fancy, but rather a permanent aspect of a classroom program. In using a bulletin board as a device for developing initial interest in new considerations, it is simply a matter of selecting items to be posted that will play up a theme that is related to a suggested case.

Dramatizations

Children show interest in whatever their classmates may be doing at a given moment. Activities that engage some members of a group often intrigue nonparticipants as well. A dramatization in which a few children assume roles as actors and actresses for a brief presentation before their classmates may constitute an effective device for drawing attention to a proposed undertaking.

Dramatizations may be used in a number of ways to develop interest initially in a new concern. It may be possible to locate suitable prepared material from which an appropriate selection may be cut or adapted for classroom staging. Or perhaps a teacher may develop a short skit to be acted out by volunteers from the class. Or a group of children, with only a minimum of teacher guidance, may develop through their own efforts a simple production — complete to script writing, directing, and acting.

Used primarily as an attention getter, a dramatization should be fairly light and informal. It is not necessary or even desirable to have elaborate costumes and stage properties. Spirited, almost spontaneous action to stimulate interest and arouse curiosity may serve the purpose better than a too obvious effort. Easy humor will generally go over well. Above all, a dramatized selection should be brief—just enough to produce a quick impression that relates clearly to a proposed consideration.

Games and Contests

As might be expected, there are both advantages and disadvantages in using a game or contest as a means of getting children initially interested in a group endeavor. On the credit side, it should be recognized that children usually are pleased to participate in recreative activities. Under certain circumstances, therefore, it might be appropriate to plan an interesting classroom session for the enjoyment of the group and, at the same time, to draw attention to a potential case. A rather obvious hazard in employing this device is that children may become so engrossed in a game or contest for its own sake that it does not channel their thoughts toward the new undertaking.

Children habitually think of games and contests as a means of deriving excitement and pleasure from their activities. Fun is likely to be seen as a worthwhile end in itself. If friendly competition is to be used as an attention getter, the game must almost invariably be modified in some way to make it peculiarly adapted to the purpose. A simple pastime or diversion may qualify very well as amusement, but in its usual form it is not likely to contribute to the introduction of a new consideration. A teacher planning to include this particular device as a motivator will, therefore, be wise to make sure that there is a definite tie-in between the game or contest and some aspect of a proposed undertaking.

Classroom Visitor

With the possible exception of pupils enrolled in a busy demonstration or experimental school in which countless visitors may be coming and going with almost routine regularity, it seems that children just naturally pay attention to a classroom visitor. Occasionally, therefore, it may be quite appropriate to invite someone to come to the classroom to speak briefly to a group or otherwise to assist in the initial introduction of a new case.

In extending an invitation to a person who is expected to make a positive contribution in stimulating the interest of a class in a proposed endeavor, a teacher should make very sure that such a visit will indeed serve a real purpose. A dynamic personality, some skill in speaking, a knowledge of some aspect of the topic, and an honest interest in children are obvious assets. A visitor may be almost anyone who is willing and able to respond to the request. A principal, another teacher, a child from a different classroom, or a parent of one of the pupils might very well qualify. Or an invitation might be extended to someone not in any way connected with the school, such as a business man, a forest ranger, a foreign visitor, or a senior citizen who can recall the early history of the community.

A few days before a scheduled visit, it is a good idea for a teacher to meet with an expected guest to discuss the purpose of the planned visit. The maturity and background of the children should be made clear so that the presentation may be appropriate. The teacher should inquire whether equipment or materials of any kind will be required for any aspect of the guest appearance. There must be agreement as to the length of the visit; a clear understanding at the outset may circumvent a potentially embarrassing situation later.

When the visitor arrives at the appointed time, the group must be immediately ready to give him complete attention. He should be welcomed either by the teacher or one of the children and properly introduced to the class. The introduction may be brief, but it should include such essential information as the name of the guest, his position, and some indication of his knowledge of the topic that he will present. An introduction also should convey the appreciation of the children and the teacher for the visitor's helpfulness. At the close of the visit, the guest should be thanked sincerely, and his name should be mentioned once more. Occasionally, it may be a thoughtful gesture to follow up the oral expression of appreciation with a short thank-you note.

In addition to the direct educational value of a classroom visitor, improved public relations and home-school understanding may result. Even busy people are often pleased to contribute a bit of their time for the direct benefit of a group of school children. And, of course, such contacts serve to increase the public understanding of what the school is striving to do. An extra benefit also accrues to children in that such guest appearances for educational purposes help them better to relate their school work to their out-of-school experiences.

Special Report

The extent of a child's personal involvement is often a contributing factor in his growing interest in a given matter. The wisdom, therefore, of arranging various opportunities for early individual participation is apparent. And, although a teacher generally expects to assume much of the responsibility for preparing motivational activities for the early introductory stages of case development, there are legitimate occasions for at least some of the children to make a unique contribution. A few such possibilities have already been suggested. Another excellent example is the special report. Its effectiveness either as an attention getter or as a means of directing and deepening interest is worth considering.

Accepting an assignment to prepare a special report for the benefit of his classmates is a challenge that a child will often relish. If he works hard and does a good job, he senses a strong feeling of satisfaction in having performed a useful service, and he enjoys the quiet expressions of appreciation that he receives from the other children. From the standpoint of a group, a special report by one of their own members brings a personal touch to a situation.

In approaching a child as a potential volunteer for such an assignment, a teacher may well take into account a number of factors. A matter of top priority, obviously, is choosing a child who is capable of doing the work satisfactorily. A second consideration is that of finding a child who is willing, if not actually eager, to accept this important task. It is desirable to offer the job to a child who will benefit significantly from the experience. Special reports ought to be included in that sensitive category of individual assignments that should be distributed judiciously over a period of time among various members of a class. To encourage the same child to respond time after time is bound to raise suspicions of favoritism. Naturally, such an eventuality would be detrimental to the individual's feelings of worth, and would jeopardize his performance as a motivator. Occasionally, the job might be given to two, or possibly even three, children.

One recommended procedure for making an assignment is for a teacher to approach a particular child privately several days prior to a certain anticipated date with a suggestion that other members of the class might enjoy a well prepared report on a given topic. Should the child already have some potential interest in the matter, he might happily volunteer for such an assignment, particularly if he receives encouragement and a sincere expression of confidence in his ability to perform adequately. On the other hand, if he seems less than responsive, a teacher may quietly drop the subject and later bring it up with another possible candidate.

Having accepted a definite assignment, a child engages in whatever research seems promising. Then, working with the advice of his teacher or a member of his family, he verifies his facts and organizes his material into a meaningful outline which is then polished into an acceptable report for presentation to his classmates. Through the investment of his own time and energy, a pupil may sense a commitment to further exploration of a topic.

The quality of a report, certainly, is important. Both for the sake of a child who takes on the responsibility and for the need of the class to be positively motivated, it is elemental that the results have an impact. A poorly prepared, carelessly delivered report is more than likely to have an unfortunate effect. For the individual's self-esteem, therefore, as well as for the usefulness of the report, certain measures must be taken to insure creditable performance.

Understandably, it is essential to avoid any semblance of pressuring a child into accepting the task. The youngster must understand that he is assuming an extra load and all that goes with it—the burden of responsibility as well as the personal satisfaction. Although his teacher will plan to assist him as much as necessary, a child should feel that the success or failure of his report will depend upon his own skill and determination. There must be adequate time for the researching and organizing of information. If a report is to be written, a teacher's helpful criticism will be appreciated. As a rule, however, a special report will be presented orally, and the delivery before his classmates will be more polished and effective if a child has had one or two private rehearsals in the presence of his teacher, a parent, or an older brother or sister.

Motion Picture Film

The importance of motion picture films both as a teaching aid and as a medium of entertainment has been well established. Films also constitute an excellent means of drawing attention to a potential case and building interest.

A film to be used as an attention getter should be selected primarily to stimulate initial interest in an area of concern. The suitability of a particular film *as an instructional device* is not pertinent at this point. In making his selection, a teacher will likely give some thought to whether a given film may be more effectively used in introducing a proposal or somewhat later, perhaps in the research and study phase. Occasionally, a certain film might be appropriately shown a second or third time during the full development of a case, but the specific purpose of each showing ought to be clearly defined.

Care should be exercised in making sure that a particular film will channel the thinking of children toward a proposed case. Whether a film is appropriate to the general maturity level of a group is another important factor. Children will not be likely to respond favorably if the approach tends either to be above their level of understanding or to be talking down to them.

Other things being equal, an ideal film to serve as an attention getter early in the step is one that requires a minimum of teacher introduction. Unlike films used primarily in instructional situations, which may necessitate advance preparation in "what to look for," a viewing of a film intended simply to attract initial interest in a potential case should be fairly casual. A soft sell is more likely to produce desired results. However, a later presentation timed specifically to foster deeper and more lasting interest will, of course, be comparatively more deliberate and purposeful.

Filmstrips and Slides

Projected still pictures are also effective in the development of interest. Filmstrips and color slides have some of the advantages of motion picture films. They can be presented to an audience of almost any size, and they command immediate attention. Still picture projections have a more intimate quality than do motion picture films, since the duration of exposure of each frame is controlled by the operator, who thus has an opportunity to make appropriate comments. If desired, children also question or comment as they view the pictures.

Commercially produced filmstrips of excellent quality are available in an almost unlimited number of subjects. Generally, the cost is reasonable, making it possible for a school to build up a sizeable library. Some titles are coordinated with sound recordings, either on tape or disc.

Prepared color slides on many subjects may be either purchased commercially or processed from the teacher's own color photography. The flexibility of color slides is at once both an advantage and a potential hazard, as their effectiveness is directly related to the judgment exercised in selecting the particular slides that are to be shown. While slides offer a convenient method of promoting initial interest in a group undertaking, they can also produce deadly boredom.

Again, the intent at this stage of case development is not primarily that of instruction, but rather that of arousing children's interest.

Single Concept Filmloops

Items of equipment that a child can operate independently in his own time and at his own pace may be quite effective in helping him to identify some definite aspect of a proposed undertaking in which he may develop a particular interest and become more deeply involved. The 8mm single concept filmloop projector is an excellent example of equipment that can be operated by even very young children without help or supervision. With a little instruction, either an individual pupil or a small group can drop a filmloop cassette into a portable projector, flip a switch, make a slight adjustment in focus, and—in a matter of seconds—be viewing a continuously-wound motion picture film that repeats its two- or three-minute message over and over to the satisfaction of the individual viewer. An obvious extra advantage of using filmloops is that, while they may be viewed on occasion by almost any child, they may be especially appreciated by those children who are among the less skillful in reading.

Recordings

Both phonograph records and prerecorded tapes offer possibilities for developing interest. Expressions in music and rhythm are frequently a useful key to cultural understanding; they may contribute to a general atmosphere to help children gain a feeling for a particular time or place. Historical events may be brought to life, and the sounds of conversation in a foreign tongue may carry children in their imaginations to a faraway land. Particularly when combined cleverly with other media, recordings can be unusually effective.

Homemade recordings may add a personal or local dimension to a proposal under consideration. Whether prepared by a teacher or by individual children, they enhance the sense of immediacy in a situation, and thus help a group to identify with it.

Transparencies and Overlays

The overhead projector has proved to be highly effective as a means of focusing the attention of a group on a projected image to point up direct instruction or to channel class discussion. With proper equipment, simple transparencies in black and white can be made easily and quickly. Multiple-sheet overlays require slightly more care. Colored drawings may be processed, and rubber cement lifts or commercially gummed plastic sheets may be used to make transparencies from pictures clipped from popular magazines. Also, it should be noted that commercially made transparencies and overlays in a variety of subjects are available. A nice element of intimacy and flexibility that should not be overlooked lies in the convenience with which an operator may point or even write upon a transparency during an actual projection.

Mockups

Although legitimate opportunities to display full-size structural models may be relatively rare, the occasional possibility of featuring a mockup should warrant its mention as an interest builder. Although it may have been created largely out of cardboard and papier mache daubed with powder paint, a space vehicle or a blinking and humming electronic computer is not likely to be ignored. Carefully constructed to scale with one or more working parts, a mockup may constitute a captivating center of interest. A realistic diesel engine or an airplane cockpit occupying a prominent spot in a classroom is likely to serve as a constant reminder of an area of concern to which it is rather directly related. A mockup may be particularly appropriate if it has been designed and constructed by two or three imaginative and skillful children who have volunteered in advance for the assignment.

Dioramas

Creating a miniaturized diorama is an activity which several children of varying artistic skills may enjoy. Although taking up very little classroom space, an imaginatively made diorama can serve as an attractive center of interest. A simple diorama may be constructed upon a low table or sandbox, with small toys and dolls incorporated into a three-dimensional foreground and a suitable background painted on a strip of cardboard curved around three sides at the rear of the scene. A somewhat more sophisticated version, of course, might challenge the best artists and craftsmen in any group.

Graphs and Diagrams

At least among children, there certainly is some truth in the adage regarding the thousand-to-one equating of words and pictures. Graphic representations, particularly when they have been prepared by members of a given class, constitute another striking means of intensifying interest. A graph or diagram can often be a challenging and fascinating way for an individual to report to his classmates the results of his library research or firsthand observation. The message can be clear, succinct, and—if appropriately posted—available at all times to an intended audience. And, for a child who finds it more productive to express his thoughts in drawings rather than in words, an occasion to design a useful diagram or graph may be an opportunity for making a satisfying and worthwhile contribution to a group concern. Also, the occasional combining of a graphic presentation with an oral or written report should be seen as a possibility.

The very nature of graphics demands, of course, that high standards of art work and accuracy of representation be strongly encouraged. Neatness is much more than a matter of visual pleasantry: it is essential to the message. Lines and figures must be drawn exactly, and lettering must be done with care. A graph or diagram requires thoughtful planning and patient execution. For this reason, it may be prudent to schedule such an undertaking as a voluntary homework assignment over a weekend. At times it may be advisable for two children to team up for a particular job.

Collections

Displaying a well organized collection as a means of pointing out certain possibilities in a particular case may entail both unusual opportunity and serious jeopardy. The physical evidence of a fascinating hobby can do much to stir the imagination of an already interested viewer and further exploit whatever motivation has been previously achieved. The very real danger, however, that a cherished collection may be damaged or lost should not be minimized.

Collecting things seems to be an almost universal trait among both people and pack rats. Children have been known to hoard quantities of bottle caps, matchbook covers, seashells, and colorful stones. Adult tastes may run all the way from monogrammed hotel towels to antique automobiles—depending upon individual scruples and plumpness of pocketbook. Tourists regularly reserve a portion of their vacation budgets for the purchase of momentos and souvenirs. And, of course, coin and stamp collectors are legion. Perhaps it is the subconscious mutual recognition of this thoroughly human characteristic that renders collections so uniquely effective as a means of building interest.

Just how best to use an attractive collection for this purpose in developing interest in a group action case may present somewhat of a dilemma. The tactile pleasure of handling certain items in a display may be for many children an important aspect of the overall enjoyment of the experience; yet, for various good reasons, this often cannot be permitted. Keeping a valuable collection in the classroom overnight may be especially risky, in consideration of the general vulnerability of schools to occasional acts of burglary or vandalism. In view of these and other limitations, it may be appropriate to restrict the showing of a particularly prized collection to a brief period of time when the owner can arrange to be present to supervise it personally. Carried to the extreme, of course, overly protective attitudes may result in more irritation than fascination. Children, it must be remembered, are basically doers—they crave active participation—and too many "don'ts" will turn them off.

Directed Reading

Reading activities continue to be viewed as highly valuable educational outcomes and as effective learning tools. Reading for pleasure and reading for information are universally recognized purposes. Reading also provides numerous opportunities for widening horizons and stimulating new interests. And, as an important means of directing and deepening children's interests to focus more sharply and intently upon a particular area of potential concern, well planned reading activities certainly ought to be included in the early stages of case development.

Generally, reading materials for this particular purpose should be selected to narrow in gradually on a specific proposal, rather than further to widen the field of vision; but there should be deeper penetration. And, while the readings will inevitably satisfy a number of questions that the children may have about an area of mutual concern, the general effect will be more to raise questions than to provide answers. In fact, it may prove intriguing if some of the answers that are supplied prove to be somewhat uncertain or even contradictory. Children may find it stimulating to be jarred out of their complacency and to realize that there is more beneath the surface that is worth digging out.

Perhaps the most obvious source of appropriate reading materials is to be found in the textbooks regularly used by children in a classroom. A teacher can easily refer to selected chapters, paragraphs, tables, or illustrations that contain an interesting or peculiar relevance to a likely group effort. As a general rule, such readings should be brief and carried out in such a way that curiosity may be more stimulated than satiated. In fact, it may be possible occasionally to introduce the germ of a controversial issue into children's thinking.

Another convenient source consists in the general reference books located in a classroom. For example, one or two children might volunteer to look up a particular topic in an encyclopedia and either read in full or summarize briefly the material for the benefit of the class. Inasmuch as an encyclopedia report will usually be rather general, there will likely remain unanswered many specific details of local or immediate application which the children may wish to pursue further. Other general references may be similarly used.

An article in a magazine or journal may have possible pertinence. Depending upon the circumstances, a teacher may ask a child to go over a given article at home, then read or review it for his classmates the following day. Or a magazine can be placed open on a table in the room where an article may be read individually by each child as he is attracted to it during two or three days.

Encouragement of children to form a habit of reading the daily newspaper certainly constitutes a worthwhile objective. And, of course, opportunities to relate something read in the newspaper at home to a topic being considered at school may be doubly rewarding.

Two other excellent sources of directed reading are the trade books that generally supply a large portion of a child's recreational reading material and the books that are in his home.

Directed reading may be assigned as the occasion may suggest. On a whole-class arrangement, every child may be responsible for his own information over the same basic material. Sometimes an assignment may be given to one or two children on an individual basis, or a child may volunteer to prepare a report or to read orally a particular article in its totality. Children should be convinced that everyone can share in the important reading responsibilities.

Library Research

As interest continues to build up, it is important that each satisfactorily answered question and each seemingly settled issue result inevitably in an ever growing concern about a proposed case. An interesting question growing out of a discussion may sometimes prompt one or two children to "look it up" in the school library, particularly in schools in which informal use of the library on an open schedule is generally encouraged. Occasionally, it may be helpful to ask for a volunteer to visit the public library for some specific bit of information that may not be immediately available. While library research may typically be thought of as an excellent means of answering questions and resolving differences of opinion, it may also deepen wonder and enliven issues. It is quite possible for a skillful teacher to incorporate the subtle influence of the library into his repertoire of curiosity builders.

Interviews

Many fascinating bits of information that might be presented at this time for the purpose of deepening children's interests in a particular consideration may not be generally available in the form of books or other published materials. Rather, they may be a part of the personal knowledge of certain individuals in the community—perhaps a local government official, a newcomer, or one of the rare old timers. Through interview techniques, it may frequently be possible to tap some of these excellent sources which might otherwise be quite inaccessible.

As the occasion may warrant or allow, a given interview may be conducted in the classroom in the presence of the entire group of children, or it may take place in the home or place of business of the subject. Brief written notes may be taken in the manner of a newspaper reporter, or a portable tape recorder may be used. At times two children may work as a team to conduct a particular interview.

There are definite advantages in using the interview as an interest builder. The person being interviewed, for example, is relieved of much of the burden of formally preparing himself for the occasion. With but a modest amount of brushing up on a few essential facts, he may appear on relatively short notice and without any qualms about either being well organized or making a good impression, inasmuch as the direction and pace will largely be set by the interviewer. Also, since interviewing requires principally oral, rather than written, communication skills, children of a wide range of abilities may participate directly. It is not unusual for a child who may not be considered particularly academic to blossom significantly when his performance is not restricted by reading or writing limitations. And, of course, the psychological effect of this upon other children may of itself be a factor in helping a group to visualize a greater variety of possibilities in a proposed case.

Some precaution may be in order to insure that an otherwise effective interview does not appear "canned." Before getting to the central concern, an interviewer and his guest may wish to engage in light conversation to the extent that they both feel at ease and relaxed in the situation. However, any strictly-adhered-to outline or semblance of an actual rehearsal should be avoided. The results will be more fruitful if the inherent elements of spontaneity and uncertainty of outcome that have established the interview as an interesting and durable technique are allowed to develop freely. Although the respective roles of the participants are defined by tradition, an ensuing dialogue hopefully may be perceived by an audience as a polite-but-spirited confrontation of two minds which cannot be easily ignored.

Letter Writing

Getting information direct from an original source can be an exhilarating and insightful experience for a young girl or boy. To receive in the mail a personal response to a written inquiry is invariably a boost to a child's self image. An increasing sense of confidence in himself and a growing interest in the subject of an exchange may come with a sudden realization that an issue or problem that has been identified by his school group also constitutes a matter of serious consideration by persons in industry or government, as well as by other adults.

Letter writing ranks among the most practical and most fruitful of possibilities for helping children become genuinely concerned about a proposed endeavor. It is clearly a two-phased activity—first, the business of writing and mailing an inquiry; and, second, the reply which comes as a welcome note of individual recognition and a subtle endorsement of the undertaking being considered by a class.

There are relatively few hazards in letter writing as an exploratory activity. In the first place, the expense is obviously minimal—an envelope, a sheet or two of paper, and a postage stamp. Of course, there is always the unhappy possibility that an answer will not be forthcoming. The likelihood of this, however, seems to be increasingly remote each year as more business concerns and public agencies continue to recognize the long-range good sense in replying promptly and frankly to questions posed by school children.

Much of the value of letter writing as an interest builder hinges directly upon the degree of individual effort. For obvious reasons, outright instances of teacher-written letters ought to be avoided as a general rule. The importance of preparing the very best letter of which he is capable can be a challenge to the most skillful writer in any elementary group. On the other hand, a child who is less proficient in written communication need not be discouraged, since there is no reason why he may not ask for whatever assistance may be necessary for turning out an acceptable job. A very young child may find it necessary to dictate his letter to a parent or an older brother or sister.

Experiments

Regardless of outcome, a bona fide experiment may usually be depended upon to hold attention and deepen interest. While some topics obviously lend themselves more readily than others to the enchanting unpredictabilities inherent in such activity, there are occasions when an appropriate experiment conducted by two or three pupils may prove surprisingly relevant in building greater concern in a proposed case and in helping certain children to visualize a variety of potential opportunities. Although there is some tendency to associate experiments only with natural science, interesting and thoroughly honest experiments may likewise be related to phenomena in virtually any other area of study or observation. As with several other categories of interest developers, the most significant benefits of a classroom experiment accrue to the children who are directly involved in the actual work; however, other members of a group also may profit in a more general way.

Informal Quizzes

An important aspect of directing and deepening interest is that of helping children to discover what they may already know about a concern that has caught their attention. The informal quiz, used with judgment and imagination, may occasionally serve this purpose. But discretion must be exercised in considering such an activity.

Depending in part upon the general attitude of a group toward various past testing practices, either a positive or a negative connotation may be inherent in any suggestion of arbitrary measurement or checkup. If there is any suspicion that it might be seen in any way as a threat or an unpleasantness, the idea of a quiz should be discarded without hesitation; the result could be hazardous to the building of greater interest and enthusiasm. On the other hand, if the purpose of the activity as a casual exploratory measure is made quite clear, and if the quiz is brief and on the light side, many children may thoroughly enjoy being momentarily on the spot.

Voluntary Homework

Regardless of the age and maturity of the children involved, and regardless of the nature of a proposed endeavor, it may be said almost axiomatically that some voluntary homework is essential to the launching of a successful case. In accepting such a homework assignment, it is especially helpful if a youngster considers his particular job important to his classmates as well as to himself. Whether obtaining some specific bit of information, making a poster, or looking for pictures in an old magazine, his task will be more delightful and challenging if he sees the larger perspective. The thought of making a worthwhile contribution to one's group can definitely spur individual effort.

Voluntary homework affords an excellent opportunity to help bridge any gap between inschool and out-of-school considerations and thereby foster a greater understanding of the total situation. As a child discusses a potentially interesting matter with his family, his own explanations of the school activity take on increased meaning and greater clarity. Questions and comments raised during the conversation may suggest new facets and possible aspects of the topic that are especially worthy of personal concern and enthusiasm.

Field Trip or Excursion

An important advantage of case-action learning is that it relates the classroom study of a child to his out-of-school learning experiences, and thereby enriches his total educational opportunities. During the development of a case, there may be several occasions on which it might be profitable to engage children actively outside of the classroom. In fact, there likely are more legitimate occasions to justify such an experience than can reasonably be scheduled in the limited time available. But it would be a serious mistake to assume that if one field trip is beneficial, a lot of them would therefore be even better. The principles relating to the use and misuse of spices in cookery apply equally well to the use or misuse of educational outings: both should be planned deliberately, sparingly, judiciously, and imaginatively.

Appropriate activity may range in complexity from a brief orientation walk in the immediate neighborhood of the school to an all day excursion or a bus trip to a farm or industrial plant. But conducting a successful away-from-school venture is never simple, and there are sound reasons for placing some reasonable limit on the number of trips in which a group of children may participate during a given period of time. A field trip is inevitably time-consuming, and school hours are far too precious to indulge in such activity just for the entertainment value. Much planning and coordination are necessary to insure that the experience will yield genuine educational dividends.

A field trip or excursion to consider possibilities and merits of a suggested undertaking will be planned somewhat differently from one that is intended simply to draw attention initially to a potential case. Although some teachers may be reluctant to use the term "excursion" on the grounds that it may connote carefree play more than honest educational effort, a field trip planned exclusively for the purpose of drawing momentary attention to a proposal should be regarded by the children in a somewhat more relaxed manner than one scheduled later. This is, of course, consistent with the general advisability of keeping attention getters somewhat on the light side. Whereas a field trip scheduled primarily for more sober considerations will require rather meticulous preparations on the part of the children, one that is mainly to stimulate immediate reaction and arouse curiosity will be treated more casually from the viewpoint of the pupils. Even though a teacher's planning may be equally detailed and purposeful, the group may view the one almost as a recreational outing. Occasionally, in fact, an activity may be precisely this. An apparently incidental detail of a school picnic, for instance, might well suffice to spark a new interest. And an away-from-school learning experience planned as a part of the serious study phase of a previous enterprise, or a research aspect of some subject matter consideration, may prove also to be a helpful attention getter for a concern that has yet to be introduced.

With the possible exception of visits that are planned purely for an immediate attention function, the specific reasons for any educational outing should be identified jointly by pupils and teacher. To the extent feasible, the youngsters should share in making arrangements with the host and in working out a tentative organization and schedule, although certain aspects will undoubtedly receive a teacher's personal treatment. Particular thought, for example, must be given to timing a visit for maximum impact.

Not to be overlooked is the matter of obtaining permission from the parents of each child who expects to participate. Whether the child carries home a standard form for the required signature or one of several other procedures is followed will likely be determined by individual school practice or district-wide policy.

Depending upon the maturity of the children, the purposes of the trip, the distance to be traveled, the weather conditions, and possibly the time available, a group may either walk or go by automobile or bus. If a school system operates its own bus service, the problem of scheduling transportation may be considerably eased. There may, however, be some nominal charge for each child; and, in any event, a work order or requisition must likely be forwarded from the principal's office several days before the occasion. If a bus must be chartered from a commercial or metropolitan line, it may be prudent to make arrangements well in advance. (Also, the cost per pupil may be a bit higher.) In certain circumstances, it may even be feasible to use taxis for intermediate distances. Legal complications alone would virtually rule out consideration of private automobiles of either parents or teachers.

Frequently it may be appropriate for one to three adults, other than the teacher, to accompany a group. With younger children, this may be considered largely a necessary safety measure, to insure that some child will not become injured or lost. But the practice may prove equally beneficial with groups of more mature pupils, for an additional person can serve as assistant guide and help them to get more out of a visit. It should be obvious that such persons must be recruited and selected judiciously and tactfully. Certainly not everyone who volunteers for such an assignment will constitute an acceptable choice. Regardless of whether he or she be a parent of one of the children, a classroom aide, an older student, the school principal, or a representative of the industry or agency which has agreed to host the children, an adult helper should be chosen with careful consideration as to potential effectiveness in helping to make a visit worthwhile and memorable. In retrospect, the overall impression made by each person accompanying a group on a field trip will become, in effect, an inseparable aspect of the total experience. Reputable character, good judgment, pleasant personality, some knowledge pertinent to the purpose of a visit, and willingness to serve are all desirable qualities.

The behavior of children on any away-from-school experience is certain to be of some concern. To begin with, there is a high level of anticipation for the specific objectives of any excursion. A feeling of excitement is almost an inevitable concomitant of the break in routine. Of course, there is some uncertainty both as to procedure and as to outcome. And many of the operative controls and guidelines that regularly obtain within a classroom will have lost much of their perspective. It may not be surprising, therefore, that the specter of grossly inappropriate pupil behavior on a field trip has been enough, on occasion, to dissuade an otherwise creative teacher from venturing beyond the security of the school plant with a group of children.

However, consistently good behavior on the part of a group of youngsters on an away-from-school assignment need not be either a matter of good luck or stern discipline. The first and most important principle to be observed is that of making sure that the children view their trip, not as a holiday from responsibility, but rather as a legitimate means of achieving one or more purposes that they have established for themselves. This premise sets the basic conditions to be considered in all aspects of planning for a visit. A teacher can help a group to recognize the need for a certain degree of formality and a high level of self discipline. In planning sessions, children may be encouraged to think ahead through all stages of a proposed visit and try to anticipate various situations that may arise. Perhaps a few special rules of behavior may be formulated and adopted. To know exactly what personal conduct is expected will help each child to be at ease and to get the most from the activity. A last-minute review by children of their agreed-upon behavioral guidelines just before departure should suffice as a positive reminder.

With such preparatory steps to care for most eventualities, the actual time away from the school area can be thoroughly enjoyable and satisfying. Travel to destination and return will be relatively safe and relaxing, and often an effective means of drawing a group together in spirit as well as in purpose. The visit itself will be conducted in an efficient businesslike manner for the optimum benefit of every member of the group.

Care must be exercised to insure that the benefits of a field trip be fully realized and preserved. Upon return to the classroom, therefore, the matter of appropriate follow-up assumes priority. Depending upon circumstances and purpose, this may take the form of an unstructured general group discussion for the casual sharing of observations and reactions. Or perhaps a more deliberate method of mutual feedback may be employed, such as individual oral or written reports, written entries in a log or diary, or drawings or diagrams.

Common courtesy, of course, suggests that a proper expression of appreciation be made to the sponsor or host, as well as to various persons who assisted. Most children will likely be eager to participate in writing thank-you notes or in making telephone calls.

Small Group Discussions

On occasion, for one or more reasons, it may be advantageous to use small group discussions either in conjunction with, or in place of, a general class discussion.

Significant benefits are inherent in small group discussion. Inasmuch as fewer individuals are interacting, each child has proportionately greater opportunity to speak during a given period of time. Also, the increased degree of informality has a salutary effect on spontaneity, and thus promotes uninhibited expression through which participants may more quickly identify whatever genuine concerns and feelings they happen to share. At least a portion of a discussion may take place independently of the immediate influence of a teacher, thereby providing subtle encouragement for children to exercise initiative and self-reliance.

There are also definite hazards which may be anticipated. In the first place, the physical characteristics of a classroom itself should be considered. A large, uncluttered area with favorable acoustical qualities, carpeting on the floor, and easily movable furniture lends itself very well to this small group activity. Conversely, a small, crowded room with poor acoustics, cumbersome furniture, and a hard surfaced floor accentuates the need for a high level of self-discipline on the part of children. The circumstances may determine whether to have several small groups engage simultaneously in independent discussion, or to limit such activity to only one or two groups at a given moment.

Because of their immaturity, children will typically experience some difficulty in buckling down to serious work when they are operating without the direct influence of a teacher. (It is not at all uncommon to observe that even a group of well educated adults meeting for a singular purpose may show this same reluctance to shatter the pleasant spell of idle small talk and tackle the business at hand.) But a bit of guidance on the part of a teacher may enable children to cope with this seemingly universal difficulty.

Occasionally, teachers have resorted to the expedient of designating one child as temporary chairman of a small discussion group. On the surface this may appear to be an effective solution, for it frequently seems to result in a reasonably businesslike session. But an assigned chairmanship automatically suggests a degree of formality that may be more inhibitive to "thinking out loud" than is appropriate to the purpose. As a rule, it is probably better to maintain a more informal procedure in a small group.

Keeping in mind both the need for some controlling framework within which to operate and the requirement for free and spontaneous expression, a teacher may take definite steps to foster productivity in the situation. Before children move into a prescribed seating arrangement, it is good to make sure that they have arrived at some general agreement as to what is to be accomplished during the forthcoming dialogue. This may be an obvious outgrowth of a just interrupted general class discussion; it may be an assigned sub-topic; or it may be a particular question that requires screening or clarifying prior to consideration by the whole class. Sometimes it may be helpful to write the question or topic on a small card to be carried to a discussion circle. The important thing, of course, is that every child know precisely what is expected to come out of the session.

Another recommended factor in guidance is a definite time limit. Knowing in advance that time is a commodity to be used efficiently is a subtle prod for each participant to carry the assignment forward to completion. Certainly, care must be taken that the time limit is reasonable. To allow quite arbitrarily what is obviously a ridiculously brief period for a discussion frustrates thoughtful workers and forces superficiality. At the other extreme, a longer period than is actually needed fosters indecisiveness and slipshod work habits. If a teacher is not sure just how much time to allow, it is probably better to err slightly on the side of too *little* time rather than too much.

A third essential to effective small group discussion is the scheduling of a "time of reckoning." Any small group splintering off temporarily must be expected to give an accounting when it later rejoins the larger group. Each small group, therefore, will plan to make a brief report or summary to the class at the conclusion of the session or at some later agreed-upon time. Thus, a whole class benefits from the efforts of a small group, and each of the discussants has the satisfaction of having made a worthwhile contribution.

General Class Discussions

At various intervals throughout the interest building step, general class discussions will likely seem to be not merely a useful notion, but perhaps almost an inevitability. One of the first of such a series may come about spontaneously as children explore ideas and questions triggered by some of the techniques and devices that were employed to get initial attention. Each child will have noticed something in a little different way, and he will naturally be anxious to share his thoughts. Succeeding full-group sessions will reflect a gradual narrowing and deepening of the concern that has been identified. Later, group discussion may become the point of easy transition between the interest building stage and an actual declaration of commitment to a particular case.

A great deal of skill on the part of a teacher is essential to productive class discussion. A teacher's overt participation will, of course, be minimal. He will need to strive for an effective balance between the degree of formality that is requisite to large-group conversation and the degree of impulsiveness essential to the purpose. Each child must be encouraged to express himself clearly and to listen thoughtfully to comments of his classmates. Some statements will undoubtedly be challenged, which is quite appropriate, provided good manners are observed. Ridicule and scoffing certainly have no place in such a discussion. Even seemingly foolish comments must be heard in good grace if the objective of the discussion is to be attained.

It must be kept in mind that the need is to identify and shape issues —not to settle them. Conclusive arguments, therefore, should generally be postponed until supporting evidence is in. Expressions of concern, wonder, uncertainty, and doubt identify aspects which ought to be studied further. Differences of opinion need not be resolved, but may be kept open for later consideration. If properly conducted, a class discussion will stimulate to a much greater extent than it settles.

Making Good Use of Unplanned Incidents

The need to respond positively to unexpected circumstances that may be realized after a potential group undertaking has been identified is vital to case-action learning. An alert mind and a keenness to seize any serendipitous opportunity are requisite to resourceful teaching. Such a teacher shows a definite eagerness to augment even the most meticulously prepared plan with appropriate improvisation. The following examples may indicate possibilities for realistic spontaneity in building interest in a proposal.

Children's Questions or Casual Observations

Perhaps one of the more delightful "facts of life" of teaching at the elementary level is the utter impossibility to anticipate many of the questions that children ask and some of the apparently offhand observations that they make. Trying to understand the immature pattern of reasoning behind such questions and comments provides a constant enigma for a teacher who is genuinely concerned with the intellectual and creative development of his young pupils. On occasion, of course, children do ask facetious questions and make comments for purely frivolous reasons. Sometimes, however, they pose an apparently foolish question in all seriousness. A seemingly ridiculous statement may, in fact, be a sage comment. An astute teacher, therefore, exercises some reticence in passing judgment as to the validity of a child's remarks.

Certainly, this does not mean that every unguarded utterance of every child in a classroom contains the germ of some hidden truth that must be pursued to its revelation. But it does imply that children's interests and concerns are frequently expressed in questions and observations that seem to come "from out of the blue." An experienced teacher will have his ear tuned, as it were, for verbal expressions that offer a legitimate tie-in with the introduction of a group action case. To pick up a potentially pertinent comment that has been casually dropped by one of the children is to take advantage of a possible windfall in drawing attention to a new consideration and in stimulating interest.

Unusual Happenings and Coincidences

The very unpredictability of certain unforeseen occurrences may give an additional impact to whatever value such a happening may have in precipitating interest in a case that is somehow related. Unusual events may spark an excitement that can sometimes be channeled to direct the children's attention toward new concerns. Likewise, the simultaneous occurrence of two or more similar, but separate, incidents—even though perhaps not particularly interesting of themselves—may serve to arouse curiosity and cause a good deal of wonder and amazement.

A centennial celebration, a scientific accomplishment, the announcement of an engineering or industrial undertaking, a political election or appointment, an important athletic championship play-off—all suggest types of unusual happenings that may take place from time to time in any sizable community. For a teacher to be alert to the possibilities of such occurrences as additional attention getters in the introduction of a new undertaking may serve the double purpose of encouraging pupil interest in a proposal and, at the same time, of helping children to relate their inschool and out-of-school learning experiences.

Perhaps an element of caution should be recommended in insuring that the spontaneity and excitement of a rare occasion are not permitted to draw the attention of children *away* from a promising area of group consideration rather than *toward* it. In making appropriate use of unusual or coincidental happenings, a teacher must be ever alert to potential hazards as well as to opportunities.

Surprise Visits

The feasibility of deliberately using classroom visitors to assist in the introduction of a new case has already been discussed as a planned technique. Most teachers are aware, however, that classroom visitors may drop in occasionally without formal invitation and with little or no advance notice. Such a visitor may be a parent, a member of a home-school committee, a university student, a representative of the local fire department, a repairman, a professional worker from the school office, or a traveler from a foreign country. As a general rule, the visitor will have reported to the principal's office for permission to enter the classroom, and his immediate objective likely is to observe routine activities for a few minutes as quietly and unobtrusively as possible. Although children are usually very much aware of a visitor's presence in the room, they likely will not interrupt their work other than to glance briefly as the guest enters the room and takes the seat that has been offered.

A well organized classroom group, under the guidance of a competent teacher, takes the matter of casual visitors in stride. Children manifest little or no interest, taking their cue from the teacher, who appears unconcerned; there are more pressing demands for their attention. However, every caller is a potential attention getter. It may take only a word from the teacher to focus the gaze of every child directly upon their guest. On a rare occasion, it may be quite appropriate—for a combination of reasons—to take advantage of the moment and to enlist on the spot the ready services of such a person in providing supplementary impetus for a new concern. This will require rather a snap judgment on the part of a teacher, for there is the obvious risk that an unexpected invitation to speak briefly to children in regard to some aspect of a proposed topic may cause the visitor some embarrassment. Also, even though he may be quite willing to respond, his comments may fall flat. Despite these hazards, the possible advantages, under certain circumstances, of a purely spontaneous reaction may be worth the gamble.

Gifts and Letters

The delivery of a wrapped-and-tied parcel or a sealed envelope is also a natural attention getter. Looking forward to the mail is an aspect of daily ritual both in homes and in offices. There are the inevitable anticipation and aroused curiosity pending revelation of the contents, then the quick development of interest and related thinking as the recipient responds to the stimulus.

Typically, several members of a class will have friends or relatives living and working in various locations throughout the nation and the world. Former classmates may have moved away or perhaps may be traveling with their parents. A lively exchange of correspondence and occasional gifts or photographs enables each party—the traveler and the stay-at-home—to sense vicariously the experiences of the other. The information received by letter may or may not be as detailed and as accurate as other, more objective, sources might provide; but there is the personal touch that adds a note of immediacy and realism.

On occasion, the receipt of a gift or letter by the classroom group or one of its members may be helpful in the introduction of a group action case. Being reasonably aware of the general nature of correspondence regularly carried on by children is a reflection of the excellent rapport that may be observed in well run elementary classrooms. Knowing when and how to blend some of the benefits of this activity into the early stages of case development is a matter of alertness and good judgment on the part of a teacher.

News Events

Keeping abreast of local, national, and world news is essential to effective living today. A positive attitude in regard to being well informed about what is constantly going on all about him should be encouraged and developed within each child from the time he enters kindergarten and throughout his school career. Many children come to school with the news habit already well ingrained by parents and older brothers and sisters. Good schools reinforce this habit both directly and indirectly. Relating appropriate events in the news to work that children are about to undertake in school is thoroughly consistent with this.

Many elementary teachers, of course, include some attempt to deal with the news of the day by various methods and with varying degrees of success. Using a particular news event to stimulate interest in a likely case will be much more effective in a classroom in which some workable plan for considering and evaluating the daily news is a routine aspect of the class program. Regularly scheduled, meaningful discussions give children an opportunity to share ideas gleaned from their out-of-school reading of daily newspapers and magazines and from newscasts presented on radio and television. Under such favorable circumstances, it becomes natural for someone in the group to point up an interesing relationship between a certain news item and some facet of a tentative group consideration.

As with other techniques and devices for interesting children in a potential case, a great deal depends upon the imagination and good judgment of a teacher. But there will be occasions on which an appropriate news event may be employed with especially good results.

Commercial Television and Neighborhood Movies

That children enjoy watching television and going to movies has been well established. In fact, the degree to which many children seem absorbed by these media—sometimes to the exclusion of other worthwhile activities— is a source of occasional concern to professional persons who work in various capacities with children. While no one ought seriously to suggest a prohibition on television and movies, the importance of helping youngsters to become more deliberately selective in their viewing has been generally accepted.

Appropriate occasions for incorporating out-of-school television and motion pictures in the introduction of a case will be relatively few. At rare times, however, an excellent show may happen to coincide with the introduction of an undertaking in the same general area of concern. The advantage of such a favorable circumstance may be realized by encouraging children to tune in a certain program or to attend a particular motion picture that happens to be showing in the neighborhood. Done with some tact and discrimination, such a suggestion by a teacher may serve a double purpose in helping to get children initially interested in a potential case and in guiding them in the development of taste in television viewing and motion picture attendance.

Accident or Disaster

An accident or a disaster is a most unfortunate incident that frequently may have costly or even tragic results. It may at first, therefore, seem crass or downright morbid to suggest that such a circumstance be exploited in the introduction of an undertaking by school children. A more objective viewpoint however, might suggest that an occasional consideration of some of life's unhappy aspects may be a means of helping children to develop a more sympathetic and understanding appreciation of other people.

An accident or disaster does command attention. It is reported in the news; it becomes a topic of general discussion in the community. Not very often, to be sure, will there likely be any significant relationship between a potential case that has been identified and an accident that has just been reported. Nevertheless, such an eventuality is possible; and, when such a coincidence does occur, a classroom teacher ought to be alert to the potential educational benefits, as well as to some of the hazards. As long as accidents continue to occur, they will capture attention, arouse curiosity, and stimulate interest. A teacher will undoubtedly exercise some restraint in channeling the thinking of children toward the area of relatedness in such a way as to move them gently beyond the purely bizarre and morbid elements of the happening in order to focus attention upon the possibilities of the new group endeavor.

Summary

The task of bringing a potential case before a group of pupils consists in helping children become interested in a particular matter of concern. Interest is built up gradually from a condition of casual attention to one of definite commitment; and appropriate planning ought to be directed toward the full range of commensurate purpose. To encourage spontaneity at the outset, it is advisable to avoid any overly serious feeling, but instead to keep the effect fairly light. Attention getters should be planned more to titillate than to satisfy. Later in the introductory stage somewhat more deliberate tactics may be employed to keep initial interest alive and foster a more serious contemplation of a proposal.

Inasmuch as all children do not necessarily respond in exactly the same way to a given incentive, and, since an individual youngster will likely react not just to one inducement, but to several, a variety of techniques and devices ought to be used in order to reach every child. The following may be regarded as suggestive examples:

1. Reading or telling a story
2. Classroom demonstration
3. Mounted flat pictures
4. Display of objects
5. Samples and specimens
6. Scale models
7. Maps and charts
8. Posters
9. Bulletin boards
10. Dramatizations
11. Games and contests
12. Classroom visitor
13. Special report
14. Motion picture film
15. Filmstrips and slides
16. Single concept filmloops
17. Recordings
18. Transparencies and overlays
19. Mockups
20. Dioramas
21. Graphs and diagrams
22. Collections
23. Directed reading
24. Library research
25. Interviews

26. Letter writing
27. Experiments
28. Informal quizzes
29. Voluntary homework
30. Field trip or excursion
31. Small group discussions
32. General class discussions

In addition to whatever interest building notions may be planned in advance, there is need to incorporate occasional unplanned circumstances to sustain a realistic level of spontaneity. Among such unanticipated possibilities are the following:

1. Children's questions or casual observations
2. Unusual happenings and coincidences
3. Surprise visits
4. Gifts and Letters
5. News events
6. Commercial television and neighborhood movies
7. Accident or disaster

Chapter Seven

Taking on
a Promising Case

At this point it is essential that the children themselves sense a powerful need to move vigorously ahead in a proposed undertaking. There should be no mistaking the manifestations of this positive readiness; the enthusiasm will plainly show. If, by any chance, the signs of eagerness are not clear and abundant, the purposes of the previous step have not yet been achieved, and further development at that level ought to be continued.

Provided that motivational activities (Chapter Six) have been planned and carried out with imagination and skill, the growing interest and deep concern that, hopefully, have been generated throughout the group will, by this time, be pressing for an appropriate outlet. The specific function of the present step is to identify and delineate that outlet—to take on a case and draw up the specifications.

Purposes

As noted earlier, a given case may be considered to be a work project, a problem solving effort, an attempt to get information, or any blend of these. Whichever category, or combination of categories, that a certain area of concern fits most easily will partially determine the unique purpose, or purposes, of this step.

The insatiable curiosity of young children is widely recognized. The need to find out about a multitude of ideas and things in their ever expanding world becomes a significant force. Not surprisingly, the great majority of considerations that might become a likely focus of children's concern consists principally of gaining desired information. An information seeking effort by a group constitutes a fairly typical example of case-action learning. Fundamental to getting such an endeavor unmistakably underway is making sure that children are given every encouragement to ask those particular questions to which they genuinely desire satisfactory answers. Obtaining those answers constitutes the major thrust in the development of that case.

The relative role of problem solving as a standard procedure for handling many of the situations encountered in daily life may have been overstated in some of the literature devoted to elementary curriculum. Nevertheless, authentic opportunities for real problem solving are often implicit in the normal experiences of any group of children. To qualify as a suitable matter of serious concern, of course, the conditions must be genuine in terms of any immediate or peculiar needs of the children themselves. That is, certain circumstances faced directly by a group require the discovery of some new way of dealing with a particular difficulty that resists presently known approaches. Setting the exact course, then, for a case that is intended to resolve such a situation calls for identifying and stating those problems that are related to a proposal and that are of significance to the children.

The work project type of case bears a striking similarity both to the various community enterprises that attract spirited public involvement and to many of the freewheeling out-of-school undertakings to which neighborhood groups of children happily devote much time and energy. The anticipated outcome of a work project is usually some thoroughly tangible evidence of the effort expended—a completed construction, a successful drive or campaign, a development or improvement, or perhaps the launching of a particular activity. A work project may generally be expected to yield results that are observable, useful, and—to an extent— measurable. Defining the direction and magnitude of a given work project, therefore, entails the establishment of specific objectives that the children see as being entirely reasonable and worthwhile. The major emphasis of a work project focuses upon neither the obtaining of new information nor problem solving in the strict sense, but the agreement upon a definite bit of work that is to be accomplished by a group.

Many group endeavors, of course, will likely be some combination of the three basic types. In such instances, the determination of an exact focus and scope will call for an appropriate combination of the respective purposes.

Briefly, then, the purposes of the present step in case-action design are one or more of the following:

1. To pose the specific questions to which the children want honest and meaningful answers.

2. To identify and state any problems that are related to a proposal and that are of genuine concern to the children.

3. To establish specific objectives that the children see as desirable, important, and obtainable.

Procedure

Regardless of whether the focus of a suggested undertaking fits precisely within one of the three types or seems more to reflect some particular combination of them, the recommended procedure at this stage need not vary to any appreciable extent. The task at hand is for a group to identify clearly and specifically just what is to be accomplished in the development of a case.

As indicated in Chapter Four, the design for case-action learning is definitely more logical than chronological. It may generally be expected, therefore, that a considerable degree of overlap in the developmental steps —especially during the earlier stages—will be normal. Thus, it is likely that certain activities related to such fundamental matters as interest building, attention getting, and possibly even case identification will be in progress to some extent even as the unique business of the new step is taken up. And, of course, from the somewhat different viewpoint of the children, no such separate planning steps even exist. The significant point to be clearly understood is that everything that is to be done now must seem to flow naturally, easily, and unbrokenly from all that has gone before.

Open Discussion to Encourage Asking of Questions

Perhaps one of the smoothest transitions comes through skillful use of general class discussion. Inasmuch as this activity will almost certainly have been an important part of the preceding step, it offers an excellent setting for the next crucial development. As a group engages itself openly in a relaxed, but spirited and—hopefully—even somewhat emotional discussion of various aspects of what seems to be shaping rapidly into an interesting and worthwhile group concern, rather strong expressions of differing points of view are virtually an inevitability.

In the process of this sort of discussion, perhaps a statement made quite unequivocally by one of the children will be challenged by a classmate. It is not unlikely, of course, that, after some further clarification by one or the other, one of the two will retract slightly. Often, however, neither individual may be immediately willing to concede; and the differences may be picked up by other members of the group. Should the point remain unresolved, it is just possible that the question might be answered satisfactorily only with authoritative information. In such instances, a teacher politely, but firmly, must resist any temptation to assume the role of classroom oracle and expound upon the subject; rather, he must lend his influence to bolstering the confidence of the group in its own ability. So there may be a brief rush to check a dictionary or other convenient source, and perhaps the matter will be concluded quickly. But many differences of opinion do not yield to such on-the-spot settlements. Some questions do not have readily available answers. Such questions can give substance and vitality to a mutual concern.

One of a teacher's most important obligations is to encourage children to think of questions in a thoroughly positive way—to view the asking of a good question with as much honest admiration as the supplying of a good answer. It is something of a truism that action frequently begins with a question and ends with an answer; and progress does require action. As the children continue their free discussion, and as the teacher openly manifests enthusiasm for unsettled differences of opinion, further questions will certainly come up, and many of these will seem to have no easy answers. Perhaps one of the children will suggest recording some of the more difficult questions. If not, the teacher, having noted the trend of conversation turning more definitely toward the raising of questions about a topic, will sense a delicacy of timing and observe that it would be a good idea to make a note of some of the concerns that have been voiced. Thus the procedure for this step may be started with reasonable smoothness and efficiency.

Recording Questions and Concerns

The manner in which questions and concerns are recorded can definitely bear upon the thoughtfulness and frankness of attitude evidenced by children in asking those questions. Since the need is to identify clearly and specifically those aspects of a topic that are of actual concern to a group, it is important that any technique for registering them have an animating, rather than an inhibiting, effect. Although a necessary note of seriousness ought to pervade the atmosphere, the situation must be lively to the extent of maintaining a high level of enthusiasm, yet paced unhurriedly in order to promote thorough consideration and deliberate expression.

Several possibilities may be considered in regard to the actual mechanics of the recording process. With a kindergarten or first-grade class, a teacher can simply write each question on the chalkboard as it is asked. Frequently it may be preferable to use chart paper and a felt-tipped marking pen or a crayon, since this variation provides permanence and portability. In a more mature group, one of the children may appropriately serve as recorder. Assuming that the volunteer for this assignment is reasonably skillful in both writing and spelling, this practice has advantages in that it further emphasizes the role of children in such proceedings and simultaneously frees the teacher to circulate among the group. Occasionally it may seem more convenient to use note paper and pencil rather than the larger materials. An obvious disadvantage of this is that the recorded questions cannot be seen by most of a group, possibly necessitating repeated oral rereadings by the recorder; however, this difficulty may sometimes be alleviated to an extent through use of an overhead projector. Also, there may be some benefit in tape recording all or portions of a session, especially if this is done in conjunction with one of the other possible methods.

Certain nuances incident to the conducting of a question asking session may affect the children either positively or negatively at this important juncture. It is highly desirable that an easy flow of questions continue unabated until the full range of concerns relative to an area of consideration has been identified and recorded. For this to obtain, it is essential that no child feel any inhibition whatsoever in saying immediately and without reservation whatever comes to mind. To foster an environment that in any way discourages such complete candor is certain to limit the ultimate potential of any group endeavor. Conversely, whatever serves to induce openness and freedom from self-consciousness will result in a more creative and thorough tabulation of the fascinating unknown that might be investigated.

Regardless of the technique employed, each question should be taken down exactly as it is asked. Some children, being relatively inexperienced in formal language usage, may phrase their questions awkwardly or ungrammatically. However, to reconstruct a question at this point or to correct obvious errors would be to run a risk of unintentionally embarrassing an individual or—even more serious—unwittingly altering an intended meaning. There will be adequate opportunity later to attend to any necessary rewriting.

Another precaution concerns dealing with the so-called "stupid" question or deliberate attempts at crude humor which may jeopardize the effectiveness of a session. Certainly there are those occasions when a child, acting possibly through ignorance or failure to pay proper attention, will innocently toss off a question that is so basically absurd or so obviously out of context as to result in either uncontrolled hilarity or open displays of disgust on the part of his classmates. This must be accepted simply as one of the hazards of the game; there is no guaranteed way of avoiding it. Such incidents occur even in the best of classrooms. Probably the most effective course is merely to accept an offbeat question at face value—just as the most serious expression of concern or wonderment. For one thing, it is not possible to discern with absolute surety whether a particular question actually stems from ignorance or from unusually deep insight. Indeed, most of the really profound questions that have stimulated the human race to significant creativity were originally deemed outbursts of stupidity. Also, there is no way to know whether a particular foolish question has been asked out of honest misunderstanding or deliberate maliciousness. Furthermore, even if it were somehow possible to know that an individual had been intentionally mischievous, the most sensible response on the part of a teacher would remain that of calm acceptance. Therefore, the best guide for a teacher is to assume that, at least in case-action learning, there simply is no such thing as a "dumb" question.

The tone of teacher reaction recommended in the two situations just discussed is not likely to draw much argument. What is principally advised in both instances is the studied avoidance of a negative posture in regard to immature or inappropriate activity. A somewhat more subtle point, however, has to do with the extent to which a teacher ought to respond in a highly *positive* manner in the instance of exemplary behavior. Should a teacher manifest great delight in a particularly profound question that has been raised by a member of the group?

Many teachers, without doubt, might scoff at any notion that there might be any possible jeopardy in showing too *much* enthusiasm for outstanding productivity on the part of an individual pupil. Educational psychology courses offered in connection with preservice programs in teacher education may seem to suggest generally more extensive applications of various forms of "positive reinforcement." Indeed, it has been well documented that a child who has been rewarded even with a smile or a nod of approval from the teacher is more likely to seize upon a future incentive to greater personal effort. In a question asking session, however, it is vital that every child be genuinely motivated to make his own unique contribution; and the hazard inherent in a certain child's being thus extolled while another is not should be apparent. It is not difficult to imagine the relative deflation of a pupil whose moderately good question is blandly received immediately following one that has been greeted with particularly high praise.

By no means should a teacher attempt to circumvent the potential difficulty by deliberately eschewing enthusiastic response to especially laudable questions. This would require a degree of reticence that is not commensurate with an adequate teacher personality. The genuine need, however, to avoid obvious disparities as he relates with different members of a group warrants a teacher's most thoughtful consideration. A reasonable pattern of response, therefore, might be based upon a fundamental respect for each child and an honest appreciation for his unique role in a group and his particular contribution to an undertaking. Thus, each question, in turn, should be accepted rather matter-of-factly as a serious point of concern, yet with a sense of sincere appreciation on behalf of the class.

Sometimes it can be interesting to speculate about the total number of questions that might eventually be brought up by a group of lively and curious children. Some adults assume that a hundred or more separate questions might be amassed in a given list. And so it might seem at the eager moment that an enthusiastic class sets out to compile a full catalog of its concerns relative to a certain topic. However, as a session gets seriously under way, it becomes rather obvious that such an estimate is grossly exaggerated. Experience suggests that a more realistic guess would place the actual number of questions somewhere between twelve and thirty, including perhaps two or three near duplicates. Recording a complete list verbatim, therefore, does not present any great difficulty.

Although a single vigorous session, if properly motivated and conducted, will likely suffice as a general rule, occasional circumstances may call for a second or possibly even a third meeting in order to ensure that the complete range of possible concerns has been identified and recorded. When every aspect of a suggested undertaking has been thoroughly considered, and the flow of comments and queries from the group has seemingly subsided, it may be helpful for the teacher to ask specifically if anyone has some further question. Not only does this emphasize the importance of including every pertinent question, but it also encourages any child who may feel that his particular contribution has not been properly understood or an unusually shy individual who has not been bold enough to squeeze his comment in earlier. With this further enticement, then, perhaps one or two additional questions will be forthcoming. When these have been duly recorded, the teacher may offer a simple compliment to the whole group, making some brief comment that a full list of questions has now been completed.

Editing and Categorizing Questions

The questions and concerns thus recorded will largely determine the remaining course of a group undertaking. In order, however, to provide
clarity and detail as to direction and coverage, all of the items must first
be carefully edited and categorized.

There is frequently a temptation not to delay obviously needed editing, but rather to modify the wording of certain questions at the instant
that they are being recorded. Nevertheless, there are valid psychological
reasons for putting off any rewriting until all of the questions have been
listed. At the precise time that it is asked, a question truly belongs to the
individual child who offers it as his voluntary contribution to a total group
effort. For a teacher to correct grammatical errors or to rephrase such a
question at this moment of personal glow is to seem less than fully appreciative in the eyes of that child. Later, after it has been properly acknowledged and has become another item in a lengthening list of mutually
shared concerns, the particular question no longer need be associated with
its author, but may properly be viewed as community property and—as
such—is subject to whatever alterations are deemed appropriate by a
group.

After the list has been completed, any reference to a question in terms
of its origin should be avoided. At this point, for example, rather than
labeling a certain item as "Mary's question" or "Fred's question," it will
be more in keeping to direct attention more objectively to "question
seven" or "question twelve." In the first place, Mary and Fred clearly
relinquished any proprietary control the instant that their personal concerns were accepted on behalf of the class. Furthermore, there is an advantage in encouraging all of the children to think of each of the questions as
the legitimate business of everyone. Such an attitude is conducive to necessary objectivity in the important editing process.

The actual editing assignment may be handled by an entire class in
general session, by a special editing committee, or possibly by the teacher
himself, provided his decisions are subject to review by the group. One of
the first tasks is to locate any pairs of duplicate or near duplicate questions
in order to eliminate useless or redundant items. Another specific job is to
make sure that each of the remaining questions is written as simply and
as clearly as possible, so as to convey the exact meaning intended. Effective
usage, spelling, and punctuation are aspects of this.

With any possible deadwood thus removed and necessary rewriting
completed, the entire list of questions is reexamined in deliberate perspective. At this time, certain questions appearing at different places throughout the list will appear to be mutually related; that is, they will tend to fall
easily into natural categories. For instance, a typical list of eighteen or

nineteen questions might break rather cleanly into four or five major categories of concern, with each such category including from three to five separate questions. Obviously, further development of a proposed case may be sharpened significantly by rearranging a question list according to such convenient categories. When this has been done, the result will be an easily understood and thoroughly useful question outline.

Identifying and Recording Major Problems

Although the situations that lend themselves to genuine problem solving develop somewhat uniquely, a workable procedure at this stage need not be basically different from that recommended in the case of an information seeking endeavor. Therefore, should the main emphasis of a proposal seem to focus upon the challenge of one or more actual problems that are immediately faced by the children, or should a particular dilemma or plight seem to be an important side issue, tactics very similar to those just described will generally suffice.

Again, a large-group discussion can serve as an effective starting place. As a group considers various facets of a topic, different points of view may bear upon circumstances that seem to block a desirable condition or course of action. Gradually, the situation becomes crystalized—some apparent difficulties quickly clear up, while those more serious aspects that do not yield so readily are isolated. Eventually, a group is able in this way to define rather precisely just what is entailed in its predicament.

The matter of recording a problem may be both an outcome and an important part of the actual identification procedure. As the business of coming to grips with vaguely understood difficulties gets started in earnest, highlights of the progress may be taken down in abbreviated form by an individual serving as recorder. These working notes can be helpful in keeping discussants effectively on the right track, thereby enhancing the efficiency of a session. As different aspects of a problem are further narrowed and refined, the progress will be reflected in the running record. Ultimately, discussion should lead almost simultaneously to a satisfactory definition and a properly written statement of the problem to guide further development of a case.

Stating and Recording Specific Objectives

While general agreement upon the central purpose of a work project may almost automatically follow the motivating activities, a more deliberate procedure may be required to pinpoint the finer details. In this type of case, just as in those that are developed around either information getting or problem solving, a class discussion may be used effectively at this stage.

The fact that anticipated results of a work project are usually tangible simplifies for many children the matter of determining a desirable objective. Perhaps the greatest concern of a teacher at this step, however, is making sure that, in their eagerness to accomplish great things, children don't undertake more than they can handle. Since halfway successes in most work projects will probably amount to nothing more than disappointment, it is crucial that commitments be realistic. At the same time, however, the work must genuinely challenge the best effort of a group. Therefore, although the essential role of a teacher in a goal setting session may be the exercise of good judgment and influence in keeping children reasonably realistic, to accomplish this without seeming to be a chronic wet blanket may call for imagination and skill.

An effective work project will generally embrace a variety of opportunities and functions that will appeal to a wide range of interests and abilities—an important point to be kept before a group during a discussion session. Encouraging a healthy degree of spontaneity in the conversation may tend to stimulate greater creativity in identifying many such possibilities.

Maintaining a running record of a discussion is, of course, recommended. Perhaps more than one recorder will be needed in order to jot down all of the many ideas. As a session progresses, many suggestions will be brought up and discarded. The few still remaining at the end of such a quick stirring and sifting should be given more thoughtful deliberation. Final considerations may then be carefully rewritten in the form of a simple prospectus, with the major objectives of a case clearly stated and the ancillary outcomes appropriately detailed.

Summary

As soon as a group of children has become genuinely concerned, they will show obvious signs of eagerness to move ahead in a proposed undertaking. The function of the step discussed in this chapter is to define the exact direction and extent of that effort.

Whether a given case consists principally of an attempt to get information, a problem solving endeavor, a work project, or some possible combination of the three types will partially determine which specific purpose or purposes will predominate.

Regardless of the particular focus, however, the procedure need not vary appreciably. Whatever is done must seem to evolve smoothly from all that has gone before. A general class discussion offers a convenient starting point at this stage of development for all three types. In the instance of an information seeking endeavor, discussion affords an easy transition in providing a natural setting for a lively question asking session. The teacher's positive attitude and enthusiasm will then encourage children to spontaneity and forthrightness. It is recommended that each question be recorded verbatim as it is asked. And, as soon as all of the questions and concerns pertinent to a proposal have been noted, the entire list must be carefully edited and the items reordered into a question outline. Should the focus be directed more toward the problem solving type of case, or perhaps a work project, large-group discussion can also lead effectively either to the identification and recording of major problems or to the stating and recording of specific objectives.

Chapter Eight

Organizing for
Action on a Case

Organization is fundamentally a matter of coordinating activities of people in relation to time, space, and things. And even the simplest human endeavors seem to require some form of it. For instance, a woman who has secured the assistance of her husband in moving the sofa while she vacuums the living room carpet has definitely organized. She has purposefully structured the situation so that her cleaning expertise and her husband's lifting proficiency coincide at a given time in a particular place to obtain a desired effect in regard to the carpet and the sofa. Basically, this is the principle involved in even the most complicated manifestations of organization. Organizing for action on a case is no exception.

Through procedures discussed in Chapter Seven, a group of children will have been helped to determine precisely what it wishes to accomplish in connection with a particular undertaking. The next developmental step in a logical sequence is deciding just how to go about it. This is the function of organization.

Purposes

Proper organization presents one of the more serious aspects of group planning. Various interrelated factors must be taken into account; several decisions will necessarily involve compromise between what is desirable and what is practical. Certainly, an objective consideration of *what* is to be done ought to suggest something about *how* to do it. An appropriate starting point, therefore, might be that particular outline of categorized questions, statement of problem, or prospectus that constituted the end product of the previous step.

An essential purpose of organization, obviously, is to delegate certain responsibilities and to assign specific jobs to various children. Important as it may be to get the work done, however, other realities must also be considered. For instance, since the undertaking is clearly an educational venture, it is vital that each child be assured a beneficial learning experience. And a thoroughly practical matter is the need to get the most out of a teacher's limited time and energy.

Getting organized also concerns such mundane requirements as making sure that general good order will obtain, despite any possible modifications in classroom routine. A group must commit itself to a reasonably challenging schedule for the completion of various aspects of the work. And thought must be given to arranging for the use of certain school facilities and items of equipment as necessary or convenient. Much of organization, it appears, consists in attempting to look deliberately into the near future and realistically to anticipate any significant details.

Briefly stated, then, purposes to be achieved in the present step include the following:

1. Planning for each child to have a profitable learning experience.
2. Insuring efficient use of a teacher's time and effort.
3. Delegating responsibilities and dividing the work to be done among available workers.
4. Maintaining an orderly, businesslike classroom atmosphere.
5. Setting limits and deadlines.
6. Planning for efficient use of available equipment and facilities.

Types of Organization

Perhaps the most obvious thought at any mention of school organization is the particular distribution of children and teachers and the relationships resulting therefrom. Certainly, this aspect of organization relates significantly to case development. Depending upon the nature of the research or work required, the maturity and needs of the children, as well as other factors, at least six distinctive organizational patterns apply either wholly or in part in a given situation.

Whole Class

The simplest and, by far, the most prevalent form of organization is the familiar arrangement whereby all of the children assigned to a given classroom section are expected to respond as a body under the immediate instruction of a teacher. Typically with a ratio of from twenty-five to thirty-five children per teacher, the situation is basically formal. The teacher is clearly in charge, and he speaks generally to the group as a whole. An individual child talks with special permission, and his comments are usually directed either to the entire class or to the teacher, rather than to a particular classmate. While multiple grade or team teaching assignments may suggest some slight modifications, the fundamental structure of such a relationship is not significantly altered.

There are, of course, both advantages and disadvantages in this, as in any, pattern. Placing a whole class under a teacher's direct guidance offers possibilities for real economies in terms of teacher time and effort, since it affords a convenient way of presenting certain information quickly and impartially to all members of a group. But it definitely limits pupil spontaneity and differentiated performance. It presents perhaps the least difficulty in maintaining an orderly classroom, but it suggests passiveness, discourages free communication, and inhibits creativity. The whole-class arrangement is particularly appropriate for looking-and-listening activities that have been planned for a group: hearing a story, viewing a film, watching a demonstration, or receiving standard instructions. Used with discretion and in balance with other recommended forms of organization, the whole-class pattern constitutes a workable option in classroom organization.

Individual Assignment

Arrangements for individual assignment of children have been featured with increasing prominence in recent years. Popular variations of contracting, private appointment, self-selection, voluntary assignment, and programmed instruction have been well publicized innovations in a number of subject matter areas at most levels of education. Individual assignment also has some application as a useful organizational structure in case-action learning.

This particular pattern is a suitable approach for supervising children engaged in a wide range of unrelated activities. In such circumstances, pupils have little, if any, need for communication with each other, what one child is attempting to accomplish is likely of no direct concern or interest to any other individual in the group. It is assumed that each pupil has accepted a fairly unique assignment according to his personal interest, need, or capability, and that his individual progress is a matter exclusively between his teacher and himself. Whatever assistance or guidance may be needed is offered privately and on the spot.

A good deal of flexibility may generally be realized in individual assignments. A work session, for example, may coincide with what would otherwise be a period of free time for a given pupil; or perhaps an entire class might be simultaneously—though independently—engaged, each child at his own separate station in the classroom. This form of organization, although economical in terms of pupil time and effort, is not especially efficient for a teacher. Since there is no requirement or opportunity for any group instruction, a teacher may circulate informally about the area, ready to lend a hand as he deems proper. Or, to the extent possible, he may try to keep himself available to render any assistance to individuals specifically requesting it.

Used with judgment and in moderation, such an organizational plan has definite value in the development of a group action case. Skillful handling of individual assignments can often do much to build enthusiasm and self-confidence in some children who may have experienced limited success in group work. There is also possible benefit for an occasional pupil who desires to explore some special interest that may be related only tangentially to a group concern. A possible shortcoming that should, of course, be considered is the obvious lack of opportunity in this arrangement for pupil-to-pupil interaction.

Team Work

Of the organizational schemes that provide for a small number of children to collaborate on a selected task, probably the least sophisticated is that of team work. Not to be confused with either the study group or the committee (despite a striking, but superficial, resemblance to both), the team constitutes a distinctive working relationship for a specific function.

In a sense, this plan may be considered somewhat as an extension of the individual assignment pattern. That is, a team will have voluntarily taken on a particular job under the immediate supervision of a teacher. The principal distinguishing factor is that, because of the magnitude or difficulty of responsibility, a certain task must necessarily be handled by two or more individuals rather than a single person. As in the individual assignment, there is no necessity for contact with classmates who are not members of the same team. Within a given squad, of course, there is obviously a genuine need for regular communication. Also as in individual assignment, the team progress is of no moment to the class as a whole, but only to the actual members and the teacher.

Since team work is less complicated and less demanding than other small-group arrangements, it is relatively simple to administer with young or otherwise immature children. It allows for some differentiation of assignment, yet enables a teacher to remain in reasonably close touch with an entire class. There is some opportunity for legitimate social interaction during work sessions, thereby affording essential practice in functional communication and basic group skills. Therefore, this type of organization facilitates the planning of enjoyable and productive small-group activity without entailing responsibilities that may be too exacting. A limiting characteristic to be kept in mind is that, being fundamentally teacher-directed, team work is not especially conducive to initiative on the part of children.

The Study Group

An intraclassroom organization plan with a surface similarity to the work team is the study group. The common feature is that both arrangements involve the combined efforts of several individuals with reference to a certain objective. The respective functions, however, are quite different.

Whereas a work team generally performs under the immediate direction of a teacher in terms of a particular assignment, a study group operates with a rather high degree of autonomy. And, while assistance and advice are not only available but likely to be requested, the assumption is that the group members have pooled their resources to achieve a mutual aim or objective of their own choosing and for their own peculiar satisfaction. Fundamentally, there is neither dependence upon, nor responsibility to, any individual or group outside its own membership. Perhaps the most familiar examples of this basic structure are the various societies and interest clubs that are maintained by people of all ages both in and out of school; such organizations will typically have been established, however, for an indefinite tenure rather than for a specifically limited period of time, as in the instance of a study group that has been formed especially for action on a particular case.

Whether the study group constitutes a workable pattern will depend upon a given set of circumstances. No doubt, the potential opportunities are limited; but there may be genuine occasions for its use. For example, should it become mutually desirable that a small number of children pursue some unique interest that—although related—has no crucial bearing upon a group endeavor, the study group offers an ideal approach. Such a group fosters pupil initiative and informal group skills, but may be viewed as an advantaged clique by others. It should also be realized that, despite the effectiveness with which a study group serves its own singular interests, its activity may be relatively unproductive with respect to the concerns shared by a whole class.

Committee Work

Of the various forms of small-group organization, committee work is undoubtedly the most demanding and perhaps the most abused. As with both teams and study groups, a committee is usually comprised of a relatively small number of individuals laboring together to achieve a certain objective. But there the resemblance ends.

Although it necessarily operates with a noticeable degree of independence and self-sufficiency, a committee must be virtually selfless in its basic function. It exists not to enhance itself, but rather to serve the plenary group from which it was formed and from which it has received its particular charge. Committees are deliberately created to perform specific jobs that have been identified as legitimate concerns of the full group; and members are generally appointed in accordance with definite strengths or talents that may be required.

In addition to whatever uniquely individual assets he may bring to the operating structure, an effective committee member must perform reasonably well in terms of group dynamics, and he must repress any personal aspirations in order to subserve the common cause. Obviously, this calls for a level of maturity and understanding which ought not be assumed in very young or inexperienced children.

The Project Chairmanship

It may be helpful to describe one further possibility for classroom organization, despite a very slight likelihood of its being used to any extent. Adaptations of the project chairmanship have considerable application in industry and voluntary community endeavors, but certain definite shortcomings make it questionable for school use. There may, however, be an infrequent occasion that will call for this particular scheme—perhaps in combination with one or two of the more practical types.

In its actual function, a project chairmanship resembles that of a committee, the chief distinction being that, in the chairmanship, the full responsibility of a given task is delegated to a single individual rather than to the combined membership of a small group. An individual designated as a "project chairman" takes on the total onus and whatever recognition may be incident to a job that has been identified by the class and exclusively assigned to him for carrying out. And, although it is typically assumed that he will enlist the help of others in various aspects of the work as necessary, he is not in any way released from the burden of responsibility for the total assignment.

The notion has obvious advantages in terms of pinpointing lines of accountability and effectively reducing buck-passing. These same features, however, generally render the plan much too demanding with respect to a relatively few individuals to suggest it as a regular pattern of classroom organization. The child who is selected to serve as chairman is definitely put on the spot, and the pressures that he will inevitably experience may exceed what he can gracefully tolerate. Conversely, children who are not so designated may feel left out of things. It should be realized, therefore, that, while it offers a possible variation, any use of the project chairmanship in a group undertaking must be considered with caution.

Decisions

Proper organization includes making a number of decisions that are crucial to further satisfactory progress of a case. To the extent feasible, all of the children who are concerned in an ultimate outcome should participate directly in this important, though perhaps unexciting, business. To circumvent any tendency toward boredom, therefore, it may be necessary for the teacher to handle this stage of development with a fair amount of enthusiasm and briskness.

Arranging for Use of School Facilities

At this point the class has to consider the availability of certain school facilities needed to reach established goals. Items of classroom hardware, supplies, audiovisual equipment and materials, use of the library, and access to any special rooms in the building cannot be taken merely for granted; all require deliberate and careful planning.

Making sure that there is the least possibility of conflict between ongoing activities of regular subject matter study and those of a particular case in progress is essential to the success of both programs. It may be desirable, consequently, to reserve a convenient corner or perhaps a table or wall area in the classroom where work in process may be kept safely between sessions. In like manner, it generally becomes advisable to anticipate any difficulties that might arise as a result of a coincidental need of another classroom group. A modest, but healthy, degree of pessimism at this stage may very well contribute to more tranquil proceedings and a happier outlook in the long run.

Delegating Responsibilities

Certainly, no other aspect of organization is more exacting than the sensitive matter of delegating responsibilities. The benefit to be derived from a group endeavor by any child will result in large measure from the quality of his personal participation, which may hinge, in turn, rather directly upon his own unique role in the proceedings and how he feels about it. Each assignment must be viewed with particular care.

For several reasons, the most promising starting point in allocating specific jobs is an objective and forthright consideration of the actual work to be done. In the first place, this constitutes a thoroughly logical approach and generally is the basis of task assignments in most daily life situations. Also, it suggests priorities that can usually be accepted by a group as necessary and fair. Children realize their own stake in a case; since they will have been instrumental in setting expected outcomes, they will sense the importance of insuring that things be handled properly. Taking a good look, therefore, at established goals and deliberating as to their most satisfactory attainment becomes an excellent point of departure.

The nature of whatever work, study, or research needs to be accomplished may determine to an extent the type of classroom organization that will predominate. As an example, one important determinant is whether it appears appropriate and feasible for every child in a given group to participate on par with other children in every aspect of a venture. This would mean, of course, that the total number of tasks and the difficulty imposed by each not exceed the personal capability of any individual. Also implied is an assumed uniform level of enthusiasm throughout the group for every facet of a group concern. Should these conditions obtain, it might be recommended that an entire class work together under a teacher's immediate direction. Understandably, for a good many undertakings geared to kindergarten or primary levels, this relatively simple and easy-to-administer pattern will likely suffice.

Complications escalate with the increasing complexities of cases that have been undertaken by older groups and with the widening range in abilities and interests manifested by more mature children. In a few instances, the need may be met quite adequately through some combination of whole-group activity and individual assignment. But there is a strong likelihood that some type of small-group effort may frequently be required to carry out various responsibilities. As discussed earlier in this chapter, there are certain fundamental differences among the three familiar forms of small-group functions. In any event, the work-to-be-done criterion ought to stand as the primary determiner as to which particular plan might be selected.

If circumstances point purely to an obvious need for simple reinforcement of manpower in terms of specific jobs, task assignments may be made according to teams or work squads. A decision to organize as teams rather than as individuals may occasionally be founded on such a bland factor as the unremarkable observation that two children can merge their energies to double a force potential or amplify a convenience. In such an uncomplicated situation, it may make little or no difference which particular children are selected for a given team; mere numbers may cover the contingency. Other occasions not quite so simple may necessitate some intragroup specialization, in which event choosing team members will involve greater deliberation. Sometimes there may be other reasons for assigning a certain child to a particular team: to equalize the total load among all of the children, to provide a desirable experience for the assigned individual, or to promote confidence in another child who may be expected to respond more positively as a future teammate. Other things being equal, it may be entirely appropriate to make an assignment strictly on the basis of individual pupil preference, although this generally merits a lower priority than some of the more practical variabilities.

With few exceptions, recommended criteria will limit any assignment of children to study groups. The characteristic self-centered function of this particular plan suggests the hazard of a manpower drain on other organizational elements which contribute directly to a total classroom effort. Therefore, while occasional use of study groups may be an attractive and worthwhile possibility, the practice must be viewed mainly as a luxury.

Delegating an important responsibility to a committee and appointing individuals as committee members are genuinely crucial matters that warrant serious deliberation. Any tendency to regard these decisions too lightly may jeopardize the ultimate success of a case. Consequently, it becomes imperative that certain principles of committee function be understood fully.

The basic relationship of a committee to its originating group implies a congruence of purpose in achieving well defined goals. Generally, the most practical juncture on which to form a committee is some recognizable facet of a concern that appears commensurate with the resources of anticipated membership. With respect to an information seeking case, for instance, a convenient and workable apportionment may be realized in whatever categories comprise a particular question outline that will have been developed in the preceding step. The specific charge to a given committee in such an instance will be to respond appropriately to each of the related questions and report the findings back to the class in an acceptable manner. Similarly, should an undertaking focus upon problem solving or a work project, a natural breakdown of established outcomes will suggest a proper magnitude for each committee responsibility. Obviously, the work-to-be-done criterion will guide committee designation.

It should never be assumed that appointing a certain child to this or that committee will be a simple matter. As already mentioned, many youngsters—in fact, a majority of pupils at the kindergarten and primary levels—lack the necessary maturity and experience to qualify for effective committee work. Furthermore, children will frequently express enthusiastic feelings as to the nature of a particular committee responsibility or perhaps in regard to other people with whom they hope to serve. In some instances, these preferences are firmly based; often, however, they stem from momentary fancy and may be founded on little or nothing of real substance. Lines of friendship rarely coincide neatly with such a unique aggregate of special strengths and interests as may be called for in a given situation. For these and other reasons, to attempt the assignment of individuals to different committees merely on the basis of personal choice is possibly to invite disaster.

A more businesslike approach to the matter of deciding committee memberships is strongly recommended. Rather than inquiring casually as to "who would like this" or "who will volunteer for that," a teacher may help children regard the decisions with some degree of objectivity. He must especially guard against any impression that assignments to certain committees are granted by him as favors or rewards. Instead, he must foster the notion that each such appointment is part of a systematic and logical response by a whole group to a definite need. Therefore, in taking up the question of various committee memberships, discussion ought first to be directed toward a deliberate cataloging of specific personnel requirements posed by each committee responsibility. Before any individual assignments are even considered, the complete picture of manpower needs for a total organizational plan should be viewed in calm perspective. Careful tabulations will show precisely the number of persons with certain talents and abilities that seem to be required. Then, an objective personnel inventory of the class will be made with respect to these same attributes. No doubt, some compromise will be indicated, since more than likely the demand for some skills will exceed the available supply. By observing recommended priorities in this way, children are given positive encouragement in placing the ultimate success of a group endeavor above personal preference, and, incidentally, enhancing the likelihood of greater satisfaction.

Whatever promotes the easiest flow of communication and smoothest working relationships among the members should largely determine the internal operation of a committee. Although opinions differ as to any possible benefits from a formalized structure, the designation of officers, whether elected by children or appointed by a teacher, undoubtedly contributes to a stultification of latent leadership. Consequently, a committee may become unnecessarily cumbersome and fail to achieve its full potential. As a general rule, it is probably better not to specify a chairman—at least at the outset. An informal, emergent pattern of operation will likely prove more productive.

When the full matter of delegating responsibilities to individuals, teams, or committees has been completed, it should be clear to every member of the class just what arrangements have been made for handling various aspects of the work. And, hopefully, each child will understand the relationship of his own particular assignment in regard to expected outcomes of the group effort, and will look forward to the challenge with confidence and enthusiasm.

Scheduling Activities and Work Sessions

Another desirable feature of good organization is dependable and convenient scheduling of activities and work sessions. Being able to plan ahead with some degree of confidence is not only conducive to peace of mind, but essential to a high level of productivity.

Since some tasks will involve only a single individual, while others will require the coordinated effort of several persons, it may appear necessary that both scheduled and unscheduled periods be arranged. But even unscheduled sessions will require planning, in a sense, in order to avoid possible conflicts. Children may need to consider a number of quite unrelated activities being conducted throughout the school. The matter of cooperating appropriately with various individuals and groups must not be taken lightly. Messy activities and noisy occasions, for example, may have to be anticipated so as not to interfere with the work of other people.

But the most exacting facet of scheduling work periods of a group undertaking is that of fitting them smoothly into a total classroom program. There is an obvious benefit in any mutual enhancement between subject matter study and a given case. Consequently, a child's duties in one of these programs should not seem to exclude him from an exciting or pleasurable work session in the other.

Building some noticeable element of routine into a work schedule contributes to efficiency. A regular schedule helps children to regard time as a useful—but limited—commodity, thus encouraging realistic budgeting of work periods. Circumstances and the nature of a particular group concern will likely determine the amount and distribution of school time allocated to a case—whether every day, twice weekly, several brief periods plus a large block of time on a certain afternoon, or some other quite unique schedule. A teacher must make sure that whatever schedule is adopted by a class be a reasonable one—allotting neither too little time nor too much. A schedule ought to be viewed somewhat as a challenge, but never as a frustration.

Setting Deadlines

For many youngsters, the ultimatums of chronometry are a fact of life not easily comprehended. Children often view the passage of time with some inaccuracies. They simply haven't experienced enough of this dimension of their existence to have developed adequate standards for its proper observance. The business, therefore, of determining necessary deadlines to pulse a case through to successful completion will undoubtedly require teacher guidance.

The importance of holding the duration of a given undertaking in case-action learning to a period of relatively high interest on the part of the children has been pointed out. Implicit in this restriction is the essentiality of concluding all work according to plan. To permit a case to run beyond a date that has been established as final is definitely hazardous to a high degree of success. Finishing on time ought not be considered merely as an option; this must be the ultimate point of closure.

In addition to settling upon a definite date for closing a case, a classroom group will need to agree upon various supportive or prefatory deadlines. In order to round out final plans for a total endeavor, the results of team and committee effort must, of course, be readied by an earlier designated time. And these, in turn, will have to be preceded by the completion of assignments that have been delegated to individuals.

The "pipeline" or "top-down" concept of logistics suggests a perspective for spacing any tributary deadlines that are antecedent to the final one. This calls for projecting backward from a selected completion date to the next-to-last collecting point, and thence—still in reverse order—to the preceding one. Planning in this fashion—that is, *from end to beginning*—has a distinct advantage over a progressive sequence, since it underscores the realism of definitely-limited time as a factor throughout a development.

To be effective, deadlines must be reasonable—both in terms of the volume and difficulty of work and with respect to various demands upon a class. A vital consideration in getting properly organized is helping children to understand that fixed reporting dates are not arbitrary demands, but are fundamental to a successful case.

Making Rules for Classroom Behavior

No single pattern of classroom behavior can be adopted in toto to guide the many and varied activities of children engaged in the work of a group action case. No two sets of circumstances will ever be identical. There are significant differences from group to group; and each undertaking will entail its peculiar requirements. Also, regardless of how adequately certain standards of conduct may have served in subject matter study, they will not likely suffice in case-action learning—even in the same classroom. The basic approach will be quite distinctive. It should be planned, therefore, that appropriate standards of personal behavior be established as a regular feature of organization in each group endeavor.

As with other aspects of development, a workable code of behavior ought to be designed by the children themselves, although—quite under-standably—a teacher's advice will be in keeping here, just as in other important decisions. Again, the work-to-be-done criterion will basically prevail. Mannerly behavior for its own sake will generally be eschewed. Rather, emphasis will be upon what best facilitates the attainment of specified goals.

One of the first considerations in setting any restrictions will proba-bly be to make sure that other classroom groups in the school are not disturbed in their own programs as a possible result of boisterousness, unlimited traffic in hallways, or noisy construction activities. Acoustical qualities of a building may partially determine acceptable levels. In any event, maintaining the good will of others is well worth a bit of consider-ation.

Other rules of conduct ought to be established to the extent that they generally serve actual purposes of a class. Specific conditions will suggest certain prohibitions, such as unlimited communication among individuals and groups, freedom to move about both in and out of the classroom, use of the library, or individual access to various items of equipment.

Left too much to their own devices, children have been observed to be overly restrictive and to legislate too many negative rules. However, a bit of encouragement from a teacher to permit the greatest degree of freedom that is practical may help to keep the situation fluid and reason-able.

Planning Homework and Out-of-School Assignments

A considerable portion of the work of any group action case will likely be handled during the normal school day. Certain sessions may involve an entire class or may require small-group coordination. Also, particular items of school equipment will be needed in some instances. It is not very likely, however, that sufficient class time can be allotted to cover all of the activities that will be undertaken. Furthermore, even if it somehow were possible to include the entire development of a given case within regular school periods, it would still be important to plan at least some homework and other out-of-school assignments in connection with responsibilities that have been delegated. One of the significant benefits to be derived from case-action learning is that of relating nonschool pursuits to inschool experiences. Opportunity to carry on an interesting project both in and out of class is consonant with this purpose.

Homework, despite possible traditional expectations to the contrary, needn't be viewed as onerous—either by children or by parents. In fact, an especially fascinating assignment that a child shares with his family can often prove to be a delightful bond between home and school. This may be especially true in case-action learning, inasmuch as an undertaking may be a direct outgrowth of an out-of-school concern. In some instances, particularly at the kindergarten or primary levels, parents and other members of the family may constitute a major source of information or assistance. An older child may enjoy explaining or demonstrating at home some facet of a consideration that has stimulated his enthusiasm at school.

Other out-of-school possibilities may also serve to extend available work time and enrich the quality of a case in progress. Potential opportunities for satisfying and worthwhile experiences will need to be identified and considered by the children in a group.

Summary

Having agreed upon specific goals of a given concern, a group of children will turn next to the matter of getting organized for effective participation. This is one of the more serious aspects of planning and developing a case. Various interrelated factors must be weighed, and some decisions will entail compromise.

Depending upon the particular circumstances, six distinctive organizational patterns may apply individually or in combination in a given situation:

1. A whole class under the immediate instruction of a teacher.
2. Individual assignment of children under the direct guidance of a teacher.
3. A work team or squad under the direction of a teacher.
4. A study group functioning autonomously.
5. A committee charged with a specific responsibility.
6. A project chairmanship with a definite responsibility charged to an individual.

Proper organization includes several crucial decisions. All of the children who are concerned in an outcome ought to participate directly in determining the following:

1. Arranging for use of school facilities.
2. Delegating responsibilities to individuals, teams, or committees.
3. Scheduling activities and work sessions.
4. Setting reasonable deadlines.
5. Making rules for classroom behavior.
6. Planning homework and out-of-school assignments.

Chapter Nine

Developing a Case

If all of the preliminary steps have been thoughtfully considered, the pupils will now be eager to get on with the actual research, study, or work. At this stage of development, a class will have identified and definitely taken on a particular case, the children will have defined specific goals, and they will have organized themselves in the best possible way to carry out various responsibilities. Such a planning sequence is basically more logical than chronological, and therefore any necessary or desirable amendments to these earlier decisions will remain in order. For all practical purposes, however, a group will have its work cut out. Now to begin in earnest.

Purposes

Although most of the total time allocated to a given case will be consumed during this step, things should move along in a straightforward manner.

Activities and procedures will be determined mainly by peculiarities of an undertaking and whatever goal-oriented tasks have been delegated. The business at hand is to complete the assignments.

From the children's point of view, the direction onward from this moment ought to be fairly clear. The mission is simply to get the work done. And, whether a case is being developed as an attempt to obtain certain information, a problem solving challenge, or a work project, there will be jobs to accomplish and difficulties to overcome. These achievements will be realized through the initiative, determination, and perseverance of the class itself.

As seen by a teacher, other benefits are also of significance. Opportunities for youngsters to work purposefully together in pursuit of mutually agreeable ends constitute a singularly valuable consequence. And the considerable commitment tacitly declared by each child provides ideal motivation for the development of efficient work and study habits. Also, the prospects are excellent that favorable attitudes toward learning experiences in general may grow out of forthcoming satisfactions.

In short, it may be hoped that the present step in case development will be commensurate with each of the following purposes:

1.   To provide opportunity for children, through their own initiative and effort, to carry out whatever research, study, or work may be necessary to achieve designated goals and objectives of a selected group endeavor.

2.   To give children meaningful experience in cooperating with others in useful and satisfying work.

3.   To help children develop efficient habits of work and study.

4.   To foster favorable attitudes toward research, study, and work.

Resources and Activities

A generally pragmatic approach will undoubtedly be taken in all aspects of the work that lies ahead. Resources and activities may be as varied as the delegated responsibilities and personal preferences of the individuals involved. Whatever yields acceptable results or whatever children want to try may be included in the class repertoire as it proceeds with its several assignments. Examples of media use described in Chapter Six (in connection with drawing attention to a likely case and considering its possibilities and merits) will also apply to the more deliberate study and research, although with a somewhat different emphasis.

Textbooks, Supplementary Books, and Library Materials

The potential of reading activities scarcely requires supporting arguments. Perhaps the most obvious source of information consists in the textbooks that have been adopted for specific subject matter areas. To make use of these very same books in case-action learning can be a subtle way of partially bridging the gap for a child between the two curriculum approaches. Supplementary books and library materials may likewise be valuable.

Reading for information calls for the development of definite attitudes and abilities. And it should not be surprising if certain on-the-spot instruction may be in order from time to time. Fortunately, research skills and library techniques may be mastered quickly when there is a clear need for immediate application.

The extent to which a teacher may think it appropriate to guide a group in its essential reading will likely vary with the situation. As a rule, whatever children may be capable of doing without frustration ought to determine the limits of any such assistance. In some instances, for example, it may be a good idea for a teacher to provide an annotated bibliography to facilitate a search for specific information; in other instances, children may find it more satisfying to do their own digging. Since an equitable distribution of expertise in research reading will presumably have been provided as an aspect of organization, it may reasonably be expected that each team or committee will enjoy some self-sufficiency.

Magazines, Newspapers, and Journals

A school library typically maintains current issues and, occasionally, bound volumes of periodicals. Magazines, newspapers, and journals certainly should not be overlooked as possible sources, nor should family subscriptions to certain publications.

Standard References

Students are aware of standard references such as dictionaries, encyclopedias, almanacs, and atlases. In fact, these may frequently be the first sources they will examine. And it may be helpful to encourage the use in precisely this way: as a first source. After reading a relatively brief, but reasonably accurate, article in an encyclopedia, for example, a child will usually have a more realistic base from which to search for more detail or particular emphases.

One possible caution which the teacher might consider is that what amounts to a thoroughly bewildering mass of related subjects may simply overwhelm an inexperienced child who has not been adequately advised in the use of standard references. A young researcher has to have a rather definite point in mind as he starts his investigation.

Maps, Globes, and Charts

Certain facts may sometimes be located most quickly and conveniently by referring to specific items of appropriate media. A particular map, globe, or chart has very likely been designed for a definite purpose. And, rather than taking it merely for granted that a group may be familiar with various cartographic projections, a teacher will often find that children appreciate learning some of the fundamentals of this fascinating science, especially as they may have direct import. A misinterpreted feature can easily result in a false concept. For example, unless a youngster is aware of the intent of the maker, a three-dimensional relief map might convey a gross exaggeration of the actual elevation of a mountain. The immediate relevance of understanding finer points basic to the use of such items should be fairly evident.

Science Materials and Equipment

Provided that there is honesty and some discretion in the procedure, there needn't be any serious concern that carrying out a delegated responsibility in connection with case-action learning might jeopardize subject matter study by "skimming the cream" from some of the more exciting aspects of a particular field. As a matter of fact, just the opposite effect might obtain: that a given subject be held in even greater esteem as a result of the personalized reference. Consequently, there should be no reluctance to make any appropriate use of materials or pieces of equipment that too often may have been regarded as indigenously and exclusively related to one of the regular subject areas. For example, many undertakings will have at least some scientific or technological emphasis, which may suggest the desirability of using supplies or apparatus designated for a science program.

Thus, various items may be utilized effectively. Animal cages, aquariums, planters, electrical devices, fans, pumps, microscopes, chemicals, burners, balances, and miscellaneous tools constitute just a few possibilities for enriching the quality of work related to a group endeavor.

Flat Pictures, Graphs, and Diagrams

As a development gets further under way, a class will generally turn to widely divergent sources to meet the challenge of its various tasks. In some instances, things that were brought into a classroom earlier for purposes of stimulating and directing pupil interest may be retained by a team or a committee for a specific use in study or research. Flat pictures, graphs, and diagrams may be valuable in several stages of development of a case. More often, however, new materials are needed. Some of these may be located in library files. Old magazines and calendars in children's homes may be harvested. And, sometimes, a needed print can be purchased at a book store. But there will be many occasions for children to photograph or design something quite original in the way of a useful graphic to facilitate or clarify a point.

Projected Still Pictures

Projected still pictures, in the form of slides, filmstrips, opaque projections, and transparencies, were discussed previously as motivators. But their potential value in research or study is fully as significant. And, although the purpose to be served at the present stage is quite different, even some of the same shots that were projected earlier might be repeated. Generally, however, the views that will be used here will be specially chosen for a particular effect; it is likely that only fresh pictures will be included in the selection.

These materials will presumably be procured from any likely source. Some items may be checked out of the library or media center. A few will undoubtedly be borrowed. Others will be purchased for the occasion. Still another possibility—and one that has interesting application—is that children themselves, with whatever teacher help may be required, will produce their own by means of photography or drawing.

Films and Filmloops

The chief value of motion-picture films and single concept filmloops during earlier stages of development consisted in their potential for arousing curiosity and directing interest; their present usefulness lies precisely in their capacity for *satisfying* curiosity and providing definite answers to specific questions. The difference, of course, is significant; and it is this distinctive purpose that should guide the selection of films and filmloops and suggest the manner of their presentation. Fundamentally, the immediate objective in choosing a film or filmloop ought to be very much like that which might determine a particular choice of any other study or research material: does it actually provide a needed answer or contribute to the solution of an identified problem.

In one sense, perhaps, selecting a certain film for its instructional merit may be somewhat more crucial than, for example, recommending a book for such a purpose. Since there is no convenient way to scan a film, selection of a suitable title is time consuming. Also, should it seem desirable for only a small group, such as the members of a team or committee, to view a given film, the matter of handling the projection without distracting other people from their own concerns is likely to prove difficult, unless a school is fortunate enough to have a separate room or booth set up specifically for such a situation. The inevitable waste of time occasioned by showing a film to children who have no definite purpose in mind, but who genuinely need to be engaged in something more directly related to their own peculiar responsibilities, is indeed critical.

Duplicated Materials

Sometimes the duplication of a set of directions or an outline facilitates a detailed discussion of a particular matter. Or it may conserve time for children to have a readily accessible list of articles, perhaps a schedule, or a bibliography when the pursuit of their assignments takes them outside the classroom or away from the building. In many instances, children will want to prepare their own materials. And, while the care and skill necessitated in making a usable stencil may rule out mimeographing, there is nothing especially difficult about preparing a master sheet for running off on a spirit duplicator. These suggestions should indicate just a few of the many ways in which duplicated materials might be used advantageously.

Objects, Specimens, and Models

Objects, specimens, and scale models will generally be appreciated by children who are not expert readers or who, possibly because of general immaturity, may have some difficulty with abstract thinking. Three-dimensional articles that can actually be handled may help such youngsters visualize a situation with remarkable clarity. Also, they frequently direct the focus of a group discussion and, thus, contribute to a good learning situation.

Television and Radio

Despite obvious limitations as to control of either content or time of presentation, both television and radio ought to be included on any list of resources for the development of a group action case. For the most part, taking full advantage of these media requires considerable flexibility and alertness at the receiving end.

Schedules published daily in local newspapers are generally accurate in indicating programs and air times of commercial radio and television stations, as well as broadcasts of educational television. And information concerning closed-circuit distribution and limited-range broadcasts of instructional television is usually available in the form of bulletins prepared by a particular producer. Working a given program into a school day, however, may require imagination and willingness to shift activities a bit.

Much of the potential value of radio and television as it may pertain directly to case development may undoubtedly be realized through giving attention to what is available for late afternoon and evening reception and encouraging children to modify their after-school viewing and listening as appropriate.

Videotape Recordings

A partial answer to the question of how to make the best use of potentially valuable programs or events that are televised or otherwise shown at inconvenient times may consist in videotape recordings. The videotape recorder has now become a fairly standard item of hardware in most school district media centers; and, in some instances, it has been installed in individual schools, as well. One of the most obvious advantages of the "VTR" is that it makes possible the recording of both audio and video portions of programs produced on either educational or commercial television for later playback in a classroom.

VTRs can also record an interview, a skit, or an experiment for further study or reporting. The zoom lens brings the viewer in very close for important detail. The fact that a videotape may be played as often as desired and stored for an indefinite period of time suggests a significant saving of time and energy. And, since the tapes are erasable and reusable, the expense need not be prohibitive. Recent developments in portable equipment allow a flexibility that will undoubtedly encourage even more imaginative employment of videotape recordings both in and out of the classroom.

Although the videotape recorder is by no means childproof at present, its operation is certainly not so difficult as to render its use impractical, after minimal training in correct procedures. Proper lighting and attention to sound level are, of course, essential; and efficient handling of the camera will generally require a few practice sessions.

Recordings and Recorders

As an aspect of research or study activities, a group may want to learn the correct pronunciation of a particular phrase in a foreign language or to hear a certain classical orchestration or the lyrics of a current song. Maybe the need is to hear a famous speech or debate, an animal call or the authentic sound of a steam locomotive, or instructions for a folk dance. These suggest just a few of the fairly obvious uses of prerecorded tapes and phonograph records.

Records and tapes can be stored and used with relative convenience, especially the newer cassette tapes. Threading one of the reel-wound tapes, of course, can be difficult for small children. Disc records may be broken or smudged. With a bit of instruction, however, these concerns may be allayed.

One of the most useful tools that generally is available for children is the portable tape recorder. This durable, compact piece of equipment is nearly foolproof in its operation, and its versatility is remarkable. In team or committee sessions, for example, it can serve as the obsequious secretary, obediently and accurately taking down for later reference everything that is said. In fact, it becomes an excellent note taker in many situations. It can be a helpful time saver in reporting. And it constitutes a particular blessing for any child whose communication needs exceed his facility in reading and writing.

Resource Persons

One of the oldest methods of obtaining information or instruction is to ask someone who knows. In both primitive and civilized societies, this has comprised a significant facet of education. But the traditional school program has generally tended, through the years, to preclude anything more than an insipid courtesy role for any nonschool personnel in the curriculum. More recently, however, the notion of making deliberate and genuine use of resource persons in children's learning activities is becoming respectable again.

Even in the smallest communities, dozens of people of varying ages and circumstances are willing and able to make an honest—and gratuitous—contribution to a worthwhile educational undertaking. And, in many instances, they need only to be asked. Perhaps there may be a reason to invite someone who is especially knowledgeable with respect to a certain consideration, but who may not be known personally by any of the children or the teacher. It may be necessary, consequently, to arrange an introduction before an actual request can be made. If the individual is a family friend, or a relative of one of the class members, the contact may be made directly.

Circumstances will probably determine whether a certain resource person ought to be invited to school to demonstrate a skill or talk to the class, or whether he should be interviewed at his home or place of business by one or two members of the group. In either event, it likely will be advisable, if not actually required by school policy, to clear the situation in advance through the principal's office.

Assistance or Advice from Families or Friends

As indicated in previous chapters, the public relations value alone might almost justify the practice of encouraging children to seek assistance or advice from their parents, families, or friends in the development of a group action case. The potential for building deeper understanding between home and school, and the benefits of relating out-of-school and inschool experiences are both obvious and significant. But, by far the most important reason for including a child's home environment in any cataloging of learning resources is simply that it is one of the most efficient and practical ways of getting the work done.

One immediate advantage of homework, of course, is that it provides additional time to complete an assigned job. Occasionally, it may be feasible for several children to get together at one of their respective homes for a pleasant and productive session. In a few instances, the home may contain certain facilities for work or study that are unavailable or in short supply at school. A member of a child's family may make a suggestion that will be carried back to the classroom for further consideration by a full group. Or perhaps a child will gain an insight into a problem merely by discussing it with a brother or sister.

Field Trips

Excursions and field trips, as attention getters and interest builders, have been discussed at some length in Chapter Six. A few additional comments, though, may be in order.

The whole question of field trips very likely constitutes one of the most controversial and crucial aspects of case development. On the one hand, direct, personal involvement is an essential element in any psychological orientation of curriculum. But an inescapable dilemma is seen in disproportionate time requirements for concrete, firsthand experiences. For, when all of the necessary preplanning and follow-up are taken into account, field trips consume immense quantities of time as compared to most other learning activities. It simply becomes out of reason to plan as many field trips as the merit of a given situation might seem to warrant. Planning a field trip invariably calls for compromise.

It is precisely by way of such compromise that an arbitrary maximum of no more than two field trips for any given undertaking is recommended. As a general rule, one of these ought to be scheduled for the present developmental stage. And, inasmuch as the unique purpose here is to carry out the necessary research, study, or work to achieve whatever objectives have been established, the peculiar emphasis of this field trip should be upon getting definite answers to questions and obtaining specific kinds of information.

If a class happens to be organized according to team or committee responsibilities, it may, occasionally, seem desirable to arrange separate field trips for each of the different work groups. Whether this will actually be advisable—or even possible—in a specific instance, however, will likely be contingent upon the anomalies of the situation.

Construction, Art Work, and Handicrafts

In accepting a responsibility for a particular job that has been delegated by a class, an individual or members of a committee may begin almost immediately to think about feasible ways in which results of the anticipated work might be reported back to the larger group. Construction, art work, and handicrafts are some of the excellent possibilities.

With certain work project endeavors, construction may well comprise the major stress of the undertaking, effectively combining product, process, and media. In such instances, the results *are* the report. And other circumstances may also suggest construction activity, although generally in conjunction with other procedures. Some children enunciate more eloquently with tools than with words, and building things can be an ideal outlet for these individuals. Especially when their work is seen as fully complementary with that achieved by other children through different forms of expression, the outcome can yield great satisfaction. Thus, in team or committee assignments, a beneficial relationship may frequently be developed among group members, with some individuals directly engaged in shaping three-dimensional raw materials into a recognizable form and others dealing with the more abstract aspects of the job in terms of reading and writing chores.

Drawings, as a medium of communication, are nearly as old as the human race. In fact, cave dwellers used this very method to report and record important events. And, today, crude attempts at art seem almost universal among young children with a message to convey. Regardless of the quality in terms of objective evaluation, self-expression through drawing, painting, or sculpting can be enormously satisfying to an individual. Various forms of art work may be included to good advantage in an assigned responsibility. For instance, a simple drawing may help a group to visualize a given situation so that it may proceed more directly with a task. A well done mural, whether painted by one person or several, will serve as a helpful illustration to accompany a formal report at the completion of an assignment. Or, perhaps, modeling or carving an appropriate figure may provide a bit of welcome variety in the work. Another potential benefit is that, in an effort to render his work as realistically and as accurately as possible, a young artist will frequently be obliged to engage in research which might prove useful, also, to other members of his group.

Since handicrafts are generally a product of a broad base of a society, it may be seen that, in many respects, they are often even more revealing of a particular culture than are the fine arts. Attempts, therefore, by children to duplicate certain artifacts may sometimes contribute to their gaining an insight into the manner and quality of living in a particular time or place. In many instances, legitimate opportunities may be found for including handicrafts as an interesting feature of research or study. And, as in art work and construction activities, they may frequently constitute a needed equalizer for children who don't perform fluently in writing.

Experiments and Demonstrations

Keeping active is vitally important to any healthy child; interest and activity are tightly interwoven in his thinking. Talking the situation over and reading about it simply will not suffice for many youngsters. In advising a group in regard to its work plan, consequently, a teacher might suggest the inclusion of several things that require real *doing*. Experiments and demonstrations both rank high on a list of such possibilities.

The extent to which either of these activities may be fitted nicely into a small group assignment will vary, of course, with the peculiarities of a particular undertaking. Although it certainly would not be recommended that a demonstration or an experiment be squeezed in without concern as to genuine function, a little exercise of imagination will likely indicate the feasibility of application in a variety of group enterprises.

School Newspapers and Bulletin Boards

Its characteristic as an indefinitely continuing, ongoing affair should generally guide any consideration of incorporating a school newspaper in any way into the development of a case. In the event, of course, that a newspaper is maintained as a fairly regular feature of a total school program, it is definitely recommended that a report of the class's progress in its interesting work be written up and submitted for publication in an early issue. If there is no existing newspaper, however, it would be well to resist any temptation to establish one merely to publicize a given case. A one-shot proposition is entirely too artificial and time consuming to warrant the effort.

A similar determination ought to obtain in regard to a school or classroom bulletin board. The central notion of a bulletin board consists in its *habitual* perusal by children. A fly-by-night arrangement is quite inconsistent with this basic assumption. But, should a well maintained posting board happen to be a more or less permanent activity of either a whole school or of a classroom alone, it will be entirely proper to list news items of individual or group work from time to time.

Oral and Written Reports

Individual reports are an established part of school routine at nearly all levels. Reports may be used in several ways in the development of a group action case. They have already been suggested in Chapter Six, both as a possible means of drawing attention to a potential undertaking and in terms of directing and deepening interest. Both oral and written reports can be useful, also, as a routine aspect of carrying out a delegated responsibility.

It should be pointed out, perhaps, that reports are not for everybody. Some children's lack of facility in either oral or written communication will make it unlikely that they might voluntarily select this method of conveying an idea when more direct or graphic means are available. Other individuals, of course, thoroughly enjoy the challenge of preparing an informative statement and the stimulation of a real audience.

Properly and purposefully used, reporting may constitute an effective study or research tool. In either an individual assignment or a work team form of classroom organization, for example, it may be interesting and convenient for one or two children to investigate a particular facet of a larger concern and to report, either orally or in writing, any findings for group deliberation. Also, individual reporting may be a time saver in small-group work. Should a committee be under pressure to meet a deadline, work might be speeded up by subcontracting specific bits of the group assignment to individual members.

One condition that has been implied should be emphasized more. As an activity for research or study, such reports are wholly an internal matter within the working group. They should, therefore, be handled informally.

Panel Discussions and Debates

Many children enjoy a stimulating exchange of ideas or conflicting points of view. And, although opportunity for much panel discussion and debate has not typified the elementary classroom, such activities can be, if controlled, an excellent study or research technique. They suggest improvisation and freewheeling to keep things loose and interesting, yet they are carried on under definitely established rules and amenities.

The purpose is to facilitate whatever investigating and deliberating may be required to fulfill an assigned responsibility. At this stage, therefore, a panel discussion or debate should be thought of as a useful device to be confined generally to the inner arena of a particular working group. Used in this way, either of these activities may be a source of pleasure and satisfaction, as well as of important information.

Physical Activities

In a work project it might be readily assumed that certain physical activities ought to be blended into any plan for fulfilling a job assignment. Such an undertaking frequently necessitates a great deal of simple, unskilled labor. Building, planting, cleaning up, surveying, improving, canvassing, collecting, and producing all connote physical exertion. But other types of cases, too, may occasion a genuine need for muscular challenge as well as intellectual opportunity. Both information seeking and problem solving endeavors, also, may at times be enhanced by appropriate physical outlets.

According to specific circumstances, any of a wide range of physical activities, in addition to various work possibilities, might complement a given study plan. These activities include both indoor and outdoor pursuits—for example, participating in sports or games, dancing, hiking, and increasing strength or agility.

Children's Responsibilities

The whole rationale of case-action learning is predicated upon the notion that, since a child is principally a seeker and a doer, much of his educationally significant experience comes through undertakings that he himself instigates and carries out in his own way and by his own resources. Basic to effective research, study, or work, therefore, are certain assumptions about pupil-teacher relationships and the various responsibilities for the success of a given case. In the main, the children must be promulgators of activity, while a teacher must be content with a more passive role.

Since little in the school program has prepared pupils for such a degree of self-reliance, some difficulty may be anticipated at the outset. However, after becoming familiar with a new situation and realizing the relevance of a distinctive alliance, a group will generally adapt quickly and with considerable enthusiasm. A class should be given every encouragement to accept as gracefully as possible the full challenge of its proper responsibilities.

Again, the work-to-be-done criterion provides a rather constant demarcation; whatever is consistent with achieving desired goals should set any limits of pupil initiative. For example, since the children will have established certain rules for classroom behavior as an aspect of organization, they also should be the ones to see that such rules are observed. For the most part, this merely calls for each individual to maintain a continuous check on his own conduct. But the situation also entails certain cautions for teams or committees. And perhaps some considerations will have to be confronted by a whole class. In any event, punishment for transgressors is neither a solution nor a partial solution. Rather, the motivation must be positive and realistic. The prevailing attitude should reflect, not "teacher's rules," but "our rules."

It is presumed, of course, that every member of a group ought to accept a proper share of responsibility for meeting whatever commitments to which the class has agreed. What constitutes a proper share, however, will differ from child to child. Each individual is unique; he has his own likes and dislikes, his own strengths and weaknesses, and his opportunities and handicaps. And each of these qualities will be revealed to some degree in his self-image. Insofar as possible, each member's participation ought to be fully commensurate with what he genuinely believes to be his rightful share of a task. Therefore, the extent to which a child will appropriately burden himself in a group effort will not necessarily be in the same ratio as his individual membership in that group. And, just as one person might volunteer for too little in terms of his actual capacity for the work at hand, another might conceivably ask for more than he can reasonably manage. Thus, every member of a responsible work group must be encouraged to take an objective view of his own potential. Although a cluster of factors may bear upon each circumstance, perhaps the principal determiner ought to be whether an individual is more capable or less capable with respect to the specific demands of a situation.

To a considerable extent, the final success of any case is contingent upon the completion of all assignments within whatever limits have been prescribed by a class. Much of the ultimate value of a particular endeavor stems precisely from the satisfaction of having laid out required work in reasonable detail and holding to a self-imposed plan of action in reaching selected objectives. Again, such benefits must be achieved by children themselves. In the process of organization, a group will have scheduled activities and work sessions that now must be maintained. Definite deadlines will have been specified, and these must be met. In addition, a class will have determined other limitations which must be respected in completing any jobs that have been delegated. And the onus of insuring that these conditions will generally obtain must necessarily fall individually upon each member of a class.

Perhaps one further element is required. Just as a machine needs lubricating oil to assure precision in its working parts, so must any group strive to avoid unnecessary friction among its members. Each child must sense the essentiality of maintaining pleasant and cooperative relations with his classmates, as well as with his teacher.

In view of these considerations, then, a list of important responsibilities of children at this stage of development of a given case will include the following:

1. To observe established rules for classroom behavior.

2. To accept a proper share of the work load.

3. To assist in maintaining schedules, holding to necessary limitations, and meeting deadlines.

4. To strive at all times to be pleasant and cooperative both with classmates and with teacher.

A Teacher's Responsibilities

Consonant with the intent and spirit of effective method is that a teacher do nothing for a pupil that the child can reasonably be expected to do for himself. While learning by *doing* is essential to all facets of curriculum, including subject matter study, it becomes especially critical in carrying out delegated responsibilities in the development of a group undertaking. Nevertheless, remaining properly reticent while a child struggles with a difficulty may be the most trying aspect of a teacher's work. A teacher must remain alert to the fine line that separates healthy challenge from debilitating frustration, as a pupil seemingly exerts his greatest effort. Sensing just when to offer assistance and when to hold back is undoubtedly one of the most important attributes of an outstanding teacher.

As children work informally together on an assignment, whatever degree of leadership might be appropriate at any point will generally emerge spontaneously to meet the demand of an occasion. But sometimes a group may find itself at dead center. In such a situation, a teacher will necessarily rely on good judgment in determining whether an apparent lack of impetus is only momentary or if, in fact, any likely approach seems utterly stymied. Should intervention be warranted, a teacher's help will be both more effective and more appreciated if he steps in quickly with just enough of a suggestion to get things moving again, and then prudently withdraws to let the children continue without the weight of outside influence.

To some extent, it will probably be necessary for a teacher to participate on a rather regular basis in terms of synchronizing disparate efforts of individuals or various working groups. Although it may occasionally be feasible to handle some of this through a coordinating committee with representation from each of the directly-functional teams or committees, there will undoubtedly remain a legitimate role for a responsible adult. There will be almost continuous call for a minimum of coordination, guidance, or advice throughout the development. However, a teacher must avoid any possibility that his involvement might become excessive.

But a teacher should be expected to provide materials, equipment, and learning resources at this step. To be sure, children ought to be encouraged to be as self-sufficient as possible. They can bring things from home. They should strive to be imaginative and creative in improvising. And they must develop study and research techniques. But there are also many things either that the children cannot supply at all or that can be obtained only with extreme effort. A group of eager youngsters will not relish the necessity of marking time while some relatively minor item is belatedly procured.

As mentioned before, children will, hopefully, take upon themselves much of the somewhat onerous business of maintaining schedules and meeting deadlines. But unforeseen circumstances can sometimes create great pressure to extend a working period or to postpone a day of reckoning. Often, it may seem to young pupils that adhering religiously to a predetermined plan is arbitrary and unimportant. At such time, a teacher may have to remind a group of the virtues of holding to a schedule or completing an assignment on time.

It is not unusual to find that a given child may not, in fact, "know his own strength." His estimate may be either too high or too low. And this situation, if existing to any appreciable degree throughout a class, might spell jeopardy to a promising case. Handling an assigned task successfully requires that every pupil be working at his own capacity. Other things being equal, most children will tend to commit themselves rather commensurately with what they reasonably can accomplish under familiar circumstances. But the strangeness of a new condition, a fear of failure, or perhaps a feeling that he must prove himself may prompt an individual to attempt too much or too little. Of course, in such a circumstance a child's classmates might help him to see things more realistically. But, ultimately, a teacher may have to encourage him to view a situation objectively and take on a more equitable load.

A teacher will constantly remind himself that it must become the children's very own show, while he must serve more or less as the efficient stage manager and prop man. He definitely will need to stand by, but always behind the scenes. In short, while restraining himself from doing things for children that they can do for themselves, a teacher is prepared at any moment to extend help when and where such help may actually be needed.

One final requisite is that a teacher maintain a demeanor of general happiness. A pleasant and cooperative attitude is much more than an optional extra; it is essential. Since joy in one's work is a basic ingredient of case-action learning, the importance of relaxed, cheerful relationships among members of a group can be realized. And it is incumbent upon a teacher to set an example.

Thus, a teacher has both general and specific responsibilities for the success of this stage of case development. Important among these concerns are the following:

1. To provide leadership wherever and whenever needed.
2. To coordinate, guide, and advise as needed.
3. To provide materials, equipment, and learning resources.
4. To see that schedules are maintained and deadlines are met.
5. To encourage children to accept responsibility commensurate with individual capability.
6. To refrain from doing things for children that they can do for themselves.
7. To be ready to give help when and where needed.
8. To be pleasant and cooperative.

Summary

At this stage in the development of a case, preliminary steps have been taken, and the actual work, study, or research, which consumes most of the allocated time, begins in earnest. In the process, a class will have opportunity to achieve the designated goals and objectives of a selected group endeavor. Furthermore, the children will have meaningful experience in cooperating with others in useful and satisfying work, will develop efficient work and study habits, and will acquire more favorable attitudes toward learning in general.

An almost unlimited variety of resources and activities, including some possibly used earlier for other reasons, may be planned here. On the whole, whatever seems promising in terms of getting the work done is appropriate. According to the circumstances of a given instance, any of the following might be recommended:

1. Textbooks, supplementary books, and library materials
2. Magazines, newspapers, and journals
3. Standard references
4. Maps, globes, and charts

5. Science materials and equipment
6. Flat pictures, graphs, and diagrams
7. Projected still pictures
8. Films and filmloops
9. Duplicated materials
10. Objects, specimens, and models
11. Television and radio
12. Videotape recordings
13. Recordings and recorders
14. Resource persons
15. Assistance or advice from families or friends
16. Field trips
17. Construction, art work, and handicrafts
18. Experiments and demonstrations
19. School newspapers and bulletin boards
20. Oral and written reports
21. Panel discussions and debates
22. Physical activities

In case-action learning, certain assumptions about pupil-teacher relationships are basic. Since much of the necessary activity ought to be instigated and carried out by a class in its own way and through its own resources, children must be given every encouragement to assume responsibility and exercise initiative commensurate with their maturity and experience. A group should be guided largely by demands that are inherent in a situation: the established goals of a particular undertaking and the requirements and limitations of whatever organizational plan will have been adopted. A teacher, on the other hand, will be obliged to assume a relatively passive role at this step, being careful to do nothing for children that they reasonably can do for themselves. His chief responsibilities will be mainly to support, advise, and encourage.

Chapter Ten

Closing a Case

There is a time to work, and there is a time to celebrate; and winding up a group-action case is definitely a time of celebration, calling for neither pretext nor apology. An appropriate conclusion is an integral part of any successful undertaking. The effort that a class will have made in attaining its goals and objectives should not be permitted to go unnoticed. There must be proper recognition of what has been accomplished.

Completion ritual is deeply rooted in tradition—indeed, in human nature. Social needs of mankind demand such acknowledgment; good fortune must be shared and, to an extent, relived. Even a bit of showing off or mild boasting—if discreetly done—may be in keeping. Adult successes are often marked by overt commendation: a housewarming, a launching ceremony, dedication of a new civic building, or a victory celebration, for example. Certainly, children's requirements are no less.

Concluding and evaluating are a vital part of any major endeavor. They are important not only per se, but also in terms of any struggle that has led to an ultimately successful completion. They develop as a natural outgrowth of work that has been done for specific goals. An evaluation consists in weighing a full inventory of benefits derived against whatever total effort and sacrifice may have been levied. A completion ceremony is an occasion for pausing briefly to look back and reflect with pride and satisfaction upon a significant group achievement.

Purposes

As specified in Chapter Two, an essential characteristic of a group action case is that it has both a definite beginning and a definite ending. Thus, the effort that goes into such an enterprise must never be allowed merely to taper off or sputter to an uneventful and uncertain halt. Rather, it must terminate in an ovation that leaves no doubt as to the absoluteness of finish. The end must be sharp and clean. Closing a case, therefore, ought to be on the order of a genuine red-letter day to which children look forward with enthusiasm and eagerness, although its actual advent may occasion some reluctance to leave the work that has been completed. To anticipate a well earned celebration may sometimes be that extra incentive needed to rally children to outstanding performance.

Significant among the purposes that are to be fulfilled in the business of concluding and evaluating a case are these three:

1. To summarize and bring a case to a satisfying and meaningful conclusion.

2. To help children realize the import of what they have accomplished in their research, study, or work.

3. To provide a teacher with additional means of evaluating a case.

Suggested Activities

A key to effectual conclusion and evaluation consists in sharing—that is, sharing *something* with *someone*. Important matters at this point, therefore, include determining, first, just what will be shared; and, second, with whom will the sharing be done. Both of these decisions need to be made in terms of what is pertinent to the goals of a particular case and consistent with the work, study, or research that will have been completed.

For the most part, celebration activities ought to evolve naturally out of various assignments in which children will have been engaged. Whatever considerations will have been in process during the preceding step will now be regarded more as finished products of that earlier effort. A case will finally have come full circle: curiosity satisfied, questions answered, a problem solved, or a project completed.

Oral or Written Reports

One of the simplest, and perhaps most obvious, forms of completion activity is a final report—either oral or written. If planned with imagination and care, this time-honored activity can be quite effective. But, conversely, it can be pretty dull if there is no real effort to make it otherwise. Certainly, an intended communication should be tied rather directly to whatever question or problem prompted the study or research in the first place. Also basic to good reporting is an appreciation of the concerns and interests of a particular listening or reading audience. Being alert to these requirements, an individual, a team, or a committee should find it possible to organize various bits of data into a meaningful outline or story that will be both informative and enjoyable.

The reception of an oral report by an audience can be a critical part of the actual presentation. As a rule, the style should stimulate, but in no way distract from the content. Whether a report is handled by one person or divided among several speakers is, of course, optional. A fairly common difficulty in either instance is that many children do not vocalize clearly and forcefully in a formal situation. A bit of coaching might improve delivery; or, possibly, amplifying equipment may be needed. Very seldom will it be appropriate for a child to read a report verbatim in its entirety, although it may occasionally be effective to present specific sections in this manner. A memorized report, unless done unusually well, will likely sound canned. Generally, an oral presentation will be brought off best if a child uses only an outline or brief notes, yet is so enthusiastic and so full of his subject that his report flows spontaneously.

At a kindergarten or early primary level, children may prefer to dictate a report to their teacher, possibly for recording on chart paper. Older children will find numerous ways in which to present a final report in writing. For instance, it may be posted on a bulletin board, bound into a single volume along with other reports, filed in an accessible place, or duplicated for distribution. Sometimes a written summary may be used in conjunction with an oral presentation. Very likely, several rough drafts will precede the final copy. And, of course, the very best talent on a given team or committee will be utilized in producing the most effectively written document.

Publishing a Pamphlet or Book

Some children may become fascinated with the notion of recording the findings of each team or committee as a separate section of a pamphlet or book to be produced jointly by all of the working groups in a class.

Undoubtedly, this constitutes one of the most permanently visible forms of completion; and, for this reason, it may suggest a special inducement for excellent workmanship both in carrying out a delegated assignment and in reporting the results.

A publication may be handled satisfactorily in either of two ways. One method, which allows each member of a group to have his own copy, consists in reproducing any desired number by means of a spirit duplicator or mimeographing. Another possibility is to create only one copy, but to take particular pains with the quality, making sure that the work will be outstanding both in content and in appearance. Illustrations, for example, are likely to be much more attractive. A class will then decide precisely what to do with the single copy—whether to retain it in the classroom, donate it to the school library, or send it to some other appropriate repository.

Tape Recordings

The familiar versatility of a tape recorder holds considerable promise with respect to closing ceremony activity. Many of the uses appropriate during previous stages in the development of a case will also have application at the final step. In fact, certain recordings that may have served an earlier need may be edited so that significant excerpts form a summary or review. Selected bits of an interview, for instance, or a sampling of the excitement that marked some incident on a field trip can create in an audience a feeling of having been present.

A recording may sometimes be used in conjunction with an oral or written report, or perhaps as a commentary to accompany a demonstration. Music to accompany a dance or other featured activity may be taped. Dramatic sound effects may be handled by this means. Or a script may be polished for a better presentation. And, of course, an unusually shy child, or perhaps one who is not a fluent writer, may wish to tape his final report or a portion of it.

Videotape Recordings

Despite the obvious fact that its relative newness and the expense of essential equipment presently militate against any widespread employment of videotape recordings in elementary schools, it should be recognized that this particular medium holds great potential. In a preceding step portable equipment may have been checked out from a school media center for the purpose of recording a certain action sequence either within a classroom or away from school. By careful planning, it will then be possible to present such a sequence in capsulated form as an effective aspect of a closing exercise. Undoubtedly, an increased use of videotape recording in elementary schools in the near future may be anticipated.

Pupil-Made Films

An interesting possibility that may have some limited application as a completion activity is a motion picture film produced by children themselves as a means of recording their progress throughout the preceding developmental stage. There are, of course, a few technical difficulties inherent in the idea, but probably no more serious than might be encountered in the shooting of 8mm home movies, with which a few children may already have been familiar. While such a film conceivably might review the activities of a class engaged in either a problem solving or an information seeking endeavor, perhaps this technique lends itself more naturally to summarizing the more visible considerations of a work project. Understandably, the chances of getting anything very professional looking may be slim; however, with a reasonable amount of instruction and a few dry runs with a camera, it might be hoped that the results will be at least tolerable.

Photographs

The very same photographs that children may have taken with their personal cameras during a case development offer one of the most convenient means available to a group for making clear to others some of the important details of interesting work just completed. Whether finished in black and white or in color, prints may be pinned in sequence on a bulletin board, mounted as helpful illustrations in a written report, or featured on a chart. In some instances, it may be worthwhile to reorder certain snapshots in quantity so that each child may have one to keep. An especially delightful aspect of using a large number of prints in connection with a completion exercise is that it enables every interested member of a class to contribute.

A few of the many other legitimate uses of photography that might be recommended at this step should also be mentioned. An enlargement of an especially interesting print can be effective in a display. Projecting several selected slides may constitute an excellent method for illustrating an oral report. Sometimes it may be good to have a color print made up from a particular slide. Or perhaps a vivid filmstrip might be produced by photographing a planned sequence with a half-frame 35mm camera.

Exhibition or Display

One can hardly imagine closing a group action case without some sort of exhibition or display. This activity serves an important purpose in bringing a major endeavor to a satisfying conclusion. It can be an inoffensive form of boasting—a clever way of showing off without really seeming to.

There are so many acceptable ways in which an effective exhibition might be planned that it may be difficult for a class to agree on any certain one. Whatever is to be displayed ought to convey a message. But unless some definite scheme is selected, a mishmash of conflicting notions will likely result. Children must be helped to realize that, if spectators are to make sense out of what is shown, a limited number of ideas must be featured with clarity and consistency. Good display consists in deliberate emphasis and sharp delineation—never merely in a jumble of exposure.

Various items that clearly reflect some significant aspect of work accomplished may be exhibited in a manner that will reveal the actual development of a case. Bulletin boards and wall pinup areas may be utilized for displaying appropriate graphics such as posters, maps, charts, graphs, diagrams, or drawings produced in connection with specific job assignments. Booths may be set up for demonstrations or explanations. Models and realia, properly labeled, may be tastefully arranged on a table, while especially fragile or valuable items may possibly be placed in a glass case for safer viewing. Perhaps written reports or descriptions may be posted or distributed for browsing. Collected materials should be identified and placed for convenient examination. It may or may not be appropriate to exhibit some things outside the classroom in locations such as a foyer, auditorium, or hallway. If decorations are used, they must support a selected theme, rather than detract from it.

Dramatization or Puppet Show

Inasmuch as some ideas may be communicated most efficiently by dramatization, it should seem reasonable to suggest that various forms of stagecraft might have occasional application in the closing of a group action case. An entertaining skit that touches sympathetically or humorously on a given matter may sometimes have sharper impact than a straight-on approach. A group will need to understand, however, that not every situation lends itself nicely to this activity. A dramatization must stem directly from the work or study of a particular undertaking. A contrived show— one without authentic roots in a concern—will inevitably miss the point and weaken the overall effect.

Assuming the existence of a legitimate reason for a show, there may be a choice as to using live actors or some type of puppets. While puppets may present a few extra problems, they also occasion some advantages— a smaller stage and greater flexibility. Some children may be less self-conscious manipulating a puppet than appearing in person. An entire script and the accompanying sound effects for a puppet show may be taped in advance. In some instances, there may even be a possibility of including music and dancing with either puppets or live performers. In any event, children ought to accept as much as possible of the full responsibility for all aspects of production—writing a script, staging, costuming, and directing.

Live Demonstrations

Certain outcomes can best be shared by identifying a particular sequential or cause-and-effect relationship that can be replicated before an audience. For example, a committee might wish to repeat an experiment that had been an aspect of its research. By referring to their working notes, these children can set up any necessary apparatus and go through a procedure any number of times. A live demonstration may also review certain facets of a construction activity or the operation of a given piece of equipment. Also, a physical activity, such as a game or dance, may be presented. Varying circumstances will likely determine whether a specific demonstration will be performed one time before a full audience or handled in a more intimate manner before several small, informal groups.

Pageantry

Pageantry thrives in every culture. It exists to an extent in much of everyday life, particularly in government, sports, and entertainment. Historical, religious, and patriotic events are relived in glorious and familiar splendor on each succeeding anniversary. More communion than communication, a pageant is an unvoiced sharing among individuals with a common heritage or cultural background.

Occasionally, a pageant can be incorporated on a modest scale into a completion celebration with highly beneficial results. It requires little or no explanation, of course. And, despite the fact that an audience may have witnessed a similar series of tableaux or listened to almost identical music on previous occasions, there need to be no lessening in appreciation. In proportion to the relatively minor effort expended, pageantry can sometimes yield a rather memorable spectacle.

Special Program

Inasmuch as children select a certain case in terms of their own particular concerns, those same interests may or may not be shared by other people. Some of the most satisfying pursuits that a class may undertake will be of little or no import to outsiders. On the other hand, there may be a few instances of widespread interest in a given enterprise, making it desirable to invite a larger number of guests to a concluding event. In such a circumstance, it may be necessary to select activities that will accommodate not merely a few visitors, but maybe even a crowd. One of the most efficient ways to prepare for a larger group is to plan a special program.

Such a program might possibly be featured as a major aspect of a completion ceremony. There must be an appropriate theme that will underscore the actual results of whatever work will have been done. Of course, a program ought not be so elaborate that it threatens to overshadow the importance of the very endeavor itself. A special program will likely be comprised of a variety of acts selected to explain different facets of a topic. Hopefully, it will be interesting—even entertaining; and, for this reason alone, it must run briskly and not too long. Several rehearsals will undoubtedly be required. Above all, such a program not only must be the actual production of a group of children, but it must reflect directly upon a case.

Creative Arts Festival

In large measure, the basic purposes and characteristics of an undertaking will determine what may be fitting as an ending activity. Accordingly, a few occasions will suggest a creative arts festival in connection with the final step in the development of a case. To be sure, this is not something that ought to be chosen in every eventuality; but, when favorable circumstances coincide, it can be a delightful note on which to bring things to a close. Should a closing occur, for instance, immediately prior to a holiday to which the respective consideration is directly related, the suitability of a festival becomes obvious. These conditions, fortunately, need not cause any additional burden in preparing an activity specifically for a closing exercise, inasmuch as the various arts—the music, dancing, drama, painting, and sculpting—that will be blended nicely into a celebration will have comprised a major product of the work already completed.

Food and Drink

It must be said categorically that some sort of food or drink is an essential element in every concluding celebration. Granted, no more than a soda cracker and a paper cup of water may sometimes be served, but they qualify—at least technically—as refreshments. Eating and drinking are an inherent part of social ritual in every culture, both primitive and civilized. "Breaking bread together" is fundamental to genuine sharing.

Insofar as may be practical, whatever is served as a completion activity ought to connote some significance with respect to a case. If a class, for example, had been studying some facet of life in a certain foreign land, a typical food of that country might be featured. Or perhaps the study of a particular farm product might suggest a food that is processed from that product. Occasionally, the preparation of a given dish may have been included in an actual work assignment. In any event, something will be served to the children and their guests. Under certain circumstances, of course, it is possible that this will become a major activity—perhaps a complete luncheon, a banquet, or a picnic. Much more frequently, however, something fairly simple will be adequate.

Gift or Dedication

Occasionally some tangible product may result directly from work that has gone into a group undertaking, particularly in a work project. For instance, a useful piece of classroom or playground equipment may have been constructed by a group. A neighborhood may have been cleaned up or otherwise beautified by enthusiastic youngsters. Perhaps scrap metal or paper has been collected and sold. A workable plan for improving some school operation may have been formulated. Maybe a book has been authored or a filmstrip developed by a class. These are a few samples of worthwhile ideas or things in which children take considerable pride, yet they may not constitute articles that can very well be carried home at the conclusion of a case. Some meaningful disposition of such a product will definitely be in order.

A recommended procedure for saving an article or an idea from limbo is to give it to someone who will actually make use of it—a community agency, a school library or playground, or possibly a charity. Should a group decide upon this course, it will be entirely appropriate to include the presentation of a particular gift or the dedication of a completed project as an activity in a completion ceremony. An official representative of the selected recipient ought to be present at this time to acknowledge acceptance. Making a useful donation of the fruits of its own labor can be a thoroughly satisfying experience for any group of children.

Field Trip or Excursion

While a field trip or an excursion as a concluding activity certainly cannot be ruled out entirely, legitimate opportunities for including one at this point in the development of a case are definitely limited. A recommended maximum of two away-from-school sessions per case is prompted in part because of the hours consumed in such ventures; and it will not be often that the necessary expenditure of time can be justified at this stage. In most instances, the impact of a field trip will be better realized during an earlier step. The need here is not to open new considerations in regard to an undertaking, but to summarize and review. However, there may exist a possibility of circumstances in which a nonschool location is unquestionably germane to purpose.

Examination

It is possible that an examination might serve a worthwhile end in connection with a case closing. But this particular activity is undoubtedly fraught with more hazard than almost any other. An expected outcome of any group undertaking is that a child's appetite for further learning endeavors be sharpened significantly. Consequently, it becomes imperative that nothing be included at the final step that offers even a slight chance of dampening enthusiasm for an area of concern. Depending upon specific circumstances and his past experience with various examining procedures, an individual may react in various ways at the prospect of being tested at this time. In some circumstances, an examination may make a child uncomfortable about his real or imagined inadequacies, and seemingly emphasize more what he is *not* than what he is. Therefore, should an examination be planned at this point, the activity must be approached with extraordinary caution.

Game or Contest

To a considerable extent, a carnival atmosphere ought to pervade the concluding step of a case. But any merrymaking must have a definite tie-in with the serious work preceding it. A diversion or pastime merely for its own sake cannot be condoned. Therefore, in selecting a game or contest in which children and their guests may wish to participate, it will be important to ascertain whether such activity will actually serve as intended.

Open House

There are a number of advantages in planning an open house in conjunction with certain other culminating activities. For example, it might be convenient to announce an informal two-hour period with perhaps a thirty-minute special program at midpoint. Invited guests may appreciate the option of coming early and leaving immediately after the program, or of showing up just in time for the formal session and remaining for a casual visit afterward. By spacing arrivals and departures over an extended period, it becomes possible to receive each caller in a more personal and friendly manner, creating somewhat of an intimate effect even with a relatively large number of visitors. During the unscheduled portion of time, guests may be encouraged to move freely about the area, talking informally with children or other visitors, viewing displays, watching demonstrations by class members, and enjoying the refreshments.

Celebrating in Good Company

When children have worked hard in achieving something worthwhile, they may want to "shout it from the rooftops." Part of the realization of a job well done is enjoying with others the resulting pleasure and satisfaction. At such a time, a need for acknowledgment or appreciation may be very real. The successful completion of a group action case is truly a time for celebrating, a time for sharing.

Need for an Audience

There are important benefits in arranging for persons other than those directly involved to participate as spectators or an audience at a closing exercise. An audience immediately constitutes a bona fide reason for children to review and summarize their work. In showing and telling other people about an undertaking, a group may appreciate more fully what it has actually accomplished. And the fact that others are obviously interested in what they have done helps children to see the significance of their work, study, or research. Also, in encouraging children to review their efforts for the enlightenment of visitors, a teacher thereby becomes a more objective observer, and, consequently, is better able to weigh all factors in a situation. Thus, an audience facilitates three important purposes of a completion observance: in bringing the case to a satisfying and meaningful conclusion; in helping children to realize the significance of their endeavor; and in providing a teacher with additional means for evaluation.

Characteristics of a Good Audience

Particularly in view of its essentiality to the success of a concluding ceremony, an audience ought to be selected in terms of what is pertinent to
the goals of a case and consistent with the nature of whatever work, study,
or research will have been completed by a class. To put it succinctly, a
genuine audience situation is needed. An assemblage must be comprised
of persons whose presence will be largely in response to actual reasons—
not simple as a courtesy or merely in token support. In order for children
to perform with sincerity and conviction, the interest and concern expressed by visitors must be real. An audience should be comprised of
persons who actually want to be in attendance.

Guests, of course, ought to be knowledgeable to the extent that they
will thoroughly understand what is to be conveyed, yet there must be no
possibility that their anticipation will be at all jaded. There ought to be
spontaneous appreciation, sympathy, and enthusiasm for the effort of the
undertaking. Preferably, an audience ought to be a "natural" gathering
made up of individuals with a basic interest in the area of concern.

Deciding Whom to Invite

Thus, the matter of deciding whom to invite to a closing exercise ought
not be taken too lightly. Although any one of several possible groups
might meet the criteria that have been suggested, certain further points
should be considered.

Generally, a choice of guests ought to be commensurately ambitious
with the case outcome that is being celebrated. For example, in concluding
a brief, fairly casual undertaking that perhaps represents less than an
all-out effort on the part of a group of children, a quite satisfactory audience situation may often be obtained very easily without carrying the
concern beyond the classroom walls. In such an event, it becomes feasible
for a portion of a group to conduct its summarizing activities while other
children function as guests. Then the roles of audience and performers may
be reversed for the remainder of the activities.

On a slightly more sophisticated plane, it may be appropriate to
invite another class in the same building to attend portions or all of a
completion exercise. In a graded school, for instance, other sections of the
same grade level may constitute an excellent audience. Should a situation
warrant a larger and wider ranging guest list, it might occasionally be
proper to ask the full enrollment of a school to be present, even though
a program might have to be repeated two or three times to accommodate
the increased number of visitors in shifts.

For several reasons, parents of children who have been working on a case will constitute a suitable assemblage in a variety of circumstances. Certainly, it is to be expected that a father or mother will have an interest in almost anything to which his or her child has been deeply committed. In many instances, this natural interest will have been further nourished by any assistance or encouragement that a youngster may have received at home. And, of course, an extra benefit to be realized in bringing parents to school—for almost any reason whatsoever—is the inevitable strengthening of home-school relations in general.

Sometimes it may be advantageous to invite people who are not connected—at least in any direct way—with school, but who nevertheless may have an interest of long standing in a concern that a class may have been pursuing. A community leader or a recognized expert may be genuinely pleased to be present at the closing of a case that relates to his own field. A manifestation of interest by such a person will undoubtedly help children to see relationships between what they do *in* school and what may be of serious concern *outside* of school.

Also, there are those rare occasions when it may be good to invite the general public of a community to a case ending. To be sure, this practice is more likely to obtain in a small, rural community than in a metropolitan area. But, given the right conditions, it might be possible almost anywhere for a group of elementary children to identify a consideration that ultimately becomes a matter of concern throughout a local citizenry.

It would appear, therefore, that there are at least six potential sources upon which to draw in selecting an appropriate audience:

1. Other members of a class
2. Another class in a building
3. The entire student body of a school
4. Parents
5. A special community group or special visitors
6. The general public of a community

Sending Invitations

Having given serious thought as to whom they will ask to attend a closing exercise, a class will probably want to make sure that guests clearly understand the details of an invitation. The enjoyment of a celebration is more pronounced when all of the expected visitors arrive at a designated location at an appointed hour on a scheduled day. In order to reduce any possibility of misunderstanding, a written invitation is strongly recommended in every instance. The format may be as plain or as fancy as the nature of the event and the skill of a particular group of children may seem to suggest, but all essential information as to what, who, when, and how long must be included. The invitations should be prepared and sent out— either by mail or hand-carried by members of a class—in plenty of time for guests to make arrangements to attend. In some instances, an R.S.V.P. may be especially helpful. In addition to its value in keeping basic information straight, the practice of sending written invitations helps to remind children of the importance of the occasion, as well as to foster a keener appreciation of their visitors.

Summary

Bringing a group action case to a successful completion calls for a celebration of what has been accomplished. A commemoration at this point is an essential aspect of a major endeavor, and it constitutes a final stage in development. Concluding and evaluating summarize an undertaking and bring it to a satisfying and meaningful ending. They also help children to realize the significance of what they have achieved. In addition, a teacher is provided with further means of evaluating a class's full effort.

Purposes of conclusion and evaluation may be effected by arranging for children to share with others a review and summarization of their work, study, or research. Activities that may be regarded here as a finished product will evolve naturally out of processes in which children will have been engaged during the preceding step.

Since a case closing ought to be viewed as a genuine occasion for celebrating, the presence of guests may be considered as essential. Consequently, it is recommended that appreciative, sympathetic, and enthusiastic visitors be invited to a concluding ceremony to participate as a bona fide audience and to enjoy the refreshments and other amenities of such an event.

Part THREE

Planning

a

Successful Case

The world is full of ideas—just waiting to be had.

Chapter Eleven

Maintaining
a Resource File

Case-action learning is planned and executed in order to relate specifically to the nature of a child and the psychological considerations of his behavioral growth. Building activities around an individual's felt needs and personal satisfactions of the moment demands constant reassessment at every step. Keeping attuned to the kaleidoscopic requirements of such a situation calls for a high degree of maneuverability in planning.

Purposes of a Resource File

A fundamental characteristic of case-action learning is that whatever is undertaken must clearly be children's choice. And, though a teacher may anticipate with remarkable accuracy what a given class will find worthy of concern, he can never be absolutely sure that a particular proposal will not be vetoed at the outset by a group's manifest disinterest. At such a time, his essential flexibility will be severely tested; he must be immediately ready to make appropriate changes in both the direction and the scope of his planning. To take things in stride, a teacher must have an organized reservoir of ideas into which he can dip at a moment's notice.

Effective planning requires ready access to numerous resources. Although a group action case may seem, from the viewpoint of the youngsters involved, to be a spontaneous happening, a successful development invariably calls for weeks—perhaps months—of purposeful groundwork. After a case has been actually started, there simply is not time to handle the preparations that are requisite to bringing it off smoothly. Most of the notions and activities that ultimately result in a satisfying outcome will have been given thoughtful consideration much earlier and held in abeyance until needed.

A teacher must have a convenient, systematic way of managing the habitual collecting and storing of a wide variety of resources that can be quickly channeled into the development of a case. Because children will be doing the work and making the decisions, there will be a number of modifications in what has been planned—even after an endeavor is well under way. The obvious good sense in beginning a case with more workable ideas than can possibly be used should prompt no serious rebuttal. For these reasons, it is essential that a resource file be established and maintained by a teacher as a permanent, ongoing, year-round activity.

Suggested Filing Procedures

Having decided that a ready supply of suggestions, references, and materials is indispensable, a teacher will likely want to establish filing and storage practices that are suited to his own particular requirements. A filing system encourages the gathering of useful resources, provides for their convenient safekeeping during an indefinite period of nonuse, and facilitates instant retrieval of a specific item when needed. To some extent, a given teacher's personality traits and individual work habits will determine an effective approach. For this reason, it may be better not to force certain procedures arbitrarily, but to let essential practices evolve more naturally.

Basic Equipment

One of the most significant factors in efficiently collecting resource materials is having a convenient place to put an item after it has been acquired. Merely having a large manila envelope appropriately labeled may make it seem more worthwhile to leaf through an old magazine in search of usable pictures. It might seem a reasonable suggestion, therefore, to attend first to the matter of setting up the physical aspects of a personal filing system.

The location of filing equipment can be important in terms of its usefulness. Often, this may be merely a matter of personal choice, since nothing very sophisticated in the way of data handling machinery will likely be necessary. While one might visualize an occasional circumstance in which punch cards or even an electronic system might be helpful, most situations, happily, will require only the simplest storage and retrieval scheme. Very probably, therefore, a teacher will wish to have his materials as convenient as possible to the place at which he normally does his preparatory work. In a good many instances, this will be in his home; in team-teaching arrangements, it may be in a team office or workroom; or perhaps it may be in a corner of a classroom.

Without doubt, the most useful item generally available is the familiar four-drawer standard or legal-size letter file with its adjustable tab-index dividers. This provides easy-access storage of plans, suggestions, and a wide variety of materials. A card file, with either 4x6 inch or 5x8 inch cards, constitutes an efficient method of handling annotated bibliographies, addresses, and directions. Certain flat materials, such as large pictures, charts, and maps, may require a chart file. And a set of uniformly sized boxes that may be labeled and stacked offers a convenient way to care for small articles. Should an austere school budget make it impossible to obtain any of these items through the usual commercial sources, it may be necessary to substitute sturdy pasteboard shipping cartons scrounged from a friendly merchant and attractively covered with self-adhesive paper or spray paint.

It may sometimes be desirable to retain an item in storage over an extended period of time, which considerably increases the incidence of normal wear and tear. Certain precautions, therefore, may be indicated. For example, a picture or cartoon that has been clipped from a newspaper or magazine and effectively preserved by either dry mounting or laminating, may be displayed several times and replaced in a file for yet another occasion. Having necessary equipment available for such processes, therefore, is of significant benefit in maintaining resource materials.

Sources of Ideas and Materials

There are many ways in which a teacher can build up his stockpile of ideas and materials over a period of several months. However, he must be a persistent and discriminating collector. To work vigorously but sporadically in accumulating useful items will not achieve the best results. Keeping at it calmly on a year-round basis is much more fruitful. But gathering too many things can be as bad as not getting enough. Without some measure of discretion, all available storage space will very quickly be so bulging with a hodgepodge of trash that whatever may be genuinely usable cannot be located.

Ideas and materials that may be incorporated to good advantage into a particular case may come from almost anywhere. In many instances, their end use will not in any wise have been visualized at the moment of acquisition. Indeed, fully as many ultimately useful items are likely gathered out of sheer habit as through deliberate search. A teacher may often seem to rely on a sixth sense in identifying something as potentially valuable, despite the fact that he may not be at all sure as to when, how, or why it might eventually be put to use.

The facilities of a school's library and media center, of course, come immediately to mind in any consideration of educational resources. In addition to the standard references that are typically checked, a library contains a variety of books, records, filmstrips, filmloops, pictures, transparencies, maps, and charts. A discussion of specific circumstances with a librarian will generally produce definite recommendations, not merely with respect to that which may actually be on hand, but to outside sources as well. A media center serves as repository for films, filmloops, pictures, transparencies, and miscellaneous models and realia. It may also be possible to check out self-contained general subject kits, complete with films, maps, slides, models, and selected reading materials. To keep himself properly reminded of any of these possibilities, a teacher may wish to place an appropriate memorandum in his resource file.

For several years, certain businesses and industries have increasingly participated in furnishing free educational materials as an aspect of their public relations activities. While a few such offerings constitute unmitigated attempts at direct advertising, many are remarkably clean in this respect and are quite acceptable for school purposes. Often, it may require only mailing in a coupon to receive a useful packet of instructional items. Community and governmental agencies, also, may be occasional providers of helpful information. In making use of these sources, it is important to anticipate future possibilities and accept any free materials at the time they are first offered. To postpone a request until a need actually arises is often to wait until the original supply has become exhausted.

Proper maintenance of a resource file is a daily habit. For instance, keeping a marking pen or a razor blade at hand as one reads the morning paper makes it possible to take advantage of anything worth clipping. Similarly, to flip quickly through an old magazine before discarding it requires but a few seconds, yet it adds up to an impressive selection of tear sheets, coupons, and articles, as well as a real saving of time. Making a bibliographical entry on a card when examining a useful book simplifies the matter of locating the volume again at a later time. Perhaps a brief note of something seen at a neighborhood shopping center may yield good returns two or three months afterward. And to jot down the name, address, and telephone number of a potential resource person on a file card as soon as possible after an introduction is both an effective reminder and a convenient locater. These few examples suggest that, with a bit of deliberate effort, a teacher can condition himself to be both persistent and discriminating in the matter of gathering practical ideas and appropriate materials to be filed away for later application in the development of a particular case.

Filing Arrangements

Deciding upon a particular system for keeping track of things is pretty much an individual consideration. Since each teacher is concerned with his own peculiar purposes in designing case-action learning, how he goes about filing resource materials is his own business and ought to be determined mainly by his personal preferences.

In most instances, a teacher will already have established some functional procedure to meet his needs in storing and retrieving items appropriate to each of the subject matter fields. This can be an excellent starting point for filing potential resources for case-action learning, since there is no reason for maintaining separate systems for the two curriculum approaches. Including a category for each school subject in a resource file is entirely practical and worthwhile.

Another fairly common practice among teachers is that of classifying ideas and materials according to general subject. What may constitute a useful category will depend upon the specifics of a given situation. A certain teacher, for instance, might find it advantageous to use such headings as "commerce," "government," "industry," "conservation," "agriculture," "transportation," "communications," "community living," "recreation and sports," "ancient civilization," "medicine and health," and any others which fit in with his particular planning practices. Such general classifications obviously, are equally applicable both in subject matter study and in case-action learning.

In addition to the commonly practiced arrangements which have been mentioned, a successful filing system for case-action design will invariably include the practice of filing according to anticipated case proposals. Perhaps a certain teacher might have useful information indexed according to such tentative titles as "Radio and Television Broadcasting in Our Community," "Wool Production in Our State," "Our Local Water Supply," "The Interstate Highway System," "Eliminating Pollution in Our Own Neighborhood," "Exploring the Moon," or whatever might occur to him as a future possibility for developing into an actual case.

It is therefore suggested that, although a filing system probably ought to be selected in accordance with the special needs and preferences of a particular teacher, headings will typically represent each of the following arrangements:

1. Resources filed according to school subject.
2. Resources filed according to general subject.
3. Resources filed according to anticipated case proposals.

Thus, having set up basic information storage equipment, having conditioned himself to a habit of persistent and discriminating collecting, and having selected an appropriate system of filing, a teacher will be well prepared to handle the numerous items that constitute much of the stock-in-trade of case-action learning design.

By going about the business deliberately and purposefully, he will become highly effective in maintaining a well filled and easily used resource file.

Summary

Because flexibility in planning is essential throughout the development of a group action case, a teacher must have a wealth of usable ideas and materials upon which he may draw at a moment's notice. It is necessary, therefore, that he establish and maintain a resource file as a permanent, ongoing, year-round activity.

An adequate filing system fosters the gathering of appropriate learning resources, provides for safe interim storage, and permits quick and accurate retrieval of a desired item. Although nothing very elaborate in the way of either apparatus or procedure is required, whatever is chosen ought to fit the particular needs and preferences of a given teacher. Filing equipment should be located in convenient proximity to the place where he usually prepares his work, whether at home or at school. Storage demands may generally be met with such familiar containers as a four-drawer letter file, card files, a chart file, and a set of sturdy boxes.

Basic to effective resource collecting is making it a regular habit. Good ideas and materials may come from almost anywhere at virtually any time, and they must be obtained and filed away at the moment of availability. The facilities of a school library and media center are rather well known. Businesses, industries, and community and governmental agencies, also, may furnish helpful materials and information. Other sources may be found in publications and through a teacher's daily contacts.

While any filing arrangement should be expected to reflect the peculiar requirements of a particular situation, it is likely that some resources will be filed according to one or more of the regular school subjects, some according to certain general subjects, and still others according to anticipated case proposals.

Chapter Twelve

Design for Success

Taking a child "from where he is," as a well worn curriculum maxim admonishes, "to where he ought to go" requires suitable transport in order to effect a safe and pleasant journey. Just as school subjects may constitute a dependable vehicle for a knowledge-based approach to elementary curriculum, so may case-action learning provide an appropriate conveyance from a child-centered starting point. In either instance, however, it takes more than wishful thinking to bring it off. And the same careful attention to preliminary preparations and honest respect for the inevitable hazards are as necessary in the one as in the other. A hopeful, optimistic outlook and realistic, down-to-earth planning are of the essence in both considerations. If—somehow—there be any such thing as a magic carpet of education, certainly it must be fueled and made ready for actual flight.

Creating a good design in case-action learning is never easy. On the contrary, it is a stern challenge to the imagination and industry of the most dedicated teacher. But, despite the many unpredictables, it is entirely possible to go about this sensitive business in a deliberate, systematic way, and with a reasonable degree of confidence in the outcome.

Six Steps to Success

While guaranteed success is fully as farfetched in case-action learning as in any other aspect of curriculum, satisfactory results in a child-centered, learning-oriented approach are caused by something more substantive than sheer good luck. Certainly, no implication is intended that the six-step design that has been discussed in Part Two constitutes the one and only scheme possible by which worthwhile learning experiences may be founded upon children's felt needs and personal satisfactions. But the procedures that have been specifically recommended are both workable and effective. Furthermore, they are common-sense-based and relatively uncomplicated to execute. Admittedly, there has been no suggestion of any surefire formula for automatic results. Nevertheless, despite what may possibly seem an incongruity in attempting a logical planning of a psychologically based evolvement, there is every good reason to believe that a teacher who earnestly observes a few basic principles is justified in anticipating a successful undertaking.

A Systematic Design for a Spontaneous Happening

Inasmuch as case-action learning is in direct response to children's own peculiar purposes, it may reasonably follow that, from the learner's viewpoint, a good case will be characterized by personal and immediate relevance, almost spontaneous activity, and full involvement in the process. Only from a teacher's vantage need the inner framework of a design take on particular significance. As responsible architect and engineer, a teacher will consider a given design according to the various structural elements of a development and the bearing of one upon another. But the children, in their quite different role, will tend to think of that same endeavor as an indivisible whole. Children may quite appropriately regard a group action case as a nondifferentiated happening. A teacher, therefore, must fit the sections of a design together so precisely that any seams or joints will be virtually invisible. The six steps, or stages, by which a teacher may systematize the building of a case need be of no concern as such to the children who will participate in the action. But it is for these very reasons that a teacher, in his own thinking, ought to observe religiously the discreteness of each separate step.

Paradoxically, the more painstaking and systematic a design has been on the part of the teacher, the greater will be the degree of spontaneity and immediacy for the children who become involved in a particular pursuit. To a considerable extent, the secret of ready sensitivity and flexibility of response lies in making a practice of overplanning at every stage of development. Having more options than conceivably can be used under any likely circumstance significantly increases a teacher's capacity to anticipate a group's interests and opportunities and to make instantaneous adjustments accordingly. By preparing well in advance for any eventuality, the desirability of keeping in tune with a freewheeling spirit of extemporaneousness need not hinge on seizing frantically upon any workable notion at the last moment. Quite the contrary, it may largely be a matter of selecting calmly from several possibilities that have already been carefully considered.

A Simultaneous Development of All Steps

Inasmuch as the recommended steps comprise more a logical than a chronological sequence, it is advisable to build up all six somewhat simultaneously. Whether to include a certain activity or learning resource in any given step must be determined with appropriate regard for the possible effect it may also have upon other phases of an undertaking. The matter of arranging a field trip may be considered as a good example. Since it is never feasible to employ an unlimited number of away-from-school activities, deciding to schedule one at a particular time will likely necessitate weighing the consequences of its equivalent loss at an earlier or later point. Thus, the planning of each phase of a group endeavor must be done in relation to the total outcome. A nice balance among the various steps may frequently be a key to an apparently natural unfolding in the development of a successful case. Also, coordination of the logical stages in a sequence may be augmented by planning them concurrently.

A Fresh Start for Every Design

It most certainly is not intended that a design for any group action case ever be regarded as engraved on bronze tablets. Quite the opposite, a good design is tentative, flexible, and expendable. In fact, it is continuously subject both to minor alterations and to major overhauls at all stages of development. After a case has been carried forward to a satisfactory closing, and subsequently has become a part of classroom history, the planning for that particular undertaking may then be regarded as final and complete —though not necessarily perfect. During the actual procedure, however, constant revision remains the norm. Even the most successful case is handled only once; and, having once served its purpose as the focus of group action, it is filed away never to be used again except as resource material. Only by starting afresh with each new undertaking by a given group of children under a particular set of circumstances may the purposes underlying case-action learning be achieved through spontaneity, relevance, and learner involvement. There are infinite ways of dealing meaningfully with an infinite number of group concerns, and each case must be truly unique.

Panic-Free Planning

It ought to be abundantly clear that enjoyment is considered an essential ingredient in case-action learning. Hopefully, children develop a positive feeling for hard work and an expectation of delight in learning as an activity in general. Fun, excitement, and an occasional surprise, of course, are all part of the process. Since a worried expression and a long face are not apt to brighten the scene, the advantages of having a happy teacher around should not require spelling out. Obviously, it is important for a teacher, as well as for children, to have a good time throughout a group undertaking. Resolving to keep the panic out of planning, therefore, is a thoroughly practical notion.

Taking It Easy

An especially helpful quality that a teacher might well cultivate is that of being fairly "unflappable." The ability to take things pretty much in stride in the midst of a little healthy confusion is an enviable asset. Many teachers—perhaps most—may need to make a deliberate effort to relax and let things evolve at a more realistic pace and in a less exact direction. In reducing any personal tendency toward rigidity in case-action planning, a teacher gains in two important ways: first, he is released from a good deal of self-imposed pressure; and, second, children are encouraged thereby to exercise their own initiative and imagination at all stages of a development, with the welcome result that a group endeavor moves along with increasing momentum.

One sample way in which a teacher may begin to relax in the situation is that of not trying too hard to "sell" a pet notion to children. If a given idea is really genuine, the children will very likely adopt it of their own accord. Or they may be more in the market for it at some future time. Or, again, perhaps it wasn't such an earthshaking thought, after all. In any event, a teacher might as well be philosophical about the virtual certainty that children will be doing some things the hard way simply because it happens to be *their* way.

This sort of unharried behavior on the part of a teacher should not be confused with an attitude of detachment or a strictly hands-off policy, for there are definite indications of honest concern for the ensuing action. But, in the final analysis, the undertaking is the children's very own, and the important decisions that must be made ought to remain their particular prerogative.

Making the Most of Long-Range Planning

Designing case-action learning can be both efficient and relatively painless if a teacher looks upon it as an ongoing aspect of the total teaching task. In all probability, there is no way to avoid much of the hard work inherent in such planning, but any show of heavy-handedness should be scrupulously avoided. A grim, now-or-never attitude serves no useful purpose; a light touch is considerably more fruitful. An important element in the secret of good planning is the maintaining of a generous backlog of workable options to render flexible response a feasibility.

Long-range planning must be seen as basic to successful design in case-action learning. At that wonderful moment when a group of children actually takes on a particular case, it is much too late for a teacher to begin planning. For a teacher to delay planning until a group has become actively involved is to rule out much of his effectiveness as consultant, guide, and resource person. His too-little-too-late efforts will likely amount to a futile jumble of fortuitous notions and gimmicks accumulated in an eleventh-hour scramble. To respond as he ought, a teacher must have immediate access to a substantial repertoire of possibilities to which children may be referred in their further considerations. Such a ready supply will undoubtedly include ideas and references that may represent weeks or even months of systematic anticipation.

The obvious advantage in having several potential cases simmering in partial readiness at any given moment ought to be fully appreciated by a teacher genuinely interested in enhancing the enjoyable aspects of a child-centered undertaking. The kind of resource filing that was considered in Chapter Eleven is recommended as a way of facilitating the unhurried, long-range planning that is so vital. While no filing system, of course, can relieve a teacher of the necessity of spending many hours in careful preparation activity, making a routine, year-round habit of collecting and filing potentially useful items is certainly a significant stride in the direction of panic-free planning in case-action learning.

Personalizing Education Through Group Action

Properly used, case-action learning can personalize education for each child. It is essential, however, that the design does not permit losing sight of the individual as he relates within the group. Although the focus is upon group intentions that are to be achieved principally through group initiative and effort, whatever is undertaken must be scrutinized and evaluated from the peculiarly personal viewpoint of each individual child. To maintain consistency with the philosophical grounding of a child-centered approach, it is especially important that each individual who takes part in such a group action be genuinely convinced within his own mind that he has become involved of his own volition, and that he is basically in pursuit of his own personal interests which happen, fortunately, to coincide with those of other members of his group.

Case-Action Learning in Various Patterns of School Organization

A basic premise in designing a group action case is that an important undertaking is to be shared in a social situation by a number of individuals, each of whom has a distinctive personality and a unique set of needs and potentialities. Such an approach need not be limited to any particular plan of school organization. Whatever the organizational pattern, there will inevitably be certain likenesses and differences among the members of a given group. And children are alike in fully as many characteristics as they are different from one another. An essential element in designing case-action learning is to focus upon the critical likenesses in identifying a concern that has mutual fascination and value for an entire group, while at the same time capitalizing upon those helpful differences that allow for an interesting variety of individual and group participation modes throughout the proceedings.

Likenesses and differences that may be found in any group of children are genuine, and they clearly transcend any trait categorizations resulting from arbitrary groupings of school organization. The special benefits of case-action learning may be realized with equal assurance and enthusiasm, regardless of whether a group of children happens to be graded, nongraded, or multigraded. Neither should any particular significance be attached to whether teachers have been assigned according to a self-contained classroom plan or according to some cooperative or team teaching arrangement.

In a typical graded, self-contained classroom, with its usual quota of one teacher and perhaps thirty children, it is entirely reasonable to expect that everyone in the group may choose to participate in a single common endeavor. For, while it is by no means an impossibility for an imaginative and well organized teacher to attend to two or three separate undertakings at a time in order to provide each child with additional options, the limited advantages are probably overshadowed by unavoidable complications. In a self-contained situation, therefore, it is ordinarily quite acceptable that no more than one case be in progress at a given moment.

There is a recognized flexibility that is inherent in either a graded or nongraded pod type classroom with three or four teachers working as a team or in a completely open school. In such a situation, it can be a relatively straightforward matter to have several group action cases under way simultaneously. For example, a team comprised of three teachers, who have been assigned to work together at an intermediate level, should occasion no unusual difficulty with as many as four different cases developing almost concurrently, and conjunctly utilizing the total efforts of the full group. The greater number of children in such an arrangement can generally provide the necessary manpower to meet the increased work load resulting from the additional undertakings. And, of course, with more children involved, a correspondingly wider range of potential interests may be satisfied through the extra outlets.

Regardless of the organizational pattern, from fifteen to thirty-five children will likely be motivated of their own free will to participate in a given case. Obviously, there will be exceptions to this. In some instances, the total enrollment of a whole pod or a combined grade level may elect to carry out the objectives of an especially interesting or particularly significant case. And, in quite unusual circumstances, virtually an entire student body of several hundred young people—each child with his own personal reasons—may plunge en masse into an extended group undertaking.

Group Action and Rugged Individualism

A question may arise as to how best to deal with the occasional rugged individualist who gives every indication of disdaining a group activity in its entirety. A conscientious teacher may feel torn between the need to respect such a child's wish to be allowed to go his own independent way and the desirability of full-group involvement in a case that perhaps all of the other children have accepted with obvious enthusiasm. The temptation to compromise conflicting values in such a situation should, of course, be anticipated. But this is not a time to let down and take the easy way out. Adhering closely to principles underlying case-action learning is a more likely means of resolving the difficulty.

In the first place, it should be sincerely hoped that *every* child might now and then manifest a bit of rugged individualism—not merely to enjoy being obstinate or unnecessarily to exercise a basic human right, but rather because his purposes at times are genuinely unique and distinct from those of any group. Firmly holding such a viewpoint as to the ultimate individuality of each child, a teacher will not be so easily taken aback when a youngster happens to declare his personal veto.

Thoughtful consideration might be given the deeper motives of a child who may seem to be dragging his heels on participating in a given group action. More than likely, the apparent negativism actually stems not so much from any real dislike of a particular group concern, but from an apprehension that getting tied up in it will deprive him of the satisfaction of pursuing something else in which he has a strong, personal interest. Seen in this light, the dilemma is considerably mollified. The child's needs are regarded in a more positive sense: his intentions seem legitimate and reasonable.

Under most circumstances, the acceptable options ought to include that of the child's actually being encouraged to go his own tangential way with the combined blessing of his teacher and classmates. A decision to splinter off a single child from the group, however, must not be arrived at capriciously. There are definite benefits to be realized from his identifying an appropriate niche in the larger undertaking, and his attention should be drawn to potential opportunities in the upcoming group action. More often than not, it may be entirely feasible to alter or slightly enlarge the scope of a particular group endeavor to make it equally attractive for the erstwhile loner. Thus, by lightly modifying the design of a proposed case, a teacher can often help a child overcome his initial doubts and embrace a group enterprise with sincere enthusiasm.

Case-Action Learning and Subject Matter Study

Basic purposes of elementary education which were identified in Chapter One can be attained through a correctly balanced curriculum for each child. Since acquisition of knowledge and intellectual development will continue to be regarded as essential ends, carefully planned subject matter will undoubtedly constitute a significant aspect of that crucial proportioning. But there are other highly desirable outcomes to which subject matter may contribute only indirectly or incidentally. Achievement of some of these equally important curriculum considerations lies within the domain of an approach that is forthrightly child centered: specifically, case-action learning. To a great extent, realization of the maximum benefits of this approach hinges upon a clear appreciation of the legitimate place of formalized knowledge in the child's curriculum and a precise understanding of an effective working relationship between subject matter study and case-action learning.

A Needed Complement

Case-action learning is not intended to supplant subject matter in any way, but rather to provide an essential component. A desirable relationship results in a vital balance in elementary curriculum which contributes significantly to a foundation of genuine scholarship in each child. Such a balance ought not be regarded as a mandatory fifty-fifty deadweight ratio, but more in terms of its dynamism. The fundamentals of a curriculum may be kept in reasonable perspective with a relatively gentle, but well-timed, counteraction. There is no necessity for a purely quantitative equating of the two basic orientations. Case-action learning does not require "equal time" for its singular benefits to be realized.

While this book has not disagreed with either a subject-focused or a child-centered approach to elementary curriculum, it has consistently opposed any significant *compromise* between the two. Instead, a dual convergence has been earnestly recommended. The scope of presentation, however, has not included a thorough consideration of the familiar logically structured, content-oriented aspects of curriculum—other than a frank recognition of their inalienable position in a balanced program. But the fact that subject matter has not been examined in detail in no way implies that a disciplinary approach is not vital as one basic dimension of elementary curriculum. Valid arguments for incorporating significant measures of formalized knowledge into a child's education have already been convincingly demonstrated.

Nothing herein should be construed, therefore, as either an apology for, or an attack upon, subject matter as it has traditionally been presented in the elementary school. That genuinely significant efforts to bring about demonstrable improvements in various subject areas are presently under way is gladly acknowledged. But, beyond this simple clarification of position, there has been no reason to deal directly and specifically with subject matter. The objective, instead, has been to present a feasible way of going about a deliberate and systematic building of important personally oriented considerations for each child's behavioral growth right into his school-based learning experiences. In promoting case-action learning, there has been no hint that subject matter in the elementary curriculum ought to be limited or restructured. The proposal, rather, has been to institute a long-needed complement to those already established curriculum aspects that are deeply rooted in formalized knowledge, and thus establish an appropriate balance between widely different approaches.

A Note of Caution

A brief, but sober, note of caution is likely in order, lest potential benefits that might normally accrue from a judicious targeting of case-action learning be lost through misuse of procedures that have been detailed in Part Two. The recommended design should never be regarded as an all-purpose teaching technique; rather it is intended for a specific facet of elementary curriculum.

However, in the exuberance of identifying an idea that has genuine merit with respect to a particular aspect of a child's education, it may often be tempting to try extending its range of usefulness. Thus, a design for case-action learning, having been demonstrated as an effective means of implementing a child-centered and learning-oriented approach to curriculum, might also be seen as equally appropriate in the handling of subject matter. It may be well, therefore, to recognize quite frankly at the outset that there are definite limitations to the circumstances in which these procedures ought to be applied. For, despite the fact that the design as herein described has been proposed *only* for case-action learning ventures, it could conceivably occur to an enterprising teacher that it might also serve as a pattern for carrying out an instructional unit in subject matter. And, perhaps to a limited extent, it just might work, although difficulties resulting from certain basic incongruities surely ought to be anticipated. For one thing, there would undoubtedly be obvious inconsistencies in applying a personally oriented teaching approach to a knowledge-based content.

The really serious hazard, however, goes deeper than simply the probability of jeopardizing a learning experience in a disciplinary area. A far more crucial error would lie in making an unwarranted assumption that, merely through borrowing the *design* of case-action learning and gearing it somehow to the teaching of subject matter, the great need for a balance between child-centeredness and subject-centeredness had thereby been automatically met. Most assuredly, it is not only the design of case-action learning that is vital to this essential balance, but also a realization of the whole philosophy of a child's being enabled to identify and achieve at least some of his own unique purposes.

It should be clearly understood, therefore, that the design for case-action learning that has been recommended in this book is intended *exclusively* as a vehicle for a child-centered, learning-oriented approach to elementary curriculum. Certainly, nothing should be construed in any manner as a suggestion that the design be used in the teaching of subject matter.

A Thought or Two in Closing

A persistent claim of this book is that case-action learning can enrich a child's school-based experiences and effectively fill a void of long standing in elementary curriculum. That this can be accomplished without either displacing valuable traditional content or requiring large expenditures of time or money is ancillary to the principal message of genuine need.

A disciplined mind and a free spirit are fundamentally characteristic of any truly educated person. Such a belief is wholly consonant with a conviction that the chief function of an elementary school ought to be the nourishing of bona fide scholarship in each and every pupil. This is a major postulate in the rationale for recommending a frankly child-centered focus as one of two distinctive approaches to elementary curriculum.

To reiterate an earlier statement, the irreducibles of the kind of scholarship that is dynamic and long lasting for each individual are a substantial fund of knowledge as a partial means and an unquenchable love of learning as a most desirable end. Unfortunately, much of traditional curriculum planning has led to a seeming reversal of such an end and such a means, thus allowing no more than an occasional or token consideration for the essential nature of real scholarship, and often promoting mere intellectual drudgery as an ineffectual substitute. True scholarship, being really more process than product, is less a matter of engaging in research, study, or investigation in order to achieve some specific objective than of pursuing learning activity purely for the delight and satisfaction of the experience itself. Implied in such achievement is not only mastery of relevant knowledge, but also a well honed facility to use acquired knowledge in ways that are gratifying and personally worthwhile to the individual.

Certainly, the more complex individual needs and the more rigorous societal demands of today and tomorrow cannot be met with only occasional instances of scholarship. Realistic opportunities for the development of a solid foundation of lifelong scholarship must be extended now to every child. This will call immediately for a significantly improved and ideally balanced curriculum in the elementary school. Surely, there is an important and unique place in that curriculum for case-action learning.

Index